KT-501-285

THE CAMBRIDGE COMPANION TO
PRIDE AND PREJUDICE

Named in many surveys as Britain's best-loved work of fiction, *Pride and Prejudice* is now a global brand, with film and television adaptations making Elizabeth Bennet and Mr Darcy household names. With a combination of original readings and factual background information, this *Companion* investigates some of the sources of the novel's power. It explores key themes and topics in detail: money, land, characters and style. The history of the book's composition and first publication is set out, both in individual essays and in the section of chronology. Chapters on the critical reception, adaptations and cult of the novel reveal why it has become an enduring classic with a unique and timeless appeal.

JANET TODD is the President of Lucy Cavendish College, Cambridge.

THE CAMBRIDGE
COMPANION TO
PRIDE AND PREJUDICE

EDITED BY
JANET TODD
Lucy Cavendish College,
University of Cambridge

 CAMBRIDGE
UNIVERSITY PRESS

CAMBRIDGE UNIVERSITY PRESS
Cambridge, New York, Melbourne, Madrid, Cape Town,
Singapore, São Paulo, Delhi, Mexico City

Cambridge University Press
The Edinburgh Building, Cambridge CB2 8RU, UK

Published in the United States of America by Cambridge University Press, New York

www.cambridge.org
Information on this title: www.cambridge.org/9780521279581

© Cambridge University Press 2013

This publication is in copyright. Subject to statutory exception
and to the provisions of relevant collective licensing agreements,
no reproduction of any part may take place without the written
permission of Cambridge University Press.

First published 2013

A catalogue record for this publication is available from the British Library

Library of Congress Cataloguing in Publication data
The Cambridge companion to Pride and prejudice / edited by Janet Todd.
p.   cm.
Includes bibliographical references and index.
ISBN 978-0-521-27958-1
1. Austen, Jane, 1775–1817. Pride and prejudice.   2. Austen, Jane,
1775–1817 – Appreciation.   3. Austen, Jane, 1775–1817 – Influence.   4. Austen,
Jane, 1775–1817 – Adaptations.   I. Todd, Janet M., 1942–
PR4034.P73C36   2013
823'.7–dc23
2012027117

ISBN 978-1-107-01015-4 Hardback
ISBN 978-0-521-27958-1 Paperback

Cambridge University Press has no responsibility for the persistence or
accuracy of URLs for external or third-party internet websites referred to
in this publication, and does not guarantee that any content on such
websites is, or will remain, accurate or appropriate.

CONTENTS

ILLUSTRATIONS

CONTRIBUTORS

EMILY AUERBACH is an award-winning Professor of English at the UW-Madison, author of *Searching for Jane Austen*, host of Wisconsin Public Radio's University of the Air, producer of Courage to Write documentaries and guides on women writers, and Director of the UW Odyssey Project (www.odyssey.wisc.edu), a free college humanities course for adults at the poverty level.

LINDA BREE is Editorial Director, Arts and Literature at Cambridge University Press. She is currently editing Maria Edgeworth's *Belinda* for Oxford University Press. She has edited a number of eighteenth- and early nineteenth-century texts including Austen's *Persuasion* (1998), Henry Fielding's *Amelia* (2011) and Daniel Defoe's *Moll Flanders* (2011), and co-edited with Janet Todd the *Later Manuscripts* volume in the Cambridge edition of the Works of Jane Austen (2008).

LAURA CARROLL is a lecturer in the English Program at La Trobe University, Melbourne. She has published widely in Jane Austen studies, including articles and chapters on adaptation in *Literature / Film Quarterly* and *Victorian Literature and Film Adaptation*. She is working on re-enactment and role-play within the Jane Austen community.

GILLIAN DOW splits her time between the University of Southampton's English Department and Chawton House Library, where she is responsible for the academic programme. Her research interests are primarily in translation and the cross-Channel exchange of ideas in the Romantic period; she has published several edited collections in this area. She co-edited with Clare Hanson *Uses of Austen: Jane's Afterlives* (2012).

ANDREW ELFENBEIN is Professor of English at the University of Minnesota – Twin Cities. He is the author of *Byron and the Victorians* (1995), *Romantic Genius: The Prehistory of a Homosexual Role* (1999) and *Romanticism and the Rise of English* (2009); he has also edited Wilde's *Picture of Dorian Gray* and Stoker's *Dracula*. His forthcoming book is *The Gist of Reading*.

THOMAS KEYMER is Chancellor Jackman Professor of English at the University of Toronto and General Editor of the *Review of English Studies*. His books include

Sterne, the Moderns, and the Novel (2002) and *Richardson's 'Clarissa' and the Eighteenth-Century Reader* (1992, paperback 2004). He co-edited with Jon Mee *The Cambridge Companion to English Literature from 1740 to 1830* (2004) and edited Johnson's *Rasselas* (2009).

PETER KNOX-SHAW is a research associate at the University of Cape Town. He has published widely on eighteenth-century and Romantic literature. He is author of 'Philosophy' in *Jane Austen in Context*, ed. Janet Todd (Cambridge University Press, 2005), and of *Jane Austen and the Enlightenment* (Cambridge University Press, 2004).

DEVONEY LOOSER is Catherine Paine Middlebush Professor of English at the University of Missouri. She is the author of *Women Writers and Old Age in Great Britain, 1750–1850* (2008) and *British Women Writers and the Writing of History, 1670–1820* (2000), editor of *Jane Austen and Discourses of Feminism* (1995) and co-editor of *Generations: Academic Feminists in Dialogue* (1997) and, since 2004, the *Journal for Early Modern Cultural Studies*. Looser is currently working on a biography, *Sister Novelists: Jane and Anna Maria Porter*.

ANTHONY MANDAL is Senior Lecturer in English Literature and Associate Director of the Centre for Editorial and Intertextual Research at Cardiff University. He is the author of *Jane Austen and the Popular Novel: The Determined Author* (2007), and co-editor of *The English Novel, 1830–1836* (2003) and *The Reception of Jane Austen in Europe* (2007). He is the developer of a number of electronic resources, among them *British Fiction, 1800–1830: A Database of Production, Circulation & Reception* (2004). He is one of the General Editors of the *New Edinburgh Edition of the Collected Works of Robert Louis Stevenson* (39 volumes, 2013–).

ROBERT MARKLEY is W. D. and Sara E. Trowbridge Professor of English, Writing Studies, and Center for East Asian and Pacific Studies at the University of Illinois at Urbana-Champaign. His books include *The Far East and the English Imagination 1600–1730* (Cambridge University Press, 2006), *Fallen Languages: Crises of Representation in Newtonian England, 1660–1740* (1993) and *Two-Edg'd Weapons: Style and Ideology in the Comedies of Etherege, Wycherley, and Congreve* (1988). He is the editor of *The Eighteenth Century: Theory and Interpretation*.

ROBERT MILES is Professor of Literature at the University of Victoria. His publications include *Gothic Writing 1750–1820: A Genealogy* (1993), *Jane Austen: Writers and their Work* (2003) and *Romantic Misfits* (2008). His current project is called 'Jane Austen and Happiness'.

JUDITH W. PAGE is Professor of English and Director of the Center for Women's Studies and Gender Research at the University of Florida, where she has also been Waldo W. Neikirk Professor of Arts and Sciences. She is the author of many articles and of *Wordsworth and the Cultivation of Women* and *Imperfect Sympathies: Jews and Judaism in British Romantic Literature and Culture* (2004) and co-author with Elise L. Smith of *Women, Literature, and the Domesticated Landscape: England's Disciples of Flora, 1780–1870* (2011).

BHARAT TANDON has taught at the Universities of Cambridge and Oxford. He is the author of *Jane Austen and the Morality of Conversation* (2003), the editor of *'Emma': An Annotated Edition* (2012) and a judge for the 2012 Man Booker Prize for Fiction.

JANET TODD is President of Lucy Cavendish College, University of Cambridge, and Emerita Professor at the University of Aberdeen. She is the author of many critical works on early women writers and a biographer of Mary and Fanny Wollstonecraft and Aphra Behn. She has edited the complete works of Wollstonecraft (with Marilyn Butler) and Aphra Behn; she is the general editor of the Cambridge edition of the works of Jane Austen.

JOHN WILTSHIRE is adjunct Professor of English at La Trobe University, Melbourne. He is editor of *Mansfield Park* in the Cambridge edition of the works of Jane Austen, and is the author, most recently, of *The Making of Samuel Johnson* (2009) and (with David Monaghan and Ariane Hudelet) *The Cinematic Jane Austen* (2009).

PREFACE

Pride and Prejudice is the Austen title everyone knows. Its opening sentence is one of the most exploited in the language. In some surveys the nation's best-loved novel, it is now a global brand and, mainly through film and television versions, the central lovers Elizabeth and Darcy have become household names.

For this extraordinary reason the chapters in this *Companion* are both about the book itself and about its immense fame, influence and legacy. They explore the critical response, the adaptations and spin-offs as well as the style and themes of the original novel and its literary and historical context. *Pride and Prejudice*, Jane Austen's second published work, is not usually selected by contemporary academic critics as her greatest achievement, but it is the book she and her friends most valued and, very early on, it became her most loved and celebrated work. Created to mark the bicentenary of the first publication of *Pride and Prejudice*, the *Companion* investigates some of the sources of the novel's power through the ages and the reason why so many readers have felt it to be true about human relations and about romance.

The *Companion* opens with Thomas Keymer's chapter on 'Narrative'. Setting the novel in a context especially of Samuel Richardson, Henry Fielding and Frances Burney, it makes the controversial argument that *Pride and Prejudice* is more likely to have been written in epistolary form than *Sense and Sensibility*, the usual candidate for a novel in letters. Touching on her fame for unmediated dialogue and slippery narrative voice, Keymer notes Austen's occasional use of intrusive explanations which provide a bed-rock of moral analysis for the reader. Free indirect style, the technique which catches in narrative prose the distinctive qualities of particular speech, was not invented by Jane Austen but she employed it very flexibly in *Pride and Prejudice* to deliver a character's idiolect, often while placing him or her within a narrator's syntax.

The delivery of character, Austen's power of creating personalities who can enter and inhabit a reader's mind, is the subject of Robert Miles's chapter.

This discusses the way fictional characters come to reveal and to know themselves. Miles argues that Austen is one of the last significant Aristotelian moralists in the English tradition; consequently self-knowledge is connected with *telos*, the end towards which our nature strives if we are to know our true place and purpose in life. Peter Knox-Shaw also associates Jane Austen with Aristotle through the notion of greatness of mind or pride as conscious worth. Moving nearer to her time, he finds her within the sceptical tradition of John Locke, whose notion of the frequently dangerous power of first impressions is related to the title of the original draft of *Pride and Prejudice*. Drawing on *Enquiry Concerning the Principles of Morals* by the philosopher David Hume, he argues that both Austen and Hume differ from many of their contemporary moralists in seeing human nature as mixed, and in refusing to celebrate good nature sentimentally. Both Miles and Knox-Shaw stress Austen's psychological realism. Miles argues that, while revealing her epistemological concerns, Austen never loses sight of the commonplace, material motivation in actions, while Knox-Shaw notes that, for Austen, ideas are organic, fluctuating, felt on the pulse, and subject to dramatic change.

In 'Composition and Publication' Anthony Mandal notes the complexity of Jane Austen's publishing career and the difficulty of compartmentalising the six novels into Steventon and Chawton works. He places *Pride and Prejudice* within a continuum of her writings, beginning with her juvenile works from 1787 and continuing through the period of original composition and redrafting of the novel until it reaches publication in 1813. He also discusses the book industry when Jane Austen entered the market and describes the literary context of women writers, especially Burney, who was such a profound influence on Jane Austen. This influence is investigated more fully in Linda Bree's chapter on the literary background. Stressing the voluminous nature of Austen's reading, Bree comments on Austen's ambivalent attitudes to the early masters of the novel, Fielding and Richardson, and her relationship to her most famous female contemporaries, Burney and Edgeworth. Bree focuses on those works that Austen singles out for special praise in *Northanger Abbey: Cecilia, Camilla* and *Belinda*. While assessing what Austen learnt and rejected in these, Bree concludes that in aims and themes Austen often followed Burney but that her wit is closer to Edgeworth's wit than to Burney's broader humour.

In his chapter on the historical background, Bharat Tandon follows Mandal in noting the changes in publishing and book-buying from the revolutionary decade when *Pride and Prejudice* began its life to the Regency when it was printed. He too argues that the novel has literary memories within it, harking back to the juvenile tales and relating securely to the late fictions. The fifteen or so years of its gestation form one of the most turbulent periods in recent English history, and Tandon argues that Austen has a 'glancing involvement' with this history rather than a direct engagement. *Pride and Prejudice* manifests some of the historical changes and continuities in, for example, the use of the militia and in the attitude to money. The concern for money and its power is the main focus of Robert Markley's chapter on the economic background of *Pride and Prejudice*. Characters view the world through a lens of finance and inheritance customs and accept the responsibilities imposed by ownership of property. Discussing the economic changes of the late eighteenth and early nineteenth centuries, Markley indicates how Austen's novels capture the sense of entitlement that many upper-class people displayed while revealing the underlying anxiety about the effect of fluctuating amounts of money on lifestyle and status. Money, social position and hierarchical values inform the worldview of Austen's characters in general, but *Pride and Prejudice* seems finally to endorse an expansive rather than a simply hierarchical view of upper-class social relations.

Two chapters concentrate on the external world of the novel. Judith W. Page investigates the estate – houses and grounds – of *Pride and Prejudice*, noting the link between characters and class on the one hand and property and landscape on the other; she comments on the way the reader is led to appreciate the value attached to the outdoors and to special places. Austen uses the picturesque aesthetic as a useful tool for viewing, as well as for conveying a more Romantic vision that emphasises the emotional effect of the natural world more than the visual effect. Andrew Elfenbein makes a similar point with reference to both inside and outside space in *Pride and Prejudice*. Seemingly engaged in an experimental minimalism, Austen often appears indifferent to setting, excluding most of what other writers would consider essential, especially in an age that loved detail and was obsessed with the aesthetic style of the picturesque. In fact in *Pride and Prejudice* Austen is closer to the Johnsonian aesthetic that prohibited minute description, although she does not follow him into stressing universality of response; instead she insists on the influence of circumstance and the interaction of bodies with social space.

In her chapter on the translations of *Pride and Prejudice*, Gillian Dow shows how the style and skill of the translator control the critical reaction of the novel in languages outside English and how theories of translation influence practice in different periods. In the nineteenth century *Pride and Prejudice* was not the most frequently translated of Austen's novels – though in adapted form it had the distinction of being the first: the Franco-Swiss version appearing in 1813 conformed the novel to the conventions of current sentimental romance fiction and largely avoided its irony and realism about marriage markets and money. Austen's later omnipresence in foreign parts is predominantly a late twentieth-century and twenty-first-century phenomenon, mirroring the Anglo-American Austen cult. The trend of romanticising her work continues globally – as the chapters of Devoney Looser and Emily Auerbach suggest.

Very different is the tradition of academic Austen criticism in the English-speaking world, the subject of my own first chapter. Although from the late nineteenth century up to the present the most serious literary comment and philosophical claims have been made for *Mansfield Park* and *Emma*, even *Pride and Prejudice*, seemingly the most escapist of Austen's works, has been found by critics to reveal a satiric edge to its comic realism, a latent hostility to a damaging society, and a deep moral seriousness. When in the twentieth century the novel was set in its supposed historical context, discussion turned on whether Austen approved or disapproved the heroine's initial rebelliousness and whether Elizabeth was in the end reduced and tamed to fit contemporary patriarchal structure. Repeatedly criticism found contradictory ethics emerging from the novel and judged it reactionary or enlightened according to desire or expectation. The debate continues in this volume and beyond.

The enormous proliferation of *Pride and Prejudice* is the subject of the final four chapters. My own second chapter, on romance, concentrates on Jane Austen's Mr Darcy as a figure differing substantially from the polite hero created in the eighteenth century by writers such as Richardson and Burney. I discuss Mr Darcy as a character who will later be reinterpreted in the light of subsequent romantic heroes created especially by Lord Byron and the Brontë novelists. Adumbrating the archetypal romantic pattern of threatening, overbearing hero and socially inferior girl who yet tames him into love, *Pride and Prejudice* had considerable influence on the genre of popular feminine romance in the twentieth century. In filmic adaptations Mr Darcy in part resembles the character Jane Austen authored and in part morphs into the more Brontësque romantic hero. The chapter considers the elements in the original novel that allow this development. Laura Carroll and John Wiltshire continue this subject by addressing screen adaptations, noting that almost as many are made of this one book as of all the other Austen novels put together. This is because it appears to encapsulate the promise of romantic love. However, Carroll and Wiltshire argue that, although the very popular film adaptations do centre on this subject, in fact they falsify the book, which is really about the nature of true marriage. Following this argument, they relate *Pride and Prejudice* to the screwball comedies of the 1930s where the chief characters quarrel, then with witty dialogue make up, learn and forgive.

Writing on the cult of Jane Austen, Devoney Looser traces the afterlife of *Pride and Prejudice* through changing sets of readers at discrete historical moments until the novel reaches near ubiquity in the late twentieth century.

Austen is known to have been associated with a male elite readership in the late nineteenth century and reputed to have given literary sustenance to men in the trenches of the First World War; Looser argues that she was also appreciated by first-wave feminists such as Rebecca West, who imagined her intentionally writing novels of energetic, proto-feminist critique. At the same time she achieved a popular readership catered for in mass-market editions of her works. Since then she has been used for a variety of purposes, repackaged for children, even toddlers, employed for contemporary self-help books on manners and dating and internet games, and reduced to pens, tea towels and mugs. Looser raises the question of how we make sense of this extraordinary exploitation of Austen and why it has occurred. Auerbach's chapter complements Looser's by describing the adaptations, permutations, sequels and prequels of *Pride and Prejudice* through various print and screen media. My chapter on romance mentions the role of Mr Darcy in the female romance tradition: in adaptations he is given a childhood, inner thoughts (some anti-semitic) and myriad sexual exploits – not only with Elizabeth but also with Bingley and Wickham, while being turned into a rock star, a rancher, a vampire and a werewolf. Other characters come out of the novel to write diaries and interact with new creations, American cowboys and French cousins for example, in the endlessly growing *Pride and Prejudice* industry. So speedy is the proliferation that, as Auerbach notes, this chapter will be out of date by the time the volume is published.

Janet Todd

Quotations from the novel are given with the abbreviation *P&P* and a page number. These numbers refer to the Cambridge Edition of the Works of Jane Austen, *Pride and Prejudice*, ed. Pat Rogers (Cambridge University Press, 2006).

Context	*Jane Austen in Context*, ed. Janet Todd (Cambridge University Press, 2005)
E	*Emma*, ed. Richard Cronin and Dorothy McMillan (Cambridge University Press, 2005)
Juvenilia	*Juvenilia*, ed. Peter Sabor (Cambridge University Press, 2006)
Letters	*Jane Austen's Letters*, ed. Deirdre Le Faye, 4th edn (Oxford University Press, 2011)
LM	*Later Manuscripts*, ed. Janet Todd and Linda Bree (Cambridge University Press, 2008)
MP	*Mansfield Park*, ed. John Wiltshire (Cambridge University Press, 2005)
NA	*Northanger Abbey*, ed. Barbara M. Benedict and Deirdre Le Faye (Cambridge University Press, 2006)
P	*Persuasion*, ed. Janet Todd and Antje Blank (Cambridge University Press, 2006)
S&S	*Sense and Sensibility*, ed. Edward Copeland (Cambridge University Press, 2006)

1764–7	Revd George Austen, rector of Steventon, marries Cassandra Leigh. Three children, James (1765), George (1766) and Edward (1767), are born.
1768	The Austens move to Steventon, Hampshire. Five more children – Henry (1771), Cassandra (1773), Francis (1774), Jane (1775) and Charles (1779) – are born.
1775 16 December	Jane Austen born at Steventon.
1781 Winter	JA's cousin, Eliza Hancock, marries Jean-François Capot de Feuillide, in France.
1782	Austen family amateur theatricals first recorded.
1783	JA's third brother, Edward, is adopted by Mr and Mrs Thomas Knight of Godmersham in Kent. Later he will take their name.
1785 Spring	JA and Cassandra attend the Abbey House School, Reading.
1786 April	JA's fifth brother, Francis, enters the Royal Naval Academy in Portsmouth.
December	JA and Cassandra leave school and return to Steventon. Between now and 1793 JA writes what will become her three volumes of *Juvenilia*.
1788 Summer	Mr and Mrs Austen, JA and Cassandra on a trip to Kent and London.
December	Francis leaves the RN Academy and sails to East Indies; does not return until Winter 1793.

1790	JA writes 'Love & Freindship'.
1791 July	JA's sixth and youngest brother Charles enters the Royal Naval Academy in Portsmouth.
27 December	Edward Austen marries Elizabeth Bridges, and they live in Rowling in Kent.
1792	JA's eldest brother, James, marries Anne Mathew; they live at Deane.
? Winter	Cassandra becomes engaged to the Revd Tom Fowle.
1793 23 January	Edward Austen's first child, Fanny, born.
1 February	War declared between Britain and France.
8 April	JA's fourth brother, Henry, becomes a lieutenant in the Oxfordshire Militia.
15 April	James Austen's first child, Anna, born.
3 June	'Ode to Pity', last item of JA's *Juvenilia*, composed.
1794 22 February	M. de Feuillide guillotined in Paris.
September	Charles goes to sea. 'Lady Susan' possibly written this year.
1795	'Elinor and Marianne' probably written.
3 May	James's wife Anne dies.
December	Tom Lefroy visits Ashe Rectory – he and JA have a brief flirtation.
1796 October	JA starts writing 'First Impressions'.
1797 17 January	James Austen marries Mary Lloyd.
February	Revd Tom Fowle dies of fever at San Domingo.
August	JA finishes 'First Impressions'. George Austen offers a JA manuscript for publication to Thomas Cadell – rejected sight unseen.

November	JA begins rewriting 'Elinor and Marianne' as *Sense and Sensibility*.
	Mrs Austen and daughters visit Bath.
31 December	Henry Austen marries his cousin, the widowed Eliza de Feuillide, in London.
1798–9	JA probably writes 'Susan' (later *Northanger Abbey*).
1800	George Austen decides to retire and move to Bath.
1801	
24 January	Henry Austen resigns commission and sets up as a banker and army agent.
May	Austen family leave Steventon for Bath.
1802	
25 March	Peace of Amiens appears to end Anglo-France war.
December	JA and Cassandra visit Steventon. Landowner Harris Bigg-Wither proposes to JA; she accepts, but declines the following day.
Winter	JA revises 'Susan' (*Northanger Abbey*).
1803	
Spring	JA sells 'Susan' (*Northanger Abbey*) to publisher Benjamin Crosby.
18 May	War with France recommences.
Summer	Austens visit Ramsgate in Kent, and possibly West Country; in November they visit Lyme Regis.
1804	JA probably starts writing 'The Watsons'.
Summer	Austens at Lyme Regis again.
1805	
January	George Austen dies.
Summer	Martha Lloyd joins Mrs Austen and her daughters.
21 October	Battle of Trafalgar.
1806	
July	Austen women visit Clifton, Adlestrop, Stoneleigh and Hamstall Ridware, before settling in Southampton in the autumn.

1808

October — Edward Austen's wife Elizabeth dies at Godmersham.

1809

April — JA tries to secure publication of 'Susan' (*Northanger Abbey*).

July — Mrs Austen, Jane and Cassandra and Martha Lloyd move to Chawton, Hants.

1810 — *Sense and Sensibility* accepted for publication by Thomas Egerton.

1811

February — JA starts planning *Mansfield Park*.

30 October — *Sense and Sensibility* published.
  JA starts revising 'First Impressions' into *Pride and Prejudice*.

1812

Autumn — JA sells copyright of *Pride and Prejudice* to Egerton.

1813

January — *Pride and Prejudice* published.

July — JA finishes *Mansfield Park*. Accepted for publication by Egerton.

1814

January — JA starts *Emma*.

5 April — Napoleon abdicates and is exiled to Elba.

May — *Mansfield Park* published.

1815

March — Napoleon escapes and resumes power in France.

March — *Emma* finished.

18 June — Battle of Waterloo ends war with France.

August — JA starts *Persuasion*.

October — Henry Austen takes JA to London; he falls ill.

November — JA visits Carlton House, is invited to dedicate future work to Prince Regent.

December — *Emma* published by John Murray, dedicated to Prince Regent (title page 1816).

1816

Spring   JA ill. Henry Austen buys back manuscript of 'Susan'
              (*Northanger Abbey*), which JA revises.

August   *Persuasion* finished.

1817

January   JA starts 'Sanditon'.

18 March   JA too ill to work.

24 May   JA goes to Winchester for medical attention.

18 July   JA dies; buried on 24 July, Winchester Cathedral.

December   *Northanger Abbey* and *Persuasion* published together, by
              Murray, with a 'Biographical Notice' added by Henry
              Austen (title page 1818).

I

THOMAS KEYMER

Narrative

One of several clever effects in the famous first sentence of *Pride and Prejudice* – 'It is a truth universally acknowledged, that a single man in possession of a good fortune, must be in want of a wife' (*P&P*, p. 3) – is the uncertainty arising about the nature and authority of the statement made. Whose voice and views are we listening to here, what status or value should we grant them, and what does Jane Austen think? In its confident declarative style, the novel's opening seems to promise uncomplicated access to authorial opinion, and adopts a formula that had been used for decades to mark moments of emphasis and assertion in polemical writing. 'It is a Truth universally acknowledged,' insists John Shebbeare in a political pamphlet of 1756, 'that *Canada* is the only part [of France's overseas dominions] which can afford these Requisites.' Or again, declares Anna Laetitia Barbauld in a religious tract of 1792, that prayer for advantages such as health may be impious 'is a truth ... universally acknowledged by all Christians'.[1] This is personal conviction in loud mode, rhetorically inflated into absolute truth. In practice readers might dispute this truth – readers such as the officials who were shortly to prosecute Shebbeare for seditious libel, or the clerics who thought Barbauld fanatical and superstitious – but the author's investment in it is impossible to mistake.

In *Pride and Prejudice*, by contrast, the same grandiose, generalising formulation is punctured by the shallowness and parochialism of the point that follows. For there is nothing even plausibly universal about this particular 'truth', and in another time or place the single man in question might just as well be in want of a hard-nosed accountant, a commitment-free fling, or a same-sex civil union. The timeless present-tense mode notwithstanding, Austen is telling us not about universal truth at all, but about a socially and

[1] John Shebbeare, *A First Letter to the People of England* (1756), p. 41; Anna Laetitia Barbauld, *Remarks on Mr. Gilbert Wakefield's Enquiry* (1792), p. 16.

historically specific set of attitudes.[2] In ways made inescapable as the novel unfolds, her words go on to suggest not reliable authorial truth-telling – the wise, supervising commentary that might guide readers through the moral complexities of George Eliot's *Middlemarch*, or even the interpretative minefield of Fielding's *Tom Jones* – but satirical invocation of a communal voice. They conjure up the shared perspective of genteel home-counties society or 'the minds of the surrounding families' (*P&P*, p. 3), and they mimic the thought and language of this society – diminished thought and impoverished language in which the petty, self-interested assumptions of Mrs Bennet and her neighbours are casually dignified into something more. A masterstroke of comic bathos and teasing plot anticipation, the trick also foreshadows the clever intricacies, strategic indeterminacies and subtle, agile ventriloquisms of the narrative to follow.

Epistolarity

A standard explanation for Austen's virtuoso handling of narrative voice in *Pride and Prejudice* and the work most closely associated with it, *Sense and Sensibility*, is that key features of her technique originate in the tradition of epistolary fiction. More than a century before Austen first drafted both novels in the 1790s, pioneering works such as Aphra Behn's *Love-Letters between a Nobleman and His Sister* (1684–7) were using fictional letters to suggest direct access to the consciousness and viewpoint of their protagonists, and classic eighteenth-century instances of the mode include Samuel Richardson's *Pamela* (1740), Frances Burney's *Evelina* (1778) and Laclos's *Les Liaisons dangereuses* (1782). Two of the best-known phrases employed by Richardson to describe his narrative practice, 'writing, to the moment' and 'writing from the heart',[3] catch the special properties of immediacy and intimacy associated with the epistolary form: first, its dramatic synchronisation of story and discourse, with narrators responding to events as they unfold; second, the revelatory character of familiar letters, addressed to friends or family members in a spirit of unguarded spontaneity. Yet in Richardson's hands the novel in letters also gives rise to more destabilising effects than these conventions suggest, above all in his multi-voiced masterpiece *Clarissa* (1747–8), where adversarial accounts of the central conflict – its causes and effects, its rights and wrongs – are put forward by competing narrators. In *Les Liaisons*

---

[2] Paradoxically, Austen may owe this move to the eighteenth century's foremost dealer in universal truths, Samuel Johnson, whose narrator in a satirical *Rambler* essay (No. 115, 23 April 1751) 'was known to possess a fortune, and to want a wife'.

[3] John Carroll (ed.), *Selected Letters of Samuel Richardson* (Oxford: Clarendon Press, 1964), p. 289; Samuel Richardson, *Clarissa*, 3rd edn, 8 vols. (1751), vol. IV, p. 269.

dangereuses, the letter becomes a vehicle not of privileged, reliably transmitted information, but instead of deception and betrayal. Laclos's novel dramatises a struggle for power – a war, one narrator finally calls it – that plays out in the epistolary medium itself.

By 1787, the year to which the earliest of Jane Austen's surviving juvenilia are normally dated, fully half the new novels published in English were narrated in letters.[4] The statistical evidence masks a creative decline, however, and with a few exceptions there was little more to the epistolary novels that now crowded the market than vapid, lumbering imitation of Richardson's last and for a time most influential work, his voluminous novel of manners *Sir Charles Grandison* (1753–4). Early fragments and skits by Austen such as 'Love and Freindship', 'Lesley Castle' and 'A Collection of Letters' deftly mock the sentimental excesses and creaking mechanics of this persistent strain of circulating-library fiction, but Austen's admiration for the towering prototype is impossible to miss. Family memoirs report her absorption in the circumstantial detail and meticulous characterisation of *Sir Charles Grandison*, and for James Edward Austen Leigh '[h]er knowledge of Richardson's works was such as no one is likely again to acquire ... all that was ever said or done in the cedar parlour, was familiar to her'.[5] In this context, *Pride and Prejudice* has been interpreted as a creative reworking of elements originating in *Sir Charles Grandison*, albeit a reworking that 'substitutes density and relation for the diffuseness of Richardson'.[6]

The influence of the scandalous Laclos is less often asserted, and would certainly have been denied by the earliest custodians of Austen's reputation. But in her longest surviving exercise in epistolary fiction, 'Lady Susan' (perhaps written as early as 1794, though other dates have been proposed), Austen is fascinated by letters as agents of duplicity and manipulation, not as vehicles of documentary realism or tokens of psychological introspection. Daringly, 'Lady Susan' entrusts much of its text to a narrator characterised above all by her ability to beguile, and to beguile specifically as a letter-writer, exerting 'a happy command of Language, which is too often used ... to make Black appear White' (*LM*, pp. 11–12). Rather than describe the 'captivating Deceit' (p. 9) of this character in secure, objective narration, 'Lady Susan' exposes readers directly to it in the hazardous medium of her writing,

---

4 Discounting translations, forty-seven new novels were published in Britain and Ireland in 1787, of which twenty-four were epistolary. See Peter Garside, James Raven, et al., *The English Novel, 1770–1829: A Bibliographical Survey*, 2 vols. (Oxford University Press, 2000), vol. I, pp. 390–415.

5 J. E. Austen-Leigh, *A Memoir of Jane Austen and Other Family Recollections*, ed. Kathryn Sutherland (Oxford University Press, 2002), p. 71 (see also p. 141).

6 Jocelyn Harris, *Jane Austen's Art of Memory* (Cambridge University Press, 1989), p. 84.

unassisted – until a short but significant third-person 'Conclusion' – by the guidance of a detached voice. The work becomes a minor masterpiece of epistolarity in the sense of the term established by Janet Altman: 'the use of the letter's formal properties to create meaning'.[7]

Other manuscripts from this early period of Austen's creativity do not survive, or survive only in the shape of radical later transformations. *Pride and Prejudice*, *Sense and Sensibility* and *Northanger Abbey*, published respectively in 1813, 1811 and 1817, all have their origins in drafts composed by Austen in her early twenties, and beyond their working titles ('First Impressions', 'Elinor and Marianne', 'Susan') little is known for certain about these drafts. It is widely accepted, however, that at least one of them was epistolary in form. 'Memory is treacherous', confessed Austen's niece Caroline in 1869, 'but I cannot be mistaken in saying that Sense and Sensibility was *first* written in letters – & *so* read to her family.'[8] Yet the residually epistolary component of *Sense and Sensibility* is by no means pronounced, and recalcitrant features of this work (notably the inseparability of Elinor and Marianne for most of the action, and the absence of eligible confidantes elsewhere) make it hard to detect the trace of a novel in letters. Some scholars have suggested instead – memory being treacherous indeed, and in this case bound up with hearsay, since Caroline Austen was not born until 1805 – that a better candidate for epistolary origins is *Pride and Prejudice*, which turns on letters as vehicles of narrative or agents of plot at several crucial junctures, and contains almost five times as much verbatim epistolary text as *Sense and Sensibility*.[9] One need only remember Mr Collins's toe-curling letters of self-introduction and faux-consolation to Mr Bennet, the pivotal account of himself that Darcy hands Elizabeth in the grove near Rosings, or the epistolary mediation of the Lydia–Wickham subplot in Volume III, to see how central letters are to the comic and dramatic effects of *Pride and Prejudice*, and especially to the dynamics of self-revelation, delayed disclosure and ongoing assessment of character and action that animate the work. Tantalising external evidence strengthens the case for an epistolary prototype. It may be relevant that when offering the manuscript to the bookseller Thomas Cadell in 1797, Austen's father compared it to Burney's *Evelina*, specifically with reference to length – length from which, Austen

---

[7] Janet Altman, *Epistolarity: Approaches to a Form* (Columbus: Ohio State University Press, 1982), p. 4.

[8] Austen-Leigh, *Memoir*, p. 185.

[9] D. W. Harding, 'The Supposed Letter Form of *Sense and Sensibility*', *Notes and Queries* 40 (1993), pp. 464–6; Joe Bray, *The Epistolary Novel: Representations of Consciousness* (London: Routledge, 2003), pp. 114–15, 124–9.

later wrote, the more streamlined *Pride and Prejudice* was 'lopt & cropt' – but perhaps also with Burney's epistolary form in mind.[10]

That said, Burney makes only limited use in *Evelina* of the rich resources of epistolary polyphony pioneered by Richardson and others, and her typical heading for each narrative letter, designed mainly to externalise the maturing consciousness of her heroine, is 'Evelina in continuation'. *Pride and Prejudice* exhibits instead a finely calibrated range of epistolary voices, voices that shift according to situation and addressee as well as from writer to writer. At first sight Austen might seem to achieve this effect within the basic conventions of epistolary immediacy, using letters as transparent windows on authentic inner lives. It is the unguarded, unpremeditated openness of Bingley's epistolary manner – 'rapidity of thought and carelessness of execution' (*P&P*, p. 53) – that is emphasised in an early chapter, and writing from the heart is always the governing assumption with guileless Jane, as when she communicates the experience of being snubbed by the Bingleys in a letter included, we are frankly told, to 'prove what she felt' (p. 167). Even in these apparently straightforward cases, however, letters cannot be taken at face value, with Bingley's vaunted artlessness challenged by Darcy as a pose, and Jane's letters anxiously scanned by her sister for signs of undeclared grief. No less important than the writing of letters is the vigilant reading of letters, which are always something more or less than the inward consciousness of the writer. They will only yield up their full meaning when read as patiently as Elizabeth reads the letters of Jane, 're-perusing' them for marks of emotional concealment, 'dwelling on' their evasions or blind spots, scrutinising every line for 'want of that cheerfulness which had been used to characterize her style' (pp. 204, 210).

It is tempting to see in the correspondence between the sisters, which culminates in Jane's breathless report of Lydia's elopement, the trace of a more fully epistolary 'First Impressions', and there may be another such trace in the correspondence that Elizabeth maintains with Charlotte following Charlotte's move to Kent. The heroine's separation from one confidante or the other for most of the action suggests, as *Sense and Sensibility* never does, the structural preconditions of a novel in letters. If so, however, Austen was writing epistolary narrative of a complex, unreliable kind, requiring that it be read between the lines for lapses in candour or assessed in the light of distortions particular to each narrator. Charlotte's marriage makes her a guarded, self-censoring writer whose letters display nothing more illuminating than 'Mr Collins's picture of Hunsford and Rosings rationally softened' (p. 166). Jane

[10] George Austen to Thomas Cadell, 1 November 1797; Jane Austen to Cassandra Austen, 29 January 1813; both quoted in Pat Rogers's introduction to *PP*, pp. xxiv, xxx.

is a deficient narrator not only from personal reticence but from her trusting nature, and as Elizabeth notes of her letter about Wickham and his honourable intentions, '[n]o one but Jane ... could flatter herself with such an expectation' (p. 308). Elsewhere Austen is drawn to correspondence less as a vehicle of dramatic representation or psychological outpouring than as a medium of cool deception or covert attack: witness the 'high flown expressions' of Miss Bingley's letters to Jane, which Elizabeth assesses 'with all the insensibility of distrust' (p. 131), or Collins's knife-twisting letter of condolence on Lydia's disgrace, inserted with tension-snapping comic timing that rivals the porter scene in *Macbeth*. The need to treat letters as a slippery, inherently untrustworthy medium, always to be analysed or decoded with care, is nowhere more fully registered than in the chapter devoted to Elizabeth's obsessive, fluctuating reading of Darcy's letter, during which '[s]he studied every sentence: and her feelings towards its writer were at times widely different' (p. 235). In attempting to undo the damage of his botched proposal, this carefully meditated letter is among the most significant and enigmatic utterances in the book, still quietly reverberating – '"Did it," said he, "did it *soon* make you think better of me?"' (p. 408) – in the closing chapters.

Authority

Yet for all Austen's evident attraction to letters, if not as reliable narration or unstudied self-portraiture then as interpretative challenges for both characters and readers, *Pride and Prejudice* also exhibits some frustration with their use as narrative vehicles. When Bingley as letter-writer thinks it 'too much, to remember at night all the foolish things that were said in the morning' (p. 53), he echoes the kind of objection that had been made since Fielding's *Shamela* to the enabling conventions of epistolary novels, with their pseudo-instantaneous delivery of implausibly particularised reports. Such objections intensified markedly throughout Austen's lifetime, and despite its ongoing currency with circulating-library audiences the novel in letters was increasingly being disparaged or discarded by leading novelists. Burney, who never resumed the mode after *Evelina*, is herself an instance of this trend, and in *Northanger Abbey* it is Burney's non-epistolary fiction that Austen singles out for praise (*NA*, p. 31). A relevant later case is Walter Scott, who conspicuously abandons letter-narrative part-way through *Redgauntlet* (1824), citing not only its cumbersome and artificial nature but also, crucially, its lack of provision for objective or heterodiegetic narrative guidance. Even multi-voiced epistolary fiction, as Scott writes on shifting to a third-person mode, 'can seldom be found to contain all in which it is necessary to instruct the reader for his full comprehension of the story'.[11] Mischievously, Scott elsewhere describes an old lady who liked to have *Grandison* read to her above other novels '"because," said she, "should I drop asleep in course of the reading, I am sure when I awake, I shall have lost none of the story, but shall find the party, where I left them, *conversing in the cedar-parlour*"'.[12]

Austen's own fondness for the cedar parlour notwithstanding, much the same joke is implied by the effect of burlesque acceleration in 'Sir Charles Grandison', a manuscript playlet that is sometimes attributed directly to her, though probably composed under her guidance by a young niece. In a neat display of amused impatience, the glacial pace of Richardson's narrative is drastically quickened to the span of an afterpiece farce, with the same frenzy of staccato dialogue, hectic stagecraft – '*Exit Bridget, exit Mr. Reeves at different doors. – calls behind the Scenes –*' (*LM*, p. 560) – and arbitrary lurches of plot. The clunky infrastructure and rhetorical constraints of epistolary fiction may also underlie Austen's arch farewell to the genre and its conventions in the third-person 'Conclusion' to 'Lady Susan', which is often considered a later addition. In her teasing declaration that '[t]his Correspondence, by a meeting between some of the Parties & a separation between the others, could not, to the great detriment of the Post office Revenue, be continued longer' (*LM*, p. 75), one hears emerge the assured, urbane voice of the mature novels, decisively intervening in the final pages to clarify and resolve the plot. No longer is there a kinship with Richardson here, and instead Austen's words bear out Claude Rawson's sense that 'in her technical habits and presentational strategies, her deepest affinities were with Fielding'.[13] In particular, the passage recalls one of Fielding's sly digs against *Pamela* in *Joseph Andrews* (1742), a novel that uses a self-consciously artificial, wittily managerial style of third-person narration to showcase a technical alternative to Richardson's method. As Fielding writes with mock regret, *Joseph Andrews* could not be an epistolary novel for one insurmountable reason: 'and this was, that poor *Fanny* [the heroine of the work] could neither write nor read'.[14]

It is a commonplace of literary history that Austen's breakthrough achievement was to unite the divergent narrative techniques of Richardson and

---

[11] Walter Scott, *Redgauntlet*, ed. Kathryn Sutherland (Oxford University Press, 2011), p. 141.
[12] Ioan Williams (ed.), *Sir Walter Scott on Novelists and Fiction* (London: Routledge, 1968), p. 31.
[13] Claude Rawson, *Satire and Sentiment, 1660–1830: Stress Points in the English Augustan Tradition* (New Haven: Yale University Press, 1994), p. 279.
[14] Henry Fielding, *Joseph Andrews*, ed. Martin C. Battestin (Oxford: Clarendon Press, 1967), p. 49.

Fielding into a flexible heterodiegetic mode that could also convey the intimacy of homodiegetic introspection. As Dorrit Cohn puts it with reference to the style of presentation she calls 'narrated monologue', 'Austen seems precisely to cast the spirit of epistolary fiction into the mold of third-person narration.'[15] Yet Austen never wholly discards the more wilfully artificial side of Fielding's practice, notably his fondness for disrupting the illusion of natural narrative with self-conscious reminders of his shaping authorial presence. *Pride and Prejudice* contains no frame-breaking gesture as overt as Austen's joke about courtship novels and their compulsory outcomes in *Northanger Abbey*, where the heroine's uncertainty about the future 'can hardly extend, I fear, to the bosom of my readers, who will see in the tell-tale compression of the pages before them, that we are all hastening together to perfect felicity' (*NA*, p. 259). But several passages in the novel come close to this, including the emphatic authorial judgment of the final chapter, in which, writes Austen with belated, head-shaking frankness about Mrs Bennet, 'I wish I could say ... that the accomplishment of her earnest desire [in marrying off several daughters] produced so happy an effect as to make her a sensible, amiable, well-informed woman for the rest of her life' (*P&P*, p. 427).

For narrative theorists and literary historians who prize Austen as a pioneer of free indirect style, these are regrettable intrusions, blemishes in a method to be praised above all for its elimination of authorial personality. 'There is a narrator who is prominent as a story-teller and moralist', Roy Pascal concedes of Austen's novels, 'but who is (with rare lapses) non-personal, non-defined, and therefore may enjoy access to the most secret privacy of the characters.'[16] Yet these 'lapses' were for Austen an important part of her creative repertoire, and there is some evidence that she felt *Pride and Prejudice* committed too few, not least her well-known comment, plainly with *Tom Jones* in mind, that the novel 'wants to be stretched out here & there' with digressive or metafictional chapters 'that would form a contrast & bring the reader with increased delight to the playfulness & Epigrammatism of the general stile' (*Letters*, p. 212). Though Austen never fully replicates the insistent authorial first person (or 'second self') of Fielding's practice, neither does she discard this register as thoroughly as theoretical textbooks sometimes suggest. In their eagerness to correct readers who claim to hear throughout the novels the companionable voice of Jane, narratologists can sound somewhat robotic in their insistence on impersonal as opposed to authorial narration, or on narrative discourse as

---

[15] Dorrit Cohn, *Transparent Minds: Narrative Modes for Presenting Consciousness in Fiction* (Princeton University Press, 1984), p. 113.

[16] Roy Pascal, *The Dual Voice: Free Indirect Speech and Its Functioning in the Nineteenth-Century European Novel* (Manchester University Press, 1977), p. 45.

opposed to a narrating voice, not least in the rhetorical move of ungendering the narrator that is sometimes made. For Pascal, who refers to Austen's narrator as 'he' in contradistinction to the historical author, 'so truly is this impersonal narrator the "spirit of the story" that one cannot ascribe him/her a sex'. Mieke Bal is likewise mindful that '[t]he narrator of *Emma* is not Jane Austen' – happily, Bal admits that 'the historical person Jane Austen is not without importance' – and makes similarly heavy weather of the issue: 'I shall here and there refer to the narrator as "it," however odd this may seem.'[17] Extreme versions of this position allow the presence of no narrator at all, only narrative as an autonomous discourse, and while there are good theoretical reasons for maintaining the author/narrator distinction as an analytic tool, to clamp it too rigidly on prose of such delicate fluidity is to risk seeming tone-deaf. Bal and Pascal by no means share the obtuseness of the early reader who responded to the penetrating intelligence of Austen's voice by declaring *Pride and Prejudice* 'too clever to have been written by a woman'.[18] But they under-estimate the convergence or even identity between shaping author and narrat-ing persona that Austen from time to time implies – a convergence, in the light of the novels' title pages (*Pride and Prejudice* is 'By the Author of "Sense and Sensibility"'; *Sense and Sensibility* is 'By a Lady'), that makes the gender reassignments of theory look odd indeed.

At times this narrating voice is a clarifying presence, and provides readers with firm guidance in matters of interpretation and judgment. The first chapter of *Pride and Prejudice* ends with a brisk but lucid character sketch of the Bennet parents, and in Volume II the analysis is amplified with a careful blend of sympathy and severity that heralds the moralising wisdom of George Eliot. Abruptly, one of the novel's running comic motifs – in which Austen has made us complicit by our laughter – is here redefined as a serious and multi-faceted moral problem. Now we must understand the marriage in new terms, as a tragedy, self-inflicted by youthful imprudence, that has blighted Mr Bennet's life, and left 'all his views of domestic happiness ... overthrown'. Yet while recognising his predicament, and deploring the contemptible shallowness of his wife, we must also deplore, as dereliction of duty to the family as a whole, the consolation he takes in mockery and teasing; far from continuing to laugh with the husband, we should now condemn 'that continual breach of conjugal obligation and decorum which, in exposing his wife to the contempt of her own children, was so highly reprehensible' (*P&P*, pp. 262–3). Later still, Austen inserts a similarly rigorous analysis of the financial catch at the novel's

[17] Pascal, *Dual Voice*, p. 45; Mieke Bal, *Narratology: Introduction to the Theory of Narrative*, 3rd edn (University of Toronto Press, 2009), p. 15.

[18] Austen-Leigh, *Memoir*, p. 149.

heart, answering, with balanced fellow feeling and blame, essential but previously unarticulated questions about the Bennets' failure to defuse the ticking time-bomb of the entailed estate – 'for, of course, they were to have a son' (p. 340). Comparable moments of more or less intrusive explanation elsewhere bring even the most unsympathetic characters within the reach, if not of the narrator's compassion, then at least of her understanding, including the appalling Mr Collins (p. 78) and the vicious Miss Bingley (p. 298).

What makes moral analysis of this directness so arresting, however, is that it arises so infrequently, and as a rule also belatedly, only once readers have had scope to make assessments of their own from the direct, neutral evidence of dialogue and action. Even by Austen's standards elsewhere, *Pride and Prejudice* contains an unusually high proportion of unmediated dialogue, some of it presented with so little narrative intervention that – for all Austen's skill in equipping her characters with distinctive idiolects – it can even be unclear who is speaking at certain points. Rereading the text in its published form, Austen was struck by the paucity of inquits in her conversation scenes, commenting that 'a "said he" or a "said she" would sometimes make the Dialogue more immediately clear – but I do not write for such dull Elves "As have not a great deal of Ingenuity themselves"' (*Letters*, p. 210).

The rationale appended at this point (adapting Scott, who presents his poem *Marmion* (1808) as incomprehensible 'to that dull elf / Who cannot image to himself') says much about Austen's general preference for coaxing readers, in the absence of full authorial explanation, to interpret and evaluate for themselves. Though willing enough to give subtle, insightful assessments of her heroine's consciousness, as when we learn that 'Elizabeth, agitated and confused, rather *knew* that she was happy, than *felt* herself to be so' (*P&P*, p. 413), Austen's narrator is pointedly non-omniscient when it comes to Bingley or Darcy. Explanations of what these characters think or feel are scarce, with emphasis placed instead on the uncertainties posed to Elizabeth and Jane by their inscrutable conduct or cryptic words. Rather than instruct us in how to understand Darcy, the narrator instead reports, in patient but noncommittal style, the conflicting conjectures he inspires in those around him, or the puzzling external signs that make him 'difficult to understand' (p. 202). In a novel concerned above all with uncertainties about true character, with the unreliability of impressions and the elusiveness of explanations, Austen's reticence – which extends to withholding key information, even to active misdirection – becomes a central technique, replicating for readers the quandaries of the heroine, and making us undertake, like her, an effort of enquiry and discovery. For D. A. Miller, the novels in general are typified by 'pseudoclosures', solutions that turn out to be 'untrue, incomplete, or merely unconfirmed',[19] and in this process the explanatory mode of the Austen narrator leaves much still to be resolved.

Free indirect discourse (FID)

Commenting on Austen's preference for the implicit indications of reported conversation over explicit commentary and analysis, Virginia Woolf suggests that, had she lived and matured, '[s]he would have trusted less (this is already perceptible in *Persuasion*) to dialogue and more to reflection to give us a knowledge of her characters'.[20] Woolf does not unpack exactly what she means by 'reflection' here. But from Henry James's concept of the 'lucid reflector' to Monika Fludernik's account of 'reflectoral narrative',[21] the term denotes the narrative illusion through which objective, third-person discourse comes to express – as though infiltrated by, or emanating from – the intimate subjectivity of the character described. It is no longer accepted that this technique for filtering or focalising narrative through the consciousness of its subject, so central to the development of the modern novel, can simply be attributed to Austen as her own invention, though assertions of this kind are still sometimes made. Sporadic instances of free indirect style – indirect because mediating a character's speech or thought through the narrator's discourse; free because able to roam from viewpoint to viewpoint – have been found in seventeenth-century texts by La Fontaine and Behn, or more systematically in Richardson and Burney. As Ann Banfield suggests, it is impossible to establish a single point of origin for the method or trace its continuous evolution, and one needs to look instead to principles of grammar that make it broadly available and apparently natural.[22] That said, it remains hard to find before Austen, or after her until Flaubert, any comparably sustained exploitation of FID, and her novels beautifully illustrate the characteristic markers of the technique in both its simple (speech) and complex (thought) modes. These include, fundamentally, an absence or suspension of reporting clauses (he said that / she thought that), and the anomalous presence within third-person, past-tense discourse of linguistic features indicating a

[19] D. A. Miller, *Narrative and Its Discontents: Problems of Closure in the Traditional Novel* (Princeton University Press, 1989), p. 53.

[20] Virginia Woolf, *The Common Reader, First Series* (New York: Harcourt, Brace, 1925), p. 206.

[21] William Veeder and Susan M. Griffin (eds.), *The Art of Criticism: Henry James on the Theory and the Practice of Criticism* (University of Chicago Press, 1984), p. 473; Monika Fludernik, *Towards a 'Natural' Narratology* (London: Routledge, 1996), pp. 35–6.

[22] Ann Banfield, *Unspeakable Sentences: Narration and Representation in the Language of Fiction* (London: Routledge, 1982), pp. 225–56.

character's perspective and voice: features such as proximal deictics (now / here / tomorrow instead of then / there / the next day); temporally backshifted exclamations ('How differently did every thing now appear in which he was concerned!' (*P&P*, p. 229)); exclamatory questions ('What could be the meaning of it? – It was impossible to imagine' (p. 81)); unshifted modals ('She must own that she was tired of great houses' (p. 267)); syntactical informalities and fragments ('A few weeks, he believed' (p. 373)); character-specific locutions or intonations, especially colloquialisms and vulgarisms ('how shocking it was to have a bad cold, and how excessively they disliked being ill' (p. 38); 'it was much better worth looking at in the summer' (p. 184)).

FID is indeed at its most prominent in Austen's last novels, and its presence in *Northanger Abbey* has been used to argue for late revision of that work.[23] Even so, it is already a pervasive resource in *Pride and Prejudice*, most obviously as a way of catching in narrative prose the distinctive qualities of a character's speech – or often its distinctive inanities, since Austen was drawn to the technique not least for its satirical potential. Consider Mr Collins's first visit to Longbourn, which opens as detached, impersonal narration before shading into mocking ventriloquism:

> During dinner, Mr. Bennet scarcely spoke at all; but when the servants were withdrawn, he thought it time to have some conversation with his guest, and therefore started a subject in which he expected him to shine, by observing that he seemed very fortunate in his patroness. Lady Catherine de Bourgh's attention to his wishes, and consideration for his comfort, appeared very remarkable. Mr. Bennet could not have chosen better. Mr. Collins was eloquent in her praise. The subject elevated him to more than usual solemnity of manner, and with a most important aspect he protested that he had never in his life witnessed such behaviour in a person of rank — such affability and condescension, as he had himself experienced from Lady Catherine. She had been graciously pleased to approve of both the discourses, which he had already had the honour of preaching before her. She had also asked him twice to dine at Rosings, and had sent for him only the Saturday before, to make up her pool of quadrille in the evening. Lady Catherine was reckoned proud by many people he knew, but *he* had never seen any thing but affability in her ... She had even condescended to advise him to marry as soon as he could, provided he chose with discretion; and had once paid him a visit in his humble parsonage; where she had perfectly approved all the alterations he had been making, and had even vouchsafed to suggest some herself, — some shelves in the closets up stairs." (*P&P*, pp. 74–5)

---

[23] Narelle Shaw, 'Free Indirect Speech and Jane Austen's 1816 Revision of *Northanger Abbey*', *SEL* 30 (1990), pp. 591–601; see also Daniel P. Gunn, 'Free Indirect Discourse and Narrative Authority in *Emma*', *Narrative* 12 (2004), pp. 35–54.

Thanks to the preparation provided for this exquisite paragraph by Collins's introductory letter and Mr Bennet's amused response, it is easy to tune in here not only to Collins's unctuous voice, but first to that of Mr Bennet himself, whose mischievous prompt might almost be reconstructed verbatim from the second sentence. Austen then shifts into narrative summary ('Mr. Collins was eloquent ...') and reported speech ('he protested that ...') before indicating the onset of Collins's effusion with an interruptive dash and two of his favourite terms for the monstrous Lady Catherine (cf. p. 178: 'She is all affability and condescension'). From this point on the oleaginous wording, though rendered in the third person and backshifted in tense, is otherwise all Collins's own, as are the sentiments expressed. For of course there is nothing in the least 'gracious' about his patron or 'humble' about his parsonage, and these terms signify not reliable narrative evaluation but Collins's self-deluding weakness for obsequy and cliché.[24] By the end of the paragraph, devoted as it is in flatulent style ('vouchsafed') to supremely pointless information ('shelves in the closets'), the text is saturated by his speaking voice – so much so that the compositor who originally typeset the paragraph (if this was not a feature of Austen's manuscript) closed it with a stray quotation mark, though no quotation ever opens.[25]

It would take a longer chapter than this one to adumbrate the much more intricate effects that arise from Austen's use of free indirect thought, which, though developed in less sustained, psychologically probing ways than in *Emma* or *Persuasion*, is handled in *Pride and Prejudice* with greater mobility and range. Not only does the technique offer an intimacy of access to the heroine's consciousness and perception that had never been achieved in such vivid style outside epistolary fiction. With startling flexibility, Austen extends the effect of telepathic insight to other characters, allowing readers to experience the world of the novel kaleidoscopically as well as from within, and to look out by turns from multiple perspectives, albeit in fleeting ways, and with blind spots. In a narrative designed to reproduce for readers the uncertainties of Elizabeth and her sister, Darcy, Bingley and Wickham are the marked exclusions, though even in the case of the enigmatic Darcy Austen

[24] 'Humble abode', which Collins uses twice in the conversation that follows, was already a grating cliché by Austen's day, though of uncertain origin. The likeliest source is Elizabeth Rowe's much-reprinted poem of 1704, 'A Pastoral on the Nativity of Our Saviour' ('But see the humble Seat, the poor Abode') – in which case Collins is implicitly comparing his house to the birthplace of Christ.

[25] For illustrative purposes I restore this closing mark (from Rogers's table of emendations in *PP*, p. 433) in the quotation above. On the uncertain status of accidentals in *Pride and Prejudice* (which one witness thought 'wretchedly printed, and so pointed as to be almost unintelligible') see Kathryn Sutherland, *Jane Austen's Textual Lives: From Aeschylus to Bollywood* (Oxford University Press, 2005), p. 303.

occasionally inflects the narrative with his voice, as in his mortifying recognition of Elizabeth's beautiful eyes and 'uncommonly intelligent' expression (*P&P*, p. 26). For William Nelles, who uses the term 'thinking parts' by analogy with the 'speaking parts' of a play, *Pride and Prejudice* filters its narrative through nineteen such thinking parts, more than any other Austen novel (*Mansfield Park*, at thirteen, is the nearest competitor).[26] Yet categorical analysis of this kind can be something of an illusion, for in Austen's hands the effect of free indirect thought is as often one of blending and blurring as of clear-cut counterpoint. By merging the idiolect of a character with a narrator's syntax, by darting from viewpoint to viewpoint in adjacent sentences, and by studding passages of objective description with clause-length fragments of FID, Austen constantly problematises the origin and authority of her narrative statements. It is for this reason that theoreticians routinely talk of the dual or composite voice in FID: a voice that sometimes suggests harmonious alignment of perspective between character and narrator, but sometimes a more disruptive effect of irony or indeterminacy. In the signature technique of her fiction, and in the deft fusion she achieves of Richardsonian interiority with Fieldingesque control, Austen remains at her most teasing as a writer, and at her most resistant to the dullness of elves.

[26] William Nelles, 'Omniscience for Atheists: or, Jane Austen's Infallible Narrator', *Narrative* 14 (2006), pp. 118–31 (p. 120).

2

ROBERT MILES

Character

'Character' is one of the language's more complex words. Besides fictional figures it encompasses an orthographic letter, a reference, moral standing, bent of mind, personality, or appearance. To understand the character of character in *Pride and Prejudice* we need to employ the word in all of the above senses. The reason Austen tests our critical mettle is that she is the great pioneer of character in the English novel, providing us with, not just characters we can understand and sympathise with, but personalities capable of taking up residence in our minds, where they flourish. While there are many factors in Austen's current popularity, a dominant one is surely her capacity to create the illusion of personality. *Pride and Prejudice* is particularly interesting in this regard, as it is the last novel of her first phase, the culmination of a twenty-year apprenticeship in the art of characterisation.

Alongside 'personality' and 'character' we need to set 'mind' in order to understand fully how Austen develops character, and to what ends:

> Mr. Bennet was so odd a mixture of quick parts, sarcastic humour, reserve, and caprice, that the experience of three-and-twenty years had been insufficient to make his wife understand his character. *Her* mind was less difficult to develop. She was a woman of mean understanding, little information, and uncertain temper. When she was discontented, she fancied herself nervous. The business of her life was to get her daughters married; its solace was visiting and news. *(P&P, p. 5)*

At first glance 'character' and 'mind' appear mere synonyms, an obvious segue that avoids awkward repetition. A second glance may give us pause. In the history of fictional representations there is a general movement from characters signifying a ruling passion, humour, vice, or virtue, to a more complex psychology. The point seemed settled enough for E. M. Forster to theorise the difference between flat characters (usually comic) and rounded, serious ones; or, if you will, between 'character' and 'mind', the former signifying a comic humour where behaviour is predictable, and the latter a layered self, where it isn't. We might therefore surmise that the order should be reversed. Mrs Bennet seems the obvious candidate for 'character', meaning a caricature in the grip of her presiding passions (greed, envy and jealousy), whereas 'mind' should modify Mr Bennet, the unreadable surface of his capricious and sarcastic behaviour registering a more deeply considered view of the world, along with a more subtle interplay between the passions. On a second reading of the novel the original order may seem appropriate after all. Despite his sarcasm, sharp perception and quick wit, Mr Bennet fails the test of 'mind'.

It was the philosopher Gilbert Ryle who first drew attention to the significance of 'mind' in Austen. He felt that her use of the word was peculiarly modern, albeit deriving, ultimately, from the seventeenth-century English moralist, the third Earl of Shaftesbury.[1] If true, this attribution is doubly noteworthy. First, it helps us understand a peculiar feature of Austen's novels: the moment of recognition and reversal, in her comic plots, turns on a moment of partial self-understanding. Second, it puts us on the path for understanding why knowing one's own mind is so difficult in Austen.

Shaftesbury reformulates the Socratic – Christianised – 'know thyself' as 'divide your-self'. Such self-division is private, and inward: one revolves back into oneself, dividing the self into two parties, with one gaining the ascendancy over the other, in point of wisdom. Through such a process a clearer moral understanding would be reached, as in this inner conversation no man would willingly appear a knave to himself.[2] In the presence of another, pride and vanity may snare us into self-deception; before our better self, such dodges aren't possible. Shaftesbury calls this process a 'soliloquy'. It is a process in which one comes to know one's own mind – one's better, more virtuous mind. On this view self-knowledge is a process, not a product: we know ourselves only to the extent that we keep this disciplined soliloquy going. Any moment of self-understanding must therefore be partial and provisional.

Following on from the work of Ryle, the Scottish moral philosopher Alasdair MacIntyre makes the case for why knowing one's own mind is so difficult in Austen, a difficulty arising from her status as one of the last significant moralists in the Aristotelian tradition.[3] Aristotelianism, MacIntyre argues, was entrenched in the pre-philosophical background of Western culture. It was a

[1] Gilbert Ryle, 'Jane Austen and the Moralists', *Oxford Review* 1 (1966), pp. 5–18.
[2] Peter Smith (ed.), *Characteristics of Men, Manners, Opinions, Times*, by A. A. C. Shaftesbury, 2 vols. (Gloucester, MA: Smith, 1963), vol. 1, pp. 113 and 115.
[3] Alasdair MacIntyre, *After Virtue*, 3rd edition (Notre Dame, IN: University of Notre Dame Press, 2007), p. 240.

framework one could know, without directly knowing Aristotle.[4] Ryle and MacIntyre both speculate the direct link might be through Shaftesbury, a key figure in Anglican literary culture. MacIntyre identifies three essential parts of the Aristotelian structure: 'untutored human-nature-as-it-happens-to-be, human-nature-as-it-could-be-if-it-realized-its-*telos*, and the precepts of rational ethics as the means for the transition from one to the other'.[5] This structure remained the same, whatever the religious form imposed upon it. While this framework was fatally damaged in the course of the Enlightenment, it survived in the Anglican culture that nurtured Austen.

By '*telos*' Aristotle means the ends towards which it is our nature to strive, so that we fully realise our nature, by realising these ends. While *telos* signifies the ends to which we strive, their attainment is not once and for all: rather it is a process always in the present continuous. One way of thinking about the selfhood of Austen's heroines, and the narrative arc of her fictions, is that the latter follows the inner potential of her heroines observed in the process of self-realisation. The arc does not terminate in the moment in which the heroine (mistakenly) believes she now knows herself, but in the moment in which the heroine's *telos* is finally 'realised', in pretty much every sense that word can bear (illumination, making real, and being instantiated as property).

MacIntyre historically locates Austen within the history of the division of labour that accompanied the rise of capitalism, especially that gendered aspect of it where women ceased to labour alongside men, with a small minority lifted into leisure, and the majority falling into different forms of drudgery. 'Her heroines must, if they are to survive, seek for economic security. But this is not just because of the threat of the outside economic world; it is because the *telos* of her heroines is a life within both a particular kind of marriage and a particular kind of household of which that marriage will be the focal point.' It is the notion of the household that gives Austen's novels their symbolic reach: 'Her heroines seek the good through seeking their own good in marriage. The restricted households of Highbury and Mansfield Park have to serve as surrogates for the Greek city-state and the medieval kingdom.'[6] As the Anglican priest Michael Giffin has argued, in Anglican theology there is crucial overlap between the notion of a household, parish, and wider community (implicating, at its widest, the nation).[7] Through realising their *telos* in a particular, virtuous, kind of marriage the heroine simultaneously redeems and renews the community (of which *Mansfield Park*

[4] Ibid., p. 52.   [5] Ibid., p. 53.   [6] Ibid., pp. 239, 240.
[7] Michael Giffin, *Jane Austen and Religion: Salvation and Society in Georgian England* (Basingstoke, Hants., and New York: Palgrave Macmillan, 2002).

is the obvious example), while failing to do so has consequences equally grave (and here we naturally think of *Emma*).

MacIntyre's reading of Austen has several consequences for how we might think about character in *Pride and Prejudice*. As he notes, Austen's primary virtue is 'constancy'. MacIntyre links this to another consequence of Aristotelian ethics, the importance of regarding the self as a narrative unity. Modernism, by way of contrast, privileges the aesthetic: thus Kierkegaard, who 'argued that the aesthetic life is one in which a human life is dissolved into a series of separate present moments in which the unity of a human life disappears from view'. As we shall see, the perils of the 'aesthetic' life loom large in Austen. 'By contrast in the ethical life the commitments and responsibilities to the future springing from past episodes in which obligations were conceived and debts assumed unite the present to past and to future in such a way as to make of human life a unity.'[8] Constancy, in Austen, is the virtue of striving to live one's life as if it were a unity, where decisions have moment and consequence as a measure of that which takes us closer to, or further from, our *telos*.

The second cardinal virtue MacIntyre notes in Austen is amiability, which she distinguishes from 'agreeableness', a false virtue implying mere show, or deceptive policy, a quality taken to self-defeating lengths by the egregious Mr Collins. Amiability, on the contrary, refers to a genuine, Christian openness to our fellows. When Elizabeth Bennet tearfully defends Darcy before her father's inquisitive gaze, the superlative she reaches for is that he is 'perfectly amiable' (*P&P*, pp. 417–18).

In Aristotle's system practical reason is brought to the fore: the moral sense is exercised, not by the hypothetical consideration of what we should do in any given situation, but through the act of making decisions as circumstances press upon us in all their concrete complexity. As numerous critics have noted, in her first two novels Austen sets up distinctions (sense and sensibility, pride and prejudice) she eventually dissolves.[9] We might think Darcy proud, and Elizabeth prejudiced, in that she is defensive about the haughtiness she projects onto him; but what is this defensiveness but another expression of pride? And isn't Darcy's hauteur naturally founded on prejudice? As this binary breaks down, Austen introduces new ones, each tested against hard circumstance. This proliferating complexity is an aspect of Austen's practical reason.

---

[8] MacIntyre, *After Virtue*, p. 242.
[9] In addition to Ryle, see Claudia L. Johnson, *Jane Austen: Women, Politics, and the Novel* (University of Chicago Press, 1988) and Marilyn Butler, *Jane Austen and the War of Ideas* (Oxford: Clarendon Press, 1975; 2nd edn 1987).

As Elizabeth discovers, she has been thinking through the wrong binary. Paradoxically it is the theoretical Mary (all precept, no practice) who supplies the correct one: 'A person may be proud without being vain. Pride relates more to our opinion of ourselves, vanity to what we would have others think of us' (*P&P*, p. 21). We are apt to remember the narrator's dismissal of Mary's book-learned, 'thread-bare morality' (p. 67), and we may easily imagine Elizabeth letting this remark pass her by, eyes momentarily lifted skyward, but the lesson is precisely the one she needs; it is also the one she learns, and acknowledges, in her first flicker of self-knowledge and self-rebuke, on reading Darcy's self-explanatory letter with its home truths: in the midst of self-mortification, Elizabeth exclaims to herself, 'But vanity, not love, has been my folly' (p. 230).

Austen carefully sets the scene for her heroine's reversal, in the process laying a trap for the reader, who has been subtly misled by the narrative's sly focalisation through the mind (and perspective) of the heroine. Elizabeth labours under her illusions, and so do we:

> 'Mr. Darcy is not to be laughed at!' cried Elizabeth. 'That is an uncommon advantage, and uncommon I hope it will continue, for it would be a great loss to me to have many such acquaintance. I dearly love a laugh.'
>
> 'Miss Bingley,' said he, 'has given me credit for more than can be. The wisest and the best of men – nay, the wisest and best of their actions – may be rendered ridiculous by a person whose first object in life is a joke.'
>
> 'Certainly,' replied Elizabeth – 'there are such people, but I hope I am not one of *them*. I hope I never ridicule what is wise or good. Follies and nonsense, whims and inconsistencies, *do* divert me, I own, and I laugh at them whenever I can. But these, I suppose, are precisely what you are without.'
>
> 'Perhaps that is not possible for any one. But it has been the study of my life to avoid those weaknesses which often expose a strong understanding to ridicule.'
>
> 'Such as vanity and pride.'
>
> 'Yes, vanity is a weakness indeed. But pride – where there is a real superiority of mind, pride will be always under good regulation.'
>
> Elizabeth turned away to hide a smile.   (*P&P*, pp. 62–3)

Elizabeth's failure to discriminate between vanity and pride is surely a part of her inattentiveness, a discrimination repeated by Darcy, but with the addition of the crucial, missing element from Mary's homily: 'real superiority of mind'. As we turn to smile with Elizabeth at Darcy's self-conceit, an important truth passes us by: there is danger in the pleasure Elizabeth takes in making sport of her acquaintance. The lesson is there before her, in her father.

As the reader quickly gathers, Mr Bennet is a charming, witty, hopeless parent. From MacIntyre's Aristotelian perspective, or Giffin's Anglican one, this hopelessness is aggravated by his abdication of authority within, and responsibility for, the household; it is a feckless turning aside from his Christian duty, and *telos*.[10] His dereliction resides, not in failing to beget a male heir, but in nurturing his private pleasure at the expense of his obligations to his wife and children. His duty is to curb his wife's silliness while helping his daughters preserve their 'respectability' (*P&P*, p. 263) in anticipation of their possible future indigence. Instead, he retreats into his study, into irony and its pleasures. Here is Mr Bennet on meeting Mr Collins (the point to recall is not that Collins is the heir of Longbourn, but that Mr Bennet is for the first time confronting the uncomfortable truth of his family's situation in its concrete form):

> Mr. Bennet's expectations were fully answered. His cousin was as absurd as he had hoped, and he listened to him with the keenest enjoyment, maintaining at the same time the most resolute composure of countenance, and, except in an occasional glance at Elizabeth, requiring no partner in his pleasure.
>
> (*P&P*, p. 76)

Of course his sarcasms are immensely enjoyable, in the manner of worldly epigrams: 'For what do we live, but to make sport for our neighbours, and laugh at them in our turn?' (p. 403). We are also apt to approve of Mr Bennet, because Elizabeth is his favourite, and because she is clearly her father's daughter. Darcy's infamous snub leads to the first real bit of information about Elizabeth's character: 'Mr. Darcy walked off; and Elizabeth remained with no very cordial feelings towards him. She told the story, however, with great spirit among her friends; for she had a lively, playful disposition, which delighted in any thing ridiculous' (p. 12).

Irony is the rock on which Elizabeth's own story may founder, her life's unity breaking up into the fleeting pleasures of the ironic consciousness, finding delight where it can, in a disconnected series. It is this temptation of the aesthetic life – the life of distance, detachment, and irony – that connects Elizabeth with her father, or other Austenian ironists, most notably *Mansfield Park*'s Mary Crawford. Self-introspection, in this context, amounts to recognising the slippery glozing of the ironic consciousness, with its subtle self-flatteries. When Elizabeth tells us she dearly loves a laugh at the expense of her acquaintance, she does more than set up the prolepsis to her father's analeptic comments about neighbours as a source of sport; she evinces, concretely, the dangers of her hubris.

Elizabeth's peril is evident in her light sparring with Darcy. When Darcy counters with the serious point that even the 'wisest and the best of men ... may be rendered ridiculous' by the determined ironist, Elizabeth defends

---

[10] MacIntyre, *After Virtue*, p. 239.

herself by saying she hopes that she never ridicules 'what is wise or good' (*P&P*, p. 62). But that presupposes she knows the difference, a presumption that very much speaks to her intellectual pride.

We are now ready to look more closely at Elizabeth's moment of *éclaircissement* that follows on from her reading of Darcy's letter in which he seeks to justify his actions. He writes – and this too is significant – because his 'character' requires it to be 'written and read' (p. 218). At first she is inclined to regard Darcy's account of his actions in ending Bingley's attachment to Jane as more of his 'pride and insolence' (p. 226) – but then her 'strong prejudice' begins to break down as she reads his account of Wickham, which she realises, to her mounting horror, is ungainsayable. In that context, Darcy's justification of his actions regarding Jane – that she displayed no evidence of deep attachment – gathers credibility, forcing Elizabeth's admission that Jane's complaisant demeanour could mislead. A second reading reveals how deep the mortification should go. As Wickham dangles the bait of his slow, amorous, reluctant character assassination of Darcy, we read: 'Elizabeth found the interest of the subject increase, and listened with all her heart; but the delicacy of it prevented farther inquiry' (p. 88). This is probably free indirect discourse; it is certainly impossible to say that it isn't. With that possibility, the ambiguity of 'all her heart' comes alive, as either simply a routine expression of eagerness, a narrator's pat phrase, or as Elizabeth's own telling expression of desire, a summoning of all that is ignoble in her character, fuelled by her wounded vanity, so that she wholeheartedly swallows scuttle-butt. In that moment, she is gripped by malice. If we have not recalled this deadly little piece of narratorial equivocation, Elizabeth evidently does:

> She grew absolutely ashamed of herself. – Of neither Darcy nor Wickham could she think without feeling she had been blind, partial, prejudiced, absurd.
>
> 'How despicably I have acted!' she cried. – 'I, who have prided myself on my discernment! – I, who have valued myself on my abilities! who have often disdained the generous candour of my sister, and gratified my vanity in useless or blameable mistrust! – How humiliating is this discovery! – Yet, how just a humiliation! – Had I been in love, I could not have been more wretchedly blind! But vanity, not love, has been my folly. – Pleased with the preference of one, and offended by the neglect of the other, on the very beginning of our acquaintance, I have courted prepossession and ignorance, and driven reason away, where either were concerned. Till this moment I never knew myself.' (*P&P*, p. 230)

The first thing to be said about this passage is that it is a 'soliloquy', Shaftesbury's term for the practice of self-division, with Elizabeth dividing herself into a better and worse self, with the worse arraigned before the better. The second is that self-knowledge is couched entirely in ethical terms: she reprobates her 'self' for failing to see others as they really are owing to her attachment to the selfish pleasures of 'vanity' and 'mistrust', character flaws linked to her failure to appreciate properly the true value of her sister's amiability (her 'candour'). Elizabeth's 'vanity' and 'mistrust' both flow from her aesthetic self, her habit of looking for the 'ridiculous' in her acquaintance for the self-gratification it affords of scoffing at it, a habit derived from her father who develops his, we are told, with the overthrow of 'all his views of domestic happiness' (p. 262), thus ending any commitment to seeing his life as a narrative (he now simply attends upon events). Pessimism, in short, is one of Elizabeth's principal vices, an aspect of her prejudiced, and, barring Calvinists, un-Christian view of the world. As she explains to her sister, 'The more I see of the world, the more am I dissatisfied with it; and every day confirms my belief of the inconsistency of all human characters, and of the little dependence that can be placed on the appearance of either merit or sense' (p. 153). Thirdly, Elizabeth still does not yet fully know her own mind.

And that is because in Austen knowing one's own mind is bound up with discerning one's *telos*, with knowing one's true place, nature, and purpose. And for Elizabeth, the developing of mind is bound up with the development of Darcy's character, but also, as MacIntyre would style it, his *character*. The central qualities of MacIntyre's theory of *character* are that *characters* are nodal points within the general background that help bring into expression 'a whole cluster of attitudes and activities' and that they 'were able to discharge this function precisely because they incorporated moral and metaphysical theories and claims'. Furthermore, 'the requirements of a *character* are imposed from the outside, from the way in which others use and regard *characters* to understand and evaluate themselves'. A *character*, then, is a public figure or archetype that 'morally legitimates a mode of social existence'; in Darcy's case, the *character* he shadows forth is that of the idealised Tory landowner.[11]

As the novel wraps up, Elizabeth teases Jane by telling her that she 'must date' her love for Darcy from 'my first seeing his beautiful grounds at Pemberley' (*P&P*, p. 414). It is part of Austen's psychological realism that she never loses sight of base, material motivation – a point honoured, not just in Charlotte's marriage to Mr Collins, but in having Elizabeth give the first inklings of her changing feeling by expressing regret, not for the man, but for his house: 'And of this place ... I might have been mistress' (p. 272). Even so,

---

[11] Ibid., pp. 29–30. MacIntyre's list of modern *characters* include the manager, rich aesthete and therapist; the 'landowner' is my example of a historically appropriate *character* for Austen; I would also add the 'sailor' and 'clergyman'. For the ideological meanings of the Tory landowner, see Beth Fowkes Tobin, 'The Moral and Political Economy of Property in Austen's *Emma*', *Eighteenth-Century Fiction* 2 (1990), pp. 229–54.

the joke is unusually accurate, for Elizabeth does indeed first become acquainted with her love on viewing Darcy's 'beautiful grounds': 'She had never seen a place for which nature had done more, or where natural beauty had been so little counteracted by an awkward taste' (p. 271). More than landscape fashion, the proper management of the estate embodied central questions about social relations.[12] In addition to being desirable property Pemberley stirs Elizabeth because it offers clues to Darcy's character and virtues.

Encompassing the first chapter of the third, concluding volume of the novel, Elizabeth's encounter with the physical representations of Darcy's character marks the beginning of the denouement, the unknotting of the lovers' feelings for each other. Each representation speaks to Darcy's virtues. From the grounds of Pemberley we move inside, where Elizabeth admires the 'taste' of the décor, which was 'neither gaudy nor uselessly fine' (p. 272), words in pointed contrast to the vulgar, aristocratic décor of Lady Catherine de Bourgh's Rosings. We are next shown the miniatures of Wickham and Darcy, followed by Miss Darcy's room, which evinces the loving attention of her brother. We then move to verbal representations as the housekeeper provides Darcy with a 'flaming character' (p. 285), as Mrs Gardiner calls it: no woman is good enough for him; he was always 'the sweetest tempered, most generous-hearted, boy in the world'; and then the *coup de grâce*: 'He is the best landlord, and the best master ... that ever lived' (p. 276).

They next move upstairs to view the gallery of family portraits: in the process, they move from the miniatures, where Wickham and Darcy are on a par, to a portrait in which Darcy is now larger than life, dwarfing Wickham, magnified in Elizabeth's mind by all of these representations of Darcy's superior character:

> At last it arrested her – and she beheld a striking resemblance of Mr. Darcy, with such a smile over the face as she remembered to have sometimes seen when he looked at her ...
>
> There was certainly at this moment, in Elizabeth's mind, a more gentle sensation towards the original than she had ever felt in the height of their acquaintance. The commendation bestowed on him by Mrs. Reynolds was of no trifling nature. What praise is more valuable than the praise of an intelligent servant? As a brother, a landlord, a master, she considered how many people's happiness were in his guardianship! – How much of pleasure or pain it was in his power to bestow! – How much of good or evil must be done by him! Every idea that had been brought forward by the housekeeper was favourable to his

[12] A. M. Duckworth, *The Improvement of the Estate: A Study of Jane Austen's Novels* (Baltimore: Johns Hopkins University Press, 1994).

character, and as she stood before the canvas, on which he was represented, and fixed his eyes upon herself, she thought of his regard with a deeper sentiment of gratitude than it had ever raised before; she remembered its warmth, and softened its impropriety of expression. (*P&P*, p. 277)

Largely free indirect discourse, the passage opens out on Elizabeth's developing mind; it is also an amazingly complex, and suggestive, piece of writing. Returning to MacIntyre's notion of a *character* will further enrich the reading, providing an explanation, as it does, for why Elizabeth's falling in love should be mediated through thoughts about her lover's role in the social network.

In Austen's fiction, the most idealised version of the landowner *character* is found in Mr Knightley, the perusal of whose grounds induces a vision in Emma that makes it transparently clear that Donwell Abbey is not just itself, but a synecdoche for an idealised England: 'It was a sweet view – sweet to the eye and the mind. English verdure, English culture, English comfort, seen under a sun bright, without being oppressive' (*E*, p. 391). In the self-same way, the household of Pemberley is a synecdoche for the nation in its idealised form. To be mistress of it involves more than luxurious pleasures (although there are those): to be its proper mistress is to embrace a *telos* that involves a vision of the virtues, of the privileges but also of the obligations and responsibilities extending from family, to community, to country.

Elizabeth comes to understand that in Darcy character, and *character*, coincide, are 'fused', as MacIntyre puts it, as false reports and impressions are dissipated, first by Darcy's own self-representation (his letter), and then by the positive representations of his household. It is these frameworks of understanding that she brings to Darcy's portrait, investing it with meaning: 'At last it arrested her – and she beheld a striking resemblance of Mr. Darcy, with such a smile over the face as she remembered to have sometimes seen when he looked at her.' She is here using and regarding Darcy's *character* as a landowner to understand and evaluate herself: 'As a brother, a landlord, a master, she considered how many people's happiness were in his guardianship!' The unspoken thought is that as his wife, and Pemberley's mistress, she too would be the responsible guardian of her own, and others', happiness, including that of her otherwise unprotected family. She is here coming to understand what her true *telos* is, as opposed to the siren call of irony and aesthetic distance. 'There was certainly at this moment, in Elizabeth's mind, a more gentle sensation towards the original than she had ever felt in the height of their acquaintance.' It is highly unusual in Austen for minds to register sensations rather than ideas. The expression speaks to the inchoate nature of Elizabeth's feelings, and that she does not quite yet understand her own mind, which must wait upon the realisation of what her life is for.

The realisation of her *telos* is bound up in the word 'regard' in the passage just quoted. On first reading the sentence (beginning 'Every idea...') seems to be saying that Elizabeth was grateful for Darcy's love, for his deep regard for her; but the predicates (warmth, impropriety) appear to be modifying the physical vehicle of that regard, his facial expression, now softened from her former misattribution of cool hauteur. This is, then, an imaginary regard, one projected by Elizabeth back onto the portrait. As she regards the picture, with its 'eyes fixed upon herself', she imagines herself caught within the actual Darcy's gaze, feeling softened, moved by his *character* (which she simultaneously projects). And a key feature of this imaginary person under whose gaze she finds herself hailed, is that he is someone who elicits gratitude for having given his regard – which considering his character as landowner includes the fulfilment of social obligation, when he, meaningfully, pays his regards. The gentle sensation in her mind is thus a prelude to knowing her own mind, including her love; but it is one thoroughly mediated by the Aristotelian framework of morality that bodies it forth. The realisation of her *telos* thus comes as an illumination as she regards Darcy's portrait; the appreciation of his household as a locus of social relations, grounding it, makes it 'real'; and in becoming mistress of Pemberley, her *telos* is realised as property.

On hearing of Lydia's delivery from seduction Elizabeth considers how 'neither *rational happiness* nor worldly prosperity could be justly expected for her sister' (*P&P*, p. 339; my italics). Elizabeth, of course, may look forward to both; as such she triangulates another binary, between the heedless Lydia, and the overly heedful Charlotte Lucas; the one reckless of self, the other, possibly, insufficiently so; both irrational, one in the conventional fashion, the other, paradoxically, through too much 'reason'. From MacIntyre's perspective, what makes Elizabeth's happiness 'rational' is that it is firmly orientated by *telos*, being in line with her 'nature'. In the ideal companionate marriage with Darcy she is free to be herself, her wittiness framed (both enabled and restricted) by her mistress-ship of an ethically freighted household whose size is commensurate with the virtues she embodies.

However, there is another reading of 'rational' available, one advanced by Vivien Jones.[13] Jones argues that *Pride and Prejudice* is a carefully judged, post-revolutionary novel: one that dialectically weighs antithetical positions emerging out of the revolutionary tumult, before forming its own, careful synthesis, one sceptical of revolutionary fervour, yet not at peace with the reactionary temper driving the war effort. While numerous voices are

---

[13] Vivien Jones (ed.), 'Introduction', *Pride and Prejudice* (Harmondsworth, Middlesex: Penguin, 1995), pp. vii–xxvii.

involved, Mary Wollstonecraft and Hannah More typify the antithetical positions, the former critiquing the irrational sensuality embedded in prevailing gender stereotypes, the latter glorifying the power delegated to women by these same gender roles in making woman the mistress of the household, a power wielded through chaste femininity.

When Elizabeth tartly commands Mr Collins – in mid proposal – to 'not consider me now as an elegant female, intending to plague you, but as a rational creature, speaking the truth from her heart' (*P&P*, p. 122), she is siding with Wollstonecraft against More and the conduct books, whose views are represented in the novel by Collins himself and Mary Bennet. Indeed, in her sallies, impertinent wit and irrepressible sense of self, Elizabeth offends nearly every point of the self-denying propriety championed by More. But in coming to focus her life's happiness entirely through marriage, Elizabeth offends against Wollstonecraft, in the process embodying More's vision of the virtuous female as the mistress of the household, and thus a 'mother of the nation'.[14] While Austen's position is dialectically related to More's and Wollstonecraft's, it is identifiable with neither, being, characteristically, 'betwixt-and-between'.[15]

From the point of view of Austen's characterisation, it is important to see how Elizabeth's sisters and acquaintance operate as minor characters throwing her own into relief. Mary talks like a conduct book; Lydia (and her mother) are the epitome of the feminine stereotype decried by Wollstonecraft, agog at the sight of an officer, without, apparently, a rational thought in their heads; while Charlotte Lucas may be considered a version of the heroine removed from the structure of desire that is the comic plot, and placed in hard, unbending, compromise-inducing reality. What all these characters have in common is lack of the wherewithal to know their own minds. Austen never explains where this 'wherewithal' comes from; it is, rather, a given of her heroines. The process of knowing their own minds is contained by the moral frameworks deeply embedded in the 'background' of Austen's time. The conflict between these frameworks and the heroine's refractory desires provides both the interest of the plot and the complexity of characterisation that comes across to us as the illusion of personality, our sense that we, somehow, know these characters. The unstated peril of the heroines is that they will fail the challenge posed by the redeeming *telos* the novel imagines for them (in becoming mistress of a richly metonymic household) and lapse into 'caricature', in the manner of Elizabeth's father, whose ironies descend into self-parody.

[14] Anne K. Mellor, *Mothers of the Nation: Women's Political Writing in England 1780–1830* (Bloomington: Indiana University Press, 2002).
[15] See Butler, *Jane Austen*, pp. 2 and 165.

3

PETER KNOX-SHAW

Philosophy

Austen's novels contain dissonances so jarring, a critic argued during the Second World War, that they pass unperceived by devotees of the anodyne Jane. The quotation from *Emma* on which D. W. Harding built his case was lifted from the sketch of Miss Bates, the penurious spinster who enjoys great popularity in her circle despite a lack of obvious assets:

> Miss Bates stood in the very worst predicament in the world for having much of the public favour; and she had no intellectual superiority to make atonement to herself, or frighten those who might hate her, into outward respect.   (*E*, p. 20)

For a generation of readers the last clause, if it did not wholly answer Virginia Woolf's challenge of catching Jane Austen in the act of greatness, served at least to capture a tartness and tough-mindedness essential to her art. Harding took the intellectual superior, better equipped to exact respect, as a ghost of the author, and biography is central to the essay he so memorably entitled 'Regulated Hatred'. Indeed the hatred of which he speaks is transferred from the textual spinster who is its object to Jane Austen herself, a writer who reserves her rancour for the perennially hateful, but with a containment that is subject to 'outlets not fully within her conscious control'.[1]

Unnoticed by Harding, the paragraph holding the notorious clause engages in a particular form of philosophical discourse, widespread by the late eighteenth century, that owes much to the writings of David Hume. Miss Bates, both as agent and recipient, demonstrates the social working of sympathy, and the reader's sympathies are implicated too, for the flattering invitation to consider someone cleverer in her circumstances is tactical, anticipating Knightley's words to Emma at Box Hill on the need to appreciate the 'character, age, and situation' of the friend she has abused (*E*, p. 407). Crucially, Miss Bates's self-esteem is seen to depend on the attitudes displayed towards her in Highbury,

---

[1] D. W. Harding, 'Regulated Hatred', in *Jane Austen: Critical Essays*, ed. Ian Watt (Englewood Cliffs, NJ: Spectrum Books, 1963), pp. 179, 173.

where her unfavourable predicament, far from drawing an unfavourable response, is counteracted by her exceptional good-will, which not only works 'wonders' on her acquaintance, but proves a 'mine of felicity to herself'. Wholly apposite here are remarks made by Hume on the redeeming effects of good-will in his discussion of benevolence from the *Enquiry Concerning the Principles of Morals* (1751). While superheroes are graced (or mercifully tamed) by the social virtues, those of 'more ordinary talents' need them:

> there being nothing eminent, in that case, to compensate for the want of them, or preserve the person from our severest hatred, as well as contempt.[2]

In the *Morals* benevolence replaces Hume's earlier choice of sympathy as the founding virtue, and yet takes on something of its character, transfusing itself, as he says, into the beholder who responds in kind, for 'to love others, will almost infallibly procure love and esteem, which are the chief circumstances in life'.[3]

Jane Austen similarly points to an almost magical reciprocity in the way Miss Bates's quick-sighted attentiveness to everybody's happiness ensures that she is herself a 'happy woman, and a woman whom no one named without good-will'. But in *Emma* we are reminded that such cheerful confederacy can be unravelled at a stroke, even by the expression of a single cruel impulse from an advocate of 'general benevolence' (*E*, p. 346). Indeed, the uneasy coexistence of natural virtue with deep-seated antagonisms is basic to the vision of both writers. If Austen is a novelist who writes about pride, contempt and hatred with supreme authority, it is because she shares Hume's understanding that 'pride and hatred invigorate',[4] and that human beings can accordingly be expected to hate wherever they can. Hume concludes his *Morals* with the plea 'that there is some benevolence, however small, infused into our bosoms; some spark of friendship for human kind; some particle of the dove, kneaded into our frame, along with elements of the wolf and serpent'.[5] Like Hume, and in contrast to many moralists, Austen believed not only that human nature was 'mixed', but that it should be represented as such.[6] Good nature has surely never been celebrated in a less sentimental way.

---

[2] David Hume, *An Enquiry concerning the Principles of Morals*, ed. Tom Beauchamp (Oxford University Press, 1998), Section 2, pp. 78–9. Hereafter *Morals*.

[3] *Morals*, p. 79; David Hume, 'Of Impudence and Modesty', in *Essays Moral, Political, and Literary*, ed. Eugene Miller (Indianapolis: Liberty Fund, 1985), pp. 552–3. Godmersham had the second edition, *Essays, Moral and Political*, 2 vols. (Edinburgh, 1742).

[4] Hume, *A Treatise of Human Nature*, ed. David and Mary Norton (Oxford University Press, 2001), 2.2.10.7, p. 252.

[5] *Morals*, p. 147.

[6] See Edgar Wind, *Hume and the Heroic Portrait* (Oxford University Press, 1986).

Even in her own era, the 'philosophical character' of Jane Austen's work was taken as a mark of what was distinctively new about her novels,[7] and while the list of philosophers with whom she has been linked has grown, Hume has emerged as the most commonly cited.[8] Though there is no extant evidence for her reading of him beyond *The History of England* (which receives warm praise from the Tilneys in *Northanger Abbey*), we can be certain, at least, that she inherited ideas that originated in his discursive writing. When Edmund Bertram is first said to be destined for the church in *Mansfield Park*, we are told that his good qualities 'bid most fairly for utility', and the same word is again foregrounded when Fanny applauds Henry Crawford's plans for bettering the housing of labourers at Everingham (*MP*, pp. 23, 470). As the *Oxford English Dictionary* notes, it was Hume's *Morals* that so propitiously launched 'utility' in its sense of the provision for general happiness, and though Austen's association of 'utility' with Edmund's vocation may have been calculated to recall Paley's explicit adoption of Hume's concept in his *Principles* (1785), a tract that was soon to become required reading for ordinands,[9] it is by no means improbable that Austen was familiar with the original herself. Owing perhaps to Hume's posthumous declaration that the *Morals* was 'incomparably the best' of his works,[10] this most informal of his treatises enjoyed a wide circulation during the 1790s. It was extensively quoted by Mary Wollstonecraft, minutely disputed by Thomas Gisborne, and respectfully deferred to by novelists as diverse as Elizabeth Hamilton, Mary Ann Hanway and Helen Craik.[11] Not even the drastic gutting of Austen's correspondence can give lasting shelter to the belief

[7] Richard Whateley, *Quarterly Review* (January 1821), *Jane Austen: The Critical Heritage*, ed. B. C. Southam, p. 88.
[8] Recent treatments of the relationship include E. M. Dadlez's comprehensive *Mirrors to One Another: Emotion and Value in Jane Austen and David Hume* (Oxford: Wiley-Blackwell, 2009); Valerie Wainwright's *Ethics and the English Novel from Austen to Forster* (New York and Aldershot: Ashgate, 2007); Karen Valihora's *Austen's Oughts: Judgment after Locke and Shaftesbury* (Newark: University of Delaware Press, 2010), ch. 2; and my *Jane Austen and the Enlightenment* (Cambridge University Press, 2004). Tony Tanner's Humean reading of *Pride and Prejudice* is of enduring value: see *Jane Austen* (Basingstoke and New York: Macmillan, 1986), ch. 4. For Aristotelian and other approaches, see 'Further Reading'.
[9] William Paley, *The Principles of Moral and Political Philosophy* (London, 1785), bk 2, chs. 4–8, bk 6, ch. 12; Irene Collins, *Jane Austen and the Clergy* (London: Hambledon Press, 1994), p. 43.
[10] David Hume, *The Life of David Hume, by himself, with a letter from Adam Smith* (London, 1777), p. 15. Godmersham had this celebratory volume.
[11] Mary Wollstonecraft, *A Vindication of the Rights of Woman*, in *Mary Wollstonecraft: Political Writings*, ed. Janet Todd (London: William Pickering, 1993), p. 131; Thomas Gisborne, *Principles of Moral Philosophy Investigated* (London, 1789), ch. 2; Elizabeth Hamilton, *Letters of a Hindoo Rajah*, 2 vols. (London, 1796), vol. I, p. 259;

that she was poorly read, still less to the view that her family lacked both the resources and appetite for intellectual debate.[12] Though little is known about the library of her father other than that he parted with 500 books on his move to Bath (*Letters*, p. 77), a catalogue of the library at Godmersham – made in 1818 but only lately come to light – reveals (among a wealth of discursive works) strong holdings in English and French philosophy.[13]

Indisputably there are broad similarities between the two writers which, if they derive from independent growth, draw on common cultural traditions, and draw out what is most innovative in Austen's work. Both novelist and philosopher were famed for the boldness and freshness of their minute observation, and however far apart the paths they took, they shared the same goal, which Jane Austen was to frame as 'the most thorough knowledge of human nature' (*NA*, p. 31). A historian has suggested that Hume's ethics were 'the first in modern philosophy to be completely secular, without reference to God's will, a divine creative plan, or an afterlife'; a contemporary complained that an overriding concern with human felicity had caused the sage '"to jump the life to come"'.[14] For her part, Jane Austen has constantly been recognised as a writer who avoids reference to the supernatural, and who keeps scrupulously within what a recent critic has termed the 'naturalistic horizon'.[15] While her Christian values were often applauded by early nineteenth-century commentators, her abstention from the doctrinal was remarked on during her lifetime ('she does not dabble in religion'), and her refusal to 'inflict retribution' at the cost of probability was glaring even to the proponents of a later realism.[16] Perhaps Elizabeth Bennet somewhat oversteps the mark when she tells Lady Catherine de Bourgh that she is 'resolved to act in that manner, which will, in my own opinion, constitute my happiness' (*P&P*, p. 396), but the individual's pursuit of happiness with due consideration to that of others is invariably defended in the six novels, and

Mary Ann Hanway, *Elinor*, 4 vols. (London, 1798), vol. III, p. 173 (cites *Morals*, VII.i); Helen Craik, *Adelaide de Narbonne*, 6 vols. (London, 1800), vol. I, p. 161.

[12] Of an estimated 3,000, 162 letters survive; see Deirdre Le Faye, 'Letters', in *Context*, p. 33. Pat Rogers casts doubt on Jane Austen's access to enlightened *raisonneurs* (*P&P*, p. xliv).

[13] The catalogue includes philosophical works by Bacon, Bayle, Bolingbroke, Butler, Condillac, Fontenelle, Gibbon (the *Essai*), Goguet, Grotius, Helvétius, Hobbes, Hume, Locke, Montesquieu, Paley, Pufendorf, Raynal, Rousseau, Saint-Évremond, Shaftesbury and Voltaire. No list of James Austen's books survives.

[14] James Fieser, 'Introduction', in his collection *Early Responses to Hume's Moral, Literary, and Political Writings*, 2 vols. (Bristol: Thoemmes, 1999), vol. I, p. xi; and William Belsham, *Essays* (1789), in Fieser, *Early Responses*, vol. I, p. 257.

[15] See Eleanor Courtemanche's important book, *The 'Invisible Hand' and British Fiction, 1818–1860* (London: Palgrave, 2011), p. 85.

[16] Unsigned notice, *British Critic* (July 1818), and W. F. Pollock, *Fraser's Magazine* (January 1860), reprinted in *Critical Heritage*, ed. Southam, pp. 71, 170.

nowhere are appeals to a transcendental realm more visibly deflated than in *Pride and Prejudice*. Lady Catherine's resounding invocation of 'reason' in support of her schemes falls on deaf ears, and the real object of the Reverend Collins's prostrations is never in doubt. Commenting on the power of the clerical profession, Hume once remarked that the parson was in possession of what Archimedes had always wanted, 'another world on which to fix his engines'.[17] Collins's other world lies securely within the palings of Hunsford until his attempt to deter Elizabeth from marrying Darcy is halted by the thought of a younger patron.

'First Impressions'

To view *Pride and Prejudice* from the vantage point of its original title is to become aware of its bearing on two conspicuous and related sceptical traditions, one specific and literary, the other extensive and epistemological. John Locke, in a foundational chapter from his famous *Essay* headed 'No Innate Principles', gave new edge to the stock phrase when he insisted on the absoluteness and tenacity of the ideas that we receive as children, for such are 'those that make the first impression ... nor will [we] find the least footsteps of any other'.[18] Locke returned to the idea of 'the first strong impression' in his treatise on education,[19] a work that went through a score of editions before the century's close, and left its imprint on a host of conduct books. These included such popular items as Lord Chesterfield's *Letters to his Son*, John Gregory's *A Father's Legacy*, James Fordyce's *Sermons to Young Women* and his brother David's more ambitious *Dialogues concerning Education*, all of which retail the doctrine of first impressions, with due acknowledgment to Locke in the case of the last.[20] All four were on the shelves of Godmersham, and Austen certainly knew the *Sermons* singled out by Collins. Unsurprisingly what Locke had originally maintained about the vulnerability of infanthood was soon extended to adolescence and

---

[17] Hume, 'Of National Characters', in *Essays*, p. 200.

[18] Locke, *Essay on Human Understanding*, in *The Works of John Locke*, 8th edn, 4 vols. (London, 1777), vol. I, p. 65. Locke's contention here that even our 'first impressions' of God were necessarily sensory was fiercely disputed, see Nicolas Brady, *A Sermon preach'd at the Chapel-Royal* (London, 1701), p. 4.

[19] Locke, *Some Thoughts Concerning Education*, 14th edn (London, 1772), pp. 165, 202. For an excellent discussion of the bearings of this work on *Northanger Abbey*, see Jocelyn Harris, *Jane Austen and the Art of Memory* (Cambridge University Press, 1989), pp. 1–26.

[20] Philip Dormer Stanhope, Lord Chesterfield, *Letters to his Son*, 4 vols. (London, 1787), vol. I, p. x; vol. II, p. 145; John Gregory, *A Father's Legacy* (London, 1792), p. 147; James Fordyce, *Sermons to Young Women*, 2 vols. (London, 1766), vol. I, p. 18; David Fordyce, *Dialogues concerning Education*, 2 vols. (London, 1745), vol. I. pp. 270, 304.

particularly to sexual relationships. When Darcy first tells Elizabeth how Wickham (his father's godson) was in a position to win the trust of his fifteen-year-old sister, his explanation is poised somewhere between the *Essay* and the later conduct books: 'he so far recommended himself to Georgiana, whose affectionate heart retained a strong impression of his kindness to her as a child, that she was persuaded to believe herself in love, and to consent to an elopement' (*P&P*, p. 224).

Locke's theory of knowledge, to which his notion of 'first impressions' is inextricably bound, arises from the recognition that our perceptions are often inadequate, or even wrong. Because knowledge comes to us exclusively through our senses, and because what we gather from them often proves to be incomplete, it is necessary to posit a mental representation of the world, consisting of 'ideas' or 'impressions' upon which our notions of reality are gradually built. While thinkers of the 'common sense' school would object, later in the century, to the 'veil' which empiricism had placed between the perceiver and the external world, there was no way round the problem other than to appoint a supernatural guarantor of sensory fidelity, or to reinstate innate ideas. For Locke, 'first impressions' are the more powerful for being imprinted on a brain that begins as a blank sheet, but their psychological primacy comes with no warrant of truth. And this sense is generally reflected in the abundant use of the formula by eighteenth-century novelists. So Fielding warns of the extreme susceptibility of the unformed mind to first impressions in *Joseph Andrews*; Richardson admonishingly includes the formula in both the contents and index of *Sir Charles Grandison*; and, a generation on, gothic novelists like Radcliffe and Lewis manage to inject the tired phrase with a streak of foreboding.[21] A usage of exactly contrary tendency was to emerge, however, when writers of romance approached the all-important scene of fateful encounter in the spirit of Marlowe's, 'Who ever loved, that loved not at first sight?'.

First impressions are seldom revoked in the novel of sensibility, and by the 1790s the light-hearted cynicism of Congreve's Lady Wishfort who dithers over whether to 'give the first impression on a couch' is left far behind.[22] We hear instead of heroines who pledge themselves, on pain of death, to be 'faithful to first impressions and first vows'.[23] And though the more serious

---

[21] With the chapter headed 'Philosophical Reflections' in *Joseph Andrews* (IV, 7), compare *Some Thoughts Concerning Education* (1693), §.s 138, 191. See Henry Fielding, *Joseph Andrews*, 2 vols. (London, 1742), vol. II, p. 216; Samuel Richardson, *Sir Charles Grandison*, 6 vols. (London, 1753–4), especially vol. I, p. 47; Ann Radcliffe, *The Mysteries of Udolpho*, 4 vols. (London, 1794), vol. I, p. 13; M. G. Lewis, *The Monk*, 3 vols. (London, 1796), vol. I, p. 38.

[22] William Congreve, *The Way of the World* (1710), IV, i.

[23] *Adeline; or the Orphan*, 3 vols. (London, 1790), vol. II, p. 80.

novelists of the decade generally steered clear of endorsing first impressions in amorous relationships, many upheld them. So Mary Hays, who issues a Lockean caveat to a heroine dangerously exposed to attraction in *Emma Courtney*, elsewhere declares that first impressions when they are deep 'come pretty near the truth'.[24] With conscious deference to genre, and an apology to devotees of realism and the circulating library, Helen Craik presents two scenes of prescient (and Platonic) first impression in her ground-breaking historical novel, *Adelaide de Narbonne* (1800). Here Charlotte Corday is struck by the 'more than mortal' appearance of the Chouan rebel-hero, and instantly senses that their mutual 'first impressions' have laid the 'foundation of a future and permanent relationship'.[25] By the end of the century the motif had travelled from its matrix in empirical epistemology to a realm of the extra-sensory.

In a passage that clearly relates to the original title, Jane Austen takes stock of the popular convention of love-at-first-blush while gesturing at Elizabeth's strangely circuitous route to recognition:

> But if otherwise, if the regard springing from such sources is unreasonable or unnatural, in comparison of what is so often described as arising on a first interview with its object, and even before two words have been exchanged, nothing can be said in her defence, except that she had given somewhat of a trial to the latter method, in her partiality for Wickham, and that its ill-success might perhaps authorise her to seek the other less interesting mode of attachment. (*P&P*, p. 308)

In comparison with those of a heroine of sensibility, Elizabeth's first impressions *vis-à-vis* Wickham are remarkably downright and robust. Charming though his manners may be, it is made abundantly clear that the core of the Lieutenant's attraction is sexual. In retrospect Elizabeth puts a firm limit on the duration, at least, of Wickham fever: 'every girl in, or near Meryton, was out of her senses about him for the first two months', but her initial susceptibility to the man who has the 'best part of beauty', 'a good figure', and grows 'handsomer than ever' is explicit (*P&P*, pp. 314, 81, 89). Her 'prepossession' (to adopt Mrs Bennet's sense of the word) lends an aura of infallibility: Wickham's good faith is evident from his 'very countenance'; there is 'truth in his looks' (pp. 79, 90, 96). Yet Elizabeth's readiness to accept the fiction that Wickham weaves round his connections with Pemberley is shaped not by her infatuation alone, but by her need for anything that will salve the damage done to her pride at the assembly. Indeed, a clue to the greater strength of that

[24] Mary Hays, *Memoirs of Emma Courtney*, 2 vols. (London, 1796), vol. 1, p. 4; *Letters and Essays* (1793), p. 117.
[25] Craik, *Adelaide de Narbonne*, vol. 1, pp. 127–9, 30–1.

earlier set of first impressions is given when we are told that what Elizabeth 'chiefly wished to hear' from Wickham, tête-à-tête, is what he has to say about Darcy (p. 86). The picture that she proceeds to build of her irresistible detractor (which we are increasingly positioned to see as a distorted one) answers to a range of her emotional needs. Where knowledge, as Locke has it, issues from the rational integration of a series of sense impressions to which the subject is essentially passive, representation in *Pride and Prejudice* is saturated with the colour of feelings and dispositions. Turning then to the central relationship of the novel, it is necessary to move from Locke to Hume, a philosopher supremely aware of the influence on thought of the body.

Pride and prejudice

Significantly, the most transformative moment in Elizabeth's understanding of Darcy occurs not only some eleven weeks after their cold parting at Hunsford, but in his absence at Pemberley. Earlier her attempts to read Darcy's character have repeatedly been compared to the sketching of a portrait (*P&P*, pp. 103, 105). Upstairs, the large oil of Darcy in the gallery brings the chequered history of this inner delineation to a climax when a surge of belief displaces her persistent stirrings of distrust:

> Every idea that had been brought forward by the housekeeper was favourable to his character, and as she stood before the canvas, on which he was represented, and fixed his eyes upon herself, she thought of his regard with a deeper senti-ment of gratitude than it had ever raised before; she remembered its warmth, and softened its impropriety of expression. (p. 277)

Usually in novels it is the painted eyes that do the roving, but Elizabeth adjusts herself to meet the pictured gaze, and proceeds to recreate as well as absorb the smiling portrait. The warm image of Darcy that Elizabeth conjures up from the past with a vividness that almost banishes the darker one, is abetted by the glowing testimony of the pointedly named Mrs Reynolds, as well as by the subliminal influence of the house and its setting. Throughout this process we effectively read over Elizabeth's shoulder, retaking our bearings on her relationship to Darcy. Though residual, her sense of an 'impropriety of expression' is enough to recall Darcy's affronts at their first encounter, and the 'indignant contempt' that he openly displays towards the Bennet family, not to mention the silences and forbidding looks that serve to license the hatred of all Meryton. The smile, on the other hand, is the tell-tale sign of a personality that has hitherto hardly entered into Elizabeth's official reckoning of her antagonist, but the reader has come to take it, along with the earnest stares or habit of rapidly averting the eyes, as the mark of a man hopelessly smitten. By contrast, the only wounds Elizabeth admits to are injuries to her pride, and Darcy's gross insensitivity makes these real enough. Yet when she replies to the massive insult meant by him as a proposal, we are made aware of a tendentiousness that is not wholly ascribable to anger:

> 'From the very beginning, from the first moment I may almost say, of my acquaintance with you, your manners impressing me with the fullest belief of your arrogance, your conceit, and your selfish disdain of the feelings of others, were such as to form the ground-work of disapprobation, on which succeeding events have built so immoveable a dislike.'   (*P&P*, p. 215)

Injured pride is pride on the offensive, and pride is not only blind, as Hume noted, but an instigator also of exaggerated narrative.[26] But the playful smiles exchanged over the pianoforte at Rosings, when Darcy is catechised for his conduct at the assembly, reveal that Elizabeth is not so fully preoccupied by the belief she has vested in Wickham's story, or even indeed by her already dawning suspicion of Darcy's role in breaking up Bingley's attachment to her sister, as to forgo the pleasure of flirting (*P&P*, pp. 196–7, 155, 160). Even so, when she is convinced, after reading and rereading Darcy's letter of exculpation, of its superior claim to truth, and recalls that Darcy may have had some cause to underestimate Jane's feelings for his friend, the collapse of her imaginative construct leaves her so spiritless that she can persuade herself that she has not the 'slightest inclination ever to see him again' (p. 236).

That ideas are organic, that they are felt on the pulse, fluctuate in intensity, and prove, above all, subject to dramatic change is a distinguishing feature of Austen's realism, and one that is particularly to the fore in *Pride and Prejudice*, where we hear of people altering so much that there is 'something new to be observed in them for ever', or – in connection with Darcy's letter – of a total reversal in the 'feelings of the person who wrote, and the person who received' (*P&P*, pp. 47, 409). This aspect of Austen's work has an interesting theoretical precedent in Hume, who claimed, not immodestly, that he was the first philosopher to investigate a matter of the plainest common experience, the question of what distinguished a *belief* from 'the simple conception of any thing'.[27] His answer to the problem was that the 'enlivening' of an idea through association and emotional state – to the point of its being raised to an approximation of what was *actually* seen, heard or felt – explained the phenomenon of conviction. As his chief example of the way in which an association (either of resemblance, contiguity or causality) can intensify an idea, he considers the case of a subject who is thinking of an absent friend:

---

[26] *Morals*, 9.1, p. 152; and 'Of Avarice', *Essays*, p. 570.
[27] See 'Abstract', in Hume, *Treatise*, p. 411.

We may, therefore, observe, as the first experiment to our present purpose, that, upon the appearance of the picture of an absent friend, our idea of him is evidently enlivened by the *resemblance*, and that every passion, which that idea occasions, whether of joy or sorrow, acquires new force and vigour. In producing this effect, there concur both a relation and a present impression.[28]

Through this progressive gain in vivacity, the idea of a thing 'approaches its impression', so that we may 'feel sickness and pain from the mere force of imagination, and make a malady real by often thinking of it'.[29]

In *Pride and Prejudice* we hear of feelings being 're-animated' or 're-kindled' by the presence of the person concerned (*P&P*, pp. 161, 373), and Elizabeth's contemplation of the portrait at Pemberley is one of several occasions on which we are reminded of the propensity of ideas to assume presence. When Elizabeth comments on the way Lydia has ransacked every imaginative resource to stoke her craze for the militia, she appeals to an unnamed but familiar psychological trait: 'She has been doing everything in her power by thinking and talking on the subject, to give greater – what shall I call it? susceptibility to her feelings; which are naturally lively enough' (p. 313). Here the parenthetical question invokes the experience of the reader whose darting recognition imparts precisely that sense of veracity that can give an immediate presence, as Hume noted, even to the feigned.[30] Within the novel we see the process at work whenever Wickham courts Elizabeth's belief in his fictions with a skilful use of consensus and circumstantiality, kindling his slander of Darcy with the oxygen of her antagonism. The realism for which Austen has long been famed has much to do with her skewering of what was often thought, but still more with her gift for voicing what is so commonplace as to have escaped attention. When Mr Bennet praises Elizabeth, after Lydia's elopement, for having shown 'greatness of mind' in attempting to stop her sister's visit to Brighton, and blames himself for not taking steps to avert the risk he has long foreseen, his apology is both heart-felt and disconcerting: 'No, Lizzy, let me once in my life feel how much I have been to blame. I am not afraid of being overpowered by the impression. It will pass away soon enough' (p. 330). From this close conjunction of two key concepts from Hume many contemporary readers would have noted Mr Bennet as a well-versed, if unavailing, reader of the philosopher.

'Greatness of mind' (a quality ascribed to Queen Elizabeth in *The History of England*) well describes the moral strength that Elizabeth constantly displays, often with fiery spirit, in standing up for her beliefs, and indeed for

---

[28] Hume, *An Enquiry concerning Human Understanding*, ed. Tom Beauchamp (Oxford University Press), 5.2, p. 127; also *Treatise*, 1.3.8.3, p. 69.
[29] Hume, *Treatise*, 2.1.11.5, pp. 207–8.   [30] Hume, *Treatise*, 1.3.9.5, p. 76.

herself.[31] Prominently placed in his roster of virtues in the *Morals*, the ancient Aristotelian ideal plays an important role in Hume's determined attempts to show just how dependent good conduct is on pride. His argument here, as in the *Essays*, falls effectively into two parts. First, without a 'high notion' of the self, a person will have nothing to live up to; and if virtue is to be esteemed it must be valued in the self as well as in others.[32] Second, if reputation is, as widely agreed, an important incentive to right action, this in its turn relies on 'self-value', for, as Hume neatly puts it, 'our regard to a character with others seems to arise only from a care of preserving a character with ourselves'.[33] As Hume was well aware, this last pragmatic take on pride derived ultimately from the Stoic tradition, and more immediately from Bernard Mandeville, who had noted that, owing to the odium of the cardinal sin, there was 'no word or expression' for the sort of pride that prompted laudable actions.[34] Regretting the absence of a 'proper name in our language' for this crucial disposition, Hume proposes 'conscious worth', which he defines as the 'self-satisfaction proceeding from a review of a man's own conduct and character'.[35] At least one novelist of the 1790s adopted this formula from Hume, and Jane Austen herself uses the phrase when she refers, in a poem, to her brother Francis, who has cause to 'Feel his Deserts with honest Glow,' after struggling to win 'the best blessing, conscious Worth' (*Letters*, p. 186).[36] Although there was no lack of conduct books that called for the total extirpation of pride on the quasi-Platonic premiss that the passions were essentially alien to the true self, which was solely manifest in the exercise of reason, the vice underwent considerable rehabilitation in the eighteenth century at the hands of both philosophers and latitudinarian divines. One enabling tactic was to appoint vanity as a whipping boy for the newly elevated sin. Whereas for a writer like Hume, vanity and pride are parts of a single faculty that can be either good or bad, vanity was increasingly seen by the run of moralists as distinct and irretrievably noxious. Pride proves to be as mixed in *Pride and Prejudice* as Austen's human protagonists,[37] but vanity too – in the sense of care for the regard of others – is seen not only as inescapable but

---

[31] Austen herself praised Elizabeth I as an exemplary and 'great' queen; To Francis Austen, 3–6 July 1813, *Letters*, p. 223.

[32] Hume, 'Of the Dignity and Meanness of Human Nature', *Essays*, p. 81; and *Morals* 7, pp. 133–4.

[33] *Morals*, 9, p. 151.

[34] Bernard Mandeville, *An Enquiry into the Origins of Honour* (London, 1732), pp. 6–7.

[35] *Morals*, app. 4, p. 177.

[36] Helen Craik's use of the phrase 'the pride of conscious worth' is shortly followed, in *Adelaide de Narbonne*, by the citation of Hume's *Morals*, see vol. I, pp. 157, 161.

[37] See especially Isobel Armstrong's discussion in her introduction to *Pride and Prejudice* (Oxford University Press, 1990), pp. xi–xx.

as essential to a sense of self. When Mary Bennet declares 'Vanity and pride are different things', she makes no great advance on Fordyce's 'Pride and vanity are different things'.[38] And with predictable inconsequence she proceeds to illustrate what Hume distinguished as the worst form of vanity ('intemperate display ... an importunate and open demand of praise and admiration'),[39] when she snatches at the first opportunity to sing, 'always impatient for display' (*P&P*, p. 27). The occasion for her dictum is Elizabeth's famous remark on Darcy, which eloquently unites what she has attempted to dissever: 'I could easily forgive *his* pride, if he had not mortified *mine*' (p. 21). Mary's well-thumbed idea that pride has to do with self, and vanity with the opinion of others, fails to deal with the obvious fact that the roots of self-esteem are inextricably social.

When Jane Austen adopted the phrase 'pride and prejudice', used by novelists like Burney and Bage, she drew attention to pride's blinkering effects, which are critical to the course of the main relationship, and subject to much illustration elsewhere – witness Mr Collins's blank disbelief that any young woman could turn him down, or Caroline Bingley's insistence that Wickham's nature can be deduced from his low descent (*P&P*, p. 106). But the touchstone most frequently applied to the novel's amalgam of vanity and pride is ethical, and centres in the natural virtue of benevolence. Like Hume, Austen seems to consider this aptitude weaker than conscious worth as a motive to action, but as a higher and purer source of morality. 'If from no better motive', Elizabeth expects that Darcy's pride should have been enough to keep him honest and just (p. 91);[40] and sympathy is repeatedly alloyed with pride to supply a mainspring of conduct, as we see when Jane doubts the evil fathered on Darcy by Wickham, 'No man of common humanity, no man who had any value for his character, could be capable of it' (p. 96). Elizabeth's detection of both 'compassion and honour' in Darcy's rescue of Lydia (p. 361) marks a critical stage in his achievement of a proper pride that is compatible with general benevolence, in marked contrast to the 'worst kind of pride' that feeds on division, or the 'family pride' that inhibits tender feelings for anyone beyond his immediate circle (pp. 209, 409). Just how deeply Darcy has been infected with a nasty strain of the toxic virtue appears from such curious manoeuvres as his attempt to persuade Elizabeth to dance a hated Scottish reel, in the hope that he can simultaneously enjoy both his scorn and her overwhelming attractions (pp. 56, 27).

To Elizabeth Darcy attributes his change of heart, and in answer to her query of what real good he ever saw in her, it is significant that he cites her

---

[38] Fordyce, *Sermons*, vol. II, p. 66   [39] *Morals*, 8, p. 142.
[40] Compare *Morals*, app. 4, p. 178.

uncompromising solicitude for Jane when ill at Netherfield (*P&P*, pp. 421–2). Elizabeth's decision to brave the three miles of mud to make the visit there gives rise to a revealing exchange:

> 'I admire the activity of your benevolence,' observed Mary, 'but every impulse of feeling should be guided by reason; and, in my opinion, exertion should always be in proportion to what is required.'
>
> 'We will go as far as Meryton with you,' said Catherine and Lydia. – Elizabeth accepted their company, and the three young ladies set off together.
>
> (*P&P*, p. 35)

Where the pursuit of self-interest (or officers) by the younger sisters saves Elizabeth from undertaking the hike alone, Mary's homily is of help to no one. Elizabeth is moved to act by her care for Jane, and has made all possible use of reason in determining that the only way to reach her, given the circumstances, is to walk at the risk of arriving dirty. The rationalism in which Mary takes refuge is mocked by the situation, for there is surely no logic by which to discover whether the limit on her sister's impulse should be set at two miles or four. But true to school, her judgments are as independent of context as her mode of collecting 'extracts' from books, a custom which Fordyce inveighs against in the very volume from which she quotes.[41] The oddly stilted phrasing of her lip-service to Elizabeth's good deed carries the imprint of Burke, no friend to the 'new-invented virtue', who had – with the pomp of sarcasm – accused Paine of harbouring 'sufficient activity in his own native benevolence' to blow the state sky high.[42] Like Hume, however, Burke doubted the executive powers of 'reason', putting his trust rather in disposition, and the refining influence of social forms.

Critics who detect a satire on the female intellectual in Mary Bennet are wide of the mark, for she has more in common with the mistress Mary of nursery rhyme than with Wollstonecraft, and falls indeed within a category then much targeted by feminists, the accomplished woman (*P&P*, pp. 12, 27, 428). *Pride and Prejudice* has much to offer on this theme, and opposes both to Mary with her modish study of 'thorough bass', and her commonplaces arranged in a shining row, and to Caroline Bingley, votary of the polyglot fashion-plate, a more 'substantial' ideal of accomplishment, involving – as Darcy has it – a mind improved by 'extensive reading' (p. 43).[43] Though on her first night at Netherfield Elizabeth denies – with a modesty characteristic of her creator – that she is a great reader, we learn later of her keen use of her father's library

---

[41] Fordyce, *Sermons*, vol. II, p. 33.

[42] See *Works of Edmund Burke*, 9 vols. (London, 1803), vol. VI, p. 33; vol. VII, p. 350.

[43] *De rigueur* for De Genlis, see *Tales of the Castle* (known to Jane Austen), 4 vols. (London, 1785), vol. III, p. 169: 'she scarcely knew the rules of Thorough Bass [!!!!]'.

(p. 186), and hear too from Darcy that a family library needs to be kept up to date – a rule well observed at Godmersham.[44] On her second night with the Bingleys, Elizabeth unostentatiously exemplifies Darcy's ideal of intellectual accomplishment in a long conversation that Hume would unhesitatingly have recognised as philosophy in the 'conversible' style, for though light, even playful in tone, it explores a serious principle (pp. 52–5). Darcy begins by provocatively declaring that when Bingley apologises for doing everything in a hurry, he is really calling attention to what he regards as a flattering trait, and cites, in addition to Bingley's reference to his careless handwriting, his remark that should he ever decide to quit Netherfield, he would be gone within minutes. When Bingley protests that he was truthful, Darcy proposes a thought experiment: if a friend had arrived and begged him to stay longer, would he not have assented? Taking Bingley's side, Elizabeth argues that his agreement would have shown him in an even more flattering light; Darcy counters that it is right to indulge the wish of a friend only if it coincides with 'propriety'. Undismayed, Elizabeth continues to argue that there is a general case to be made for obliging a friend, but gradually all parties are brought to recognise that the rival claims of sympathy and of the impartial stance can only be resolved in the knowledge, as Bingley facetiously puts it, of 'all particulars, not forgetting their comparative height and size'. Beneath this fecund dialogue many of Austen's contemporaries would have recognised the contours of recent philosophical debate. Witness Reid's insistence on the inadequacy of 'attuning our conduct to the tone of other men's passions', or, closer still, Smith's contention that the sympathy of the spectator should be governed by evaluation of the situation of the agent.[45] Though Hume is in both these cases the subject of critique, he himself – while celebrating the 'dominion of the beneficent affections' entered into by those who serve a friend – acknowledged the paramount importance of a holistic reckoning, and of deriving a 'common point of view'.[46]

The tenets upheld by Elizabeth and Darcy in the course of their argument prove to be neither entirely disinterested nor of long standing. To the veteran reader it is clear that Darcy, after a full morning of exposure to Mrs Bennet, is in no mood to see his friend remain in Meryton, and already has thoughts of protecting him from the sort of affectionate intercession that Elizabeth supports. In the event, however, it is Elizabeth who has cause to renege on that

[44] Well tempered, as well as up to date: hence Burke's *Reflections* (1790) was followed by T. F. Hill's *Observations on the Politics of France and their Progress* (London, 1792).
[45] See Thomas Reid, *Essays on the Active Powers of Man* (Edinburgh, 1788), V, iv, p. 408; and Adam Smith, *The Theory of Moral Sentiments* (London: A. Millar, and Edinburgh: A. Kincaid and J. Bell, 1759), IV, 1 and 2.
[46] *Morals*, pp. 170, 160–1, 148.

plea for loyalty between friends which she has so nearly elevated to a principle, and Darcy who grievously offends against his own axiom of general
'propriety', when, without due cognisance of his wish for a brother-in-law, he
hastily misjudges Jane's feelings for Bingley, and seizes the role of intercessor
himself.

The dispute at Netherfield provides an early focus for the novel's preoccupation with both benevolence and impartiality. It leads, as the plot of Bingley
and Jane's frustrated courtship at last plays out, to a final reminder of how
dependent moral judgment is on accurate observation when the reformed
Darcy admits to having subjected Jane to scrutiny on two occasions, before
finding the words to turn his friend's diffidence into 'immediate conviction'
(*P&P*, p. 412). In place of a rationalist ethics, and in common with Hume,
Austen upholds the experimental method in matters of morality. Sympathy
and propriety are built into the very ordonnance of her narration through the
alternation of multiple points of view and their exposure to omniscient commentary, but tidy moral saws of the sort cherished by Mary Bennet (and even
those 'universally acknowledged') prove to be fallible guides. Elizabeth is not
wholly to be relied on when she rules, 'we all love to instruct, though we can
teach only what is not worth knowing' (p. 380). *Pride and Prejudice* does,
however, show how vulnerable precepts are to specific contexts, without
diminishing the difficulty experienced by the subject in constructing these.
After reviewing a dozen maxims of consolation (a form relished by Mary
much to Elizabeth's dismay), Hume compared the genre to quack medicine,
'equally good for a diabetes and a dropsy'.[47] He foresaw that beyond the reach
of even the most refined generalisation there lay a territory of fine discrimination in ethics, 'left by nature to baffle all the pride of philosophy'.[48] That surely
was the realm Jane Austen made her own.

---

[47] Mary's words on Lydia (*P&P*, p. 319) resemble the opening of *Hermione, or the Orphan
Sisters* (1791); see 'The Sceptic', *Essays*, p. 175.
[48] *Morals*, 8, p. 143.

4

ANTHONY MANDAL

Composition and publication

In the autumn of 1797, the prominent London publishers Cadell & Davies received a letter from an elderly clergyman from Hampshire, offering them a new novel for publication:

> Sirs,
> I have in my possession a Manuscript Novel, comprised in three Vols. about the length of Miss Burney's Evelina. As I am well aware of what consequence it is that a work of this sort should make its' first appearance under a respectable name I apply to you. Shall be much obliged therefore if you will inform me whether you chuse to be concerned in it; what will be the expense of publishing at the Author's risk; & what you will venture to advance for the Property of it, if on a perusal it is approved of?
>   Should your answer give me encouragement I will send you the work.
> I am, Sirs, Yr. obt. hble. Servt:
> Geo Austen
> Steventon, near Overton
> Hants
> 1st Novr. 1797[1]

The offer of the unseen manuscript was rejected, with the phrase 'declined by Return of Post' written on the returned letter that had been sent by George Austen on behalf of his second daughter, Jane. It is possible that this novel was an early version of what would be published sixteen years later as *Pride and Prejudice*, Jane Austen's best-loved and most successful novel.[2]

    Despite a published canon of only six novels, Austen's literary career is a complex one, spanning four decades that witnessed much drafting and

---

[1] Cited in George Holbert Tucker, *A History of Jane Austen's Family*, revised edition (Stroud: Sutton, 1998), p. 34.

[2] See J. E. Austen-Leigh, *Memoir of Jane Austen and Other Family Recollections*, ed. Kathryn Sutherland (Oxford University Press, 2002), p. 105. In 'A Tentative Jane Austen Query', Janet Todd suggests the proffered novel might have been an early version of *Sense and Sensibility*, *Notes and Queries* 59 (2012), pp. 105–6; doi: 10.1093/notesj/gjr280.

redrafting of her *œuvre*. Austen scholarship has typically divided her novels into two distinct phases, based on her residence when she composed them. The earlier 'Steventon novels' – *Sense and Sensibility* (1811), *Pride and Prejudice* (1813) and *Northanger Abbey* (1818) – were first drafted between 1795 and 1799 before being finally published in the 1810s. The later 'Chawton novels' – *Mansfield Park* (1814), *Emma* (1816) and *Persuasion* (1818) – were written and published in rapid succession. As well as the compositional differences, critics have also identified tonal distinctions between the Steventon and Chawton novels. The former are seen as breezier comedies written by an Austen in her early twenties looking expectantly to the opportunities of adulthood; while the latter are darker, more complex studies by an author approaching her forties after an unsettled middle period characterised by bereavement and dependency.

While substantial differences in purpose and execution do indeed exist between the earlier and later novels, a fuller examination of the chronology of Austen's works demonstrates that they occupied a continuum of writing which proceeded over a thirty-year period virtually without interruption. The juvenilia of 1787–93 gave way to longer experiments resulting in the ambitious 'Lady Susan' around 1794–5, just before she began composing her Steventon novels (1795–9). During the 1800s, Austen continued to work on her fiction, albeit less intensively, selling the copyright of what would later become *Northanger Abbey* (then titled 'Susan') in 1803 to Benjamin Crosby, a trade publisher of circulating-library fare. Around 1804, she drafted the abortive 17,500-word fragment now called 'The Watsons'; and in 1805, she wrote out a fair copy of 'Lady Susan', possibly adding a conclusion to the piece at this time. By 1809, Austen was ensconced in Chawton and began that final and fruitful period of redrafting and original composition that would culminate in the publication of six novels. It becomes clear, then, that trying to tease out 'phases' of writing as distinct moments in Austen's writing career is not as simple as it may initially appear.

Unlike a number of her female peers, Austen's literary world was a circumscribed one. While other novelists such as Frances Burney, Maria Edgeworth and Amelia Opie could partake of the buzz of literary circles in and around the metropolis, Austen's life was a provincial one, marked out with visits to family members that might occasionally include more cosmopolitan areas such as London. It was, in essence, Austen's closely knit, active family network, along with some close friends, that characterised her own literary domain – one which allowed for some early flirtations with literary excitement. A close relative on Austen's mother's side, Cassandra Cooke, was a neighbour of Frances Burney and had published a poorly received novel entitled *The Traditions* in 1799, to which Austen herself made reference

(*Letters*, p. 17). Perhaps the most significant connection Austen formed to fiction during these early years, however, was her subscription to Burney's best-selling third novel, *Camilla; or, a Picture of Youth* (1796): the earliest of Austen's surviving letters (dated September 1796) are filled with references to *Camilla*, clearly demonstrating Austen's lively engagement with Burney's novel. Despite the relatively restricted nature of her immediate literary environment, it is evident that this five-year period at the end of the century represents a clear moment in her literary development, marking a transition from playful experimentation to more sophisticated practice.

'First Impressions': first rejection

No manuscripts of the six published novels survive, other than two cancelled chapters from *Persuasion*, and we must rely on other evidence to give a clearer picture of Austen's writing practices. There is no mention of the composition of the earliest version of *Pride and Prejudice* – originally titled 'First Impressions' – in Austen's surviving letters, but we do have circumstantial information, primarily in the form of family anecdotes and a retrospective memorandum of publication of the six novels written by Cassandra shortly after Austen's death.[3] After preparing in 1795 a first draft of 'Elinor and Marianne', a novel-in-letters that would later be refashioned into the third-person *Sense and Sensibility*, Austen began work on her new novel 'First Impressions' between October 1796 and August 1797. Kathryn Sutherland observes that '[w]e do not know whether Jane Austen followed a general practice in writing and what it might have been. Long periods of gestation and of critical attention post-composition are mentioned within the immediate family and can be adduced from the record of dates.'[4] Austen herself commented on the creative process in 1798, noting that 'an artist cannot do anything slovenly' (*Letters*, p. 21). Although Brian Southam has argued that 'First Impressions' was also epistolary in its original composition,[5] there is persuasive evidence to suggest that it was written in direct narrative from its inception, with Jan Fergus pointing to the clear influence of the third-person *Camilla* over Austen at the time she was composing 'First Impressions'.[6]

'First Impressions' was a firm favourite with the Austen family circle, and evidently continued to be circulated among friends and family. Austen's niece

---

[3] Cassandra's memorandum is reproduced in Jane Austen, *Minor Works*, ed. R. W. Chapman, revised B. C. Southam (London: Oxford University Press, 1969), facing p. 242.

[4] Kathryn Sutherland, 'Chronology of Composition and Publication', in *Context*, p. 20.

[5] Brian Southam, *Jane Austen's Literary Manuscripts: A Study of the Novelist's Development through the Surviving Papers* (London and New York: Athlone Press, 2001), pp. 57–60.

[6] Jan Fergus, *Jane Austen: A Literary Life* (Basingstoke: Macmillan, 1991), p. 81.

Anna recalled being told later in life that, when the manuscript was read aloud in James's family home by its author, the three-year-old Anna 'was in the room, & not expected to listen – Listen however I did, with so much interest, & with so much talk afterwards about "Jane & Elizabeth" that it was resolved, for prudence sake, to read no more of the story aloud in my hearing.'[7] Austen herself makes references to it in two letters to Cassandra, neither of which demonstrates dissatisfaction with the work, despite the fact that both letters were written after the rejection by Cadell & Davies. The first mention occurs in a letter to Cassandra dated 9 January 1799; set amidst gossipy sketches about neighbours and acquaintances, Austen offers a teasing remonstrance to her sister: 'I do not wonder at your wanting to read *first impressions* again, so seldom as you have gone through it, & that so long ago' (*Letters*, p. 36). The following June, she makes a second reference to the novel in another letter to her sister, alongside domestic matters and references to other reading matter: 'I would not let Martha read First Impressions again upon any account, & am very glad that I did not leave it in your power. – She is very cunning, but I see through her design; – she means to publish it from Memory, & one more perusal must enable her to do it' (*Letters*, p. 46). Once again, the tone is playful and acknowledges the esteem in which 'First Impressions' was held within the Austen circle.

It seems that the high reputation of 'First Impressions' with Austen's family and friends led to its being offered for publication to Cadell & Davies four months after completion. Deirdre Le Faye identifies Austen's father as the prime mover behind this application,[8] although it is just as likely that Austen herself instigated the approach, with George simply conveying his daughter's wishes. There is no documented reason why the London firm was chosen, although an obvious one lies in association with Burney: George Austen's reference to Burney's *Evelina* might signal an attempt to link his daughter's manuscript with the recently published *Camilla*, to which she had subscribed. Whatever initiated the approach, it is interesting to note the serious belief that 'First Impressions' would be accepted, demonstrated by George's mention of the usual methods of publication: either at the author's expense or through sale by copyright.[9]

The origins of Cadell & Davies lay in Bristol with Thomas Cadell, a minor bookseller who apprenticed his son Thomas to the successful London publisher Andrew Millar in 1758. By 1767, Thomas had become the sole

---

[7] Anna Lefroy, 'Recollections of Aunt Jane' (1864), in Austen-Leigh, *Memoir*, p. 158.

[8] Deirdre Le Faye, *Jane Austen: A Family Record*, 2nd edition (Cambridge University Press, 2004), p. 104.

[9] See Fergus, *Literary Life*, pp. 14–19 for a useful summary of the various methods of publication an author could undertake during Austen's lifetime.

proprietor, consolidating the firm's position as a leading publisher based in the fashionable West End. This second Thomas Cadell enjoyed connections with pre-eminent authors such as Henry Fielding, Edward Gibbon and Samuel Johnson. In 1793, he passed on the business to his son, the third Thomas Cadell (also known as 'Cadell the Younger'), in partnership with William Davies, who had been a senior assistant at the firm. By 1797, the Cadell imprint was an indicator of quality status, and although the firm did not issue fiction heavily, they had accumulated a substantial backlist of noteworthy novels over the years – among them Henry Mackenzie's *Man of Feeling* (1771), Burney's *Cecilia* (1782) and *Camilla* (1796), six of Charlotte Smith's novels and Ann Radcliffe's *The Italian* (1797). Despite this, fiction formed a relatively minor part of their literary investment, and their output was typical of an eighteenth-century publisher: principally religious works, then poetry, historiography, belletristic works (essays, dictionaries, the classics) and political commentaries. Compared with this, fiction itself was low in the firm's publishing priorities, amounting to less material than either travel writing or medical studies.

So, why did Cadell & Davies reject George Austen's proposition? If we consider his letter more closely, it becomes apparent that, despite displaying some knowledge of publishing practices, it is in some other respects clumsy and unbusinesslike, requesting an immediate response regarding the terms under which they would publish the (unseen) manuscript. It is hardly likely that Cadell & Davies would find this anything but intrusive. Perhaps the Burney link was supposed to invoke their recent success with *Camilla*, but this possibly misfired, pointing to *Evelina*, an already old-fashioned epistolary novel. James Raven provides figures that demonstrate publication of epistolary novels fell from 41.7 per cent in the 1780s to 18.3 per cent the following decade, with direct-narrative fictions gaining ascendancy – particularly the sentimental novels of Smith and gothic romances of Radcliffe.[10] Considering the high standing of the firm in the book trade at this time, George Austen – an unknown clergyman from the provinces – appears somewhat naïve (if not arrogant) in his attempt to gain anything tangible on the basis of a few lines. We might even surmise that a clash of personalities might have occurred. George Austen's parochial attitude typifies the eighteenth-century opinion that publishers were tradesmen. Assisting her cousin James Edward Austen Leigh in preparing his *Memoir of Jane Austen* (1870), his sister Caroline

---

[10] James Raven, 'Historical Introduction: The Novel Comes of Age', in *The English Novel, 1770–1829: A Bibliographical Survey of Prose Fiction Published in the British Isles*, ed. Peter Garside, James Raven and Rainer Schöwerling, 2 vols. (Oxford University Press, 2000), vol. I, pp. 31–2.

observed: 'The letter does not do much credit to the tact or courtesy of our good Grandfather for Cadell was a great man in his day, and it is not surprising that he should have refused the *favour* so offered from an *unknown*.'[11] It is not surprising that the metropolitan firm may indeed have had its own sense of hauteur, having dealt with established authors for many years: as Theodore Besterman notes, 'Cadell & Davies could reasonably feel that they belonged to at least a third generation of the highest aristocracy of the Trade.'[12]

Arguments that restrict themselves solely to these dynamics only tell one side of a complex story. Whatever the letter's inadequacies, there are other, external circumstances that might have inhibited the success of the proposal. It was not typical for an important publisher to consider, let alone accept, a novel by an unknown author the first time around: *Evelina* had itself been rejected when first offered. A fuller explanation for Cadell & Davies's rejection lies in the broader dynamics of the literary marketplace at the close of the eighteenth century. By 1797, the novel was a problematised genre, a result most especially of the antagonism towards radical fiction that occurred in the wake of the French Terror. Additionally, the novel had accumulated unsavoury associations, not least as a consequence of the scandal caused by Matthew Lewis's gothic potboiler, *The Monk* (1796), and its imitators. Respectable publishers such as Cadell & Davies likely wished to avoid uncertain ventures at such an anxious time: in fact, the firm's publication of fiction indeed fell around the turn of the century. It would seem, then, that Austen had indeed approached the most suitable publishers for her fiction, but at the most inauspicious moment possible.

As Fergus has argued, if Austen had swallowed her pride and applied to another publisher, 'First Impressions' may have marked an earlier commencement for Austen's publishing career.[13] For instance, publication would have been much likelier had she approached the more prolific publishers of fiction during the period. The Minerva Press, which kept the circulating libraries steadily supplied with new fiction, might have been an option, given the diversity and breadth of its output of novels. However, the Austens' sense of respectability probably militated against such an arrangement: as Austen had facetiously noted nearly two years earlier, 'I write only for Fame, and without any view to pecuniary Emolument' (*Letters*, p. 3). Another option might have been a publisher like Longmans, who were certainly supportive of

[11] Austen-Leigh, *Memoir*, p. 185. James Edward (Edward) and Caroline were the children of Austen's eldest brother, James.
[12] Theodore Besterman, *The Publishing Firm of Cadell & Davies: Select Correspondence and Accounts, 1793–1836* (London: Oxford University Press, 1938), p. viii.
[13] Fergus, *Literary Life*, pp. 9–14.

first-time authors of respectable novels; however, the Austens' provincial life at this time most likely prevented them from recognising the firm as a possible option. Facing rejection, then, it is conceivable that Austen was not willing to publish with a lesser firm, deciding instead to let the matter rest. Despite this setback, Austen returned to work on 'Elinor and Marianne', applying the lessons learned in composing 'First Impressions'.

One wonders why Austen desisted from trying to publish what remained a popular work in her circles. Although no compelling explanation exists, two coincidental episodes may have encouraged Austen to discard 'First Impressions' for the time being. The first concerns the domestic disruption that occurred after George Austen's unexpected retirement from the living at Steventon Rectory. This move led them to Bath in 1801, which may well have stymied Austen's creative facility: according to family anecdotes, she had fainted when learning about the planned relocation.[14] The second circumstance was the publication of Margaret Holford's *First Impressions* in 1801: far from being a domestic comedy with Burneyesque touches, this novel is a melodramatic sentimental tale, which contains the clichéd phrase 'vortex of dissipation' towards which Austen felt such distaste – perhaps the appearance of the phrase in this *First Impressions* was the original cause of that prejudice.[15]

Published at last

According to Henry Austen's 'Biographical Notice of the Author' which prefaced the posthumous edition of *Northanger Abbey* and *Persuasion* in 1817, '[i]t was with extreme difficulty that her friends, whose partiality she suspected whilst she honoured their judgement, could prevail on her to publish her first work', *Sense and Sensibility*.[16] Despite her supposed reservations, Austen had in fact made a second unsuccessful attempt to secure publication, with the sale of 'Susan' to Crosby in 1803.[17] Nevertheless, the move to Chawton in 1809 seems to have given Austen more purpose in seeking publication once again, and in 1811 she was finally successful in her attempts. *Sense and Sensibility* was issued by the London publisher

[14] Le Faye, *Family Record*, p. 128.
[15] In a letter to her niece Anna in September 1814, Austen commented on the hackneyed use of the phrase 'vortex of dissipation': 'I cannot bear the expression; – it is such thorough novel slang – and so old, that I dare say Adam met with it in the first novel he opened' (*Letters*, p. 289).
[16] Austen-Leigh, *Memoir*, p. 140.
[17] A full account of the attempt can be found in Anthony Mandal, 'Making Austen MAD: Benjamin Crosby and the Non-Publication of *Susan*', *Review of English Studies*, new series, 57 (September 2006), pp. 507–25.

Thomas Egerton in October 1811, published on commission: in other words, Austen herself (with the assistance of Henry) paid Egerton the costs of producing the book as well as a 10 per cent commission on profits. The first edition sold steadily by July 1813 and garnered Austen 'a reasonable profit for the period' of £140,[18] as well as positive reviews from the *British Critic* and *Critical Review*.[19] In many ways, while the mid-1790s period during which Austen had commenced writing her first drafts was a key period in the history of women's writing, the 1810s amplified the role played by female novelists in propelling the literary marketplace. During this latter decade, women authored at least half of the new fiction published, compared to just under one-third by men: clearly, Austen's success in finally securing publication can be contextualised under the auspices of a literary marketplace favourable to female writers.[20]

Thomas Egerton seems an odd choice of publisher for a novelist: although established and respectable, the firm issued mainly military and political documents rather than fiction, along with historical treatises and travel writing. Around 1782–3, Thomas and John (possibly Thomas's brother) Egerton acquired the 55-year-old business of John Millan; when John Egerton died in 1795, Thomas continued as sole proprietor for over forty years. Egerton's publishing business and subscription library was situated opposite the Admiralty offices at Charing Cross. While the proximity of Egerton to the Admiralty might suggest a connection to Austen's seafaring brothers, Francis and Charles, neither was in fact based in London around 1809. A likelier contact is Henry, who had been from 1801 a banker and army agent in London. The relationship might be further explicable through a publishing arrangement made some twenty years earlier: from January 1789 to March 1790, first James (Jane's oldest brother) and then Henry, both students at Oxford, issued a short-lived weekly entitled the *Loiterer*, which ran to sixty issues. From the fifth instalment, Egerton's name appears on the imprint as one of its publishers; perhaps some recent dealings with Egerton over Army affairs or even a decision to settle upon a publisher he already knew (however little) led Henry to Egerton sometime in 1809.

This personal connection seems the most likely, as Egerton was hardly a publisher of novels, unlike either of Austen's previous choices. Identifying himself on some imprints as a 'military bookseller', Egerton seems rather

---

[18] Le Faye, *Family Record*, p. 189.
[19] See David Gilson, *A Bibliography of Jane Austen*, new edition (Winchester: St Paul's Bibliographies, and New Castle, DE: Oak Knoll Press, 1997), pp. 6–12.
[20] See Anthony Mandal, *Jane Austen and the Popular Novel: The Determined Author* (Basingstoke and New York: Palgrave, 2007), pp. 3–40.

untypical of the eighteenth-century publisher: theological matter, by far the largest element of many publishers' catalogues at the time, hardly appears in his output. It is unsurprising that fiction features lightly, considering literary writings in general form a disproportionately small fraction of Egerton's output, which comprised mainly reissues and anthologies of older plays and poems. Egerton's audience more likely fell into a very specific niche, mainly consisting of professional men drawn from the Armed Forces. Neither an upmarket publisher like Cadell & Davies nor a populist bookseller like Crosby and Co., Egerton was rather a competent tradesman. Following the poor treatment she received from two notable publishers of fiction, Austen may indeed have preferred to enter into business with a firm less preoccupied with the nuances of the novel market.

Between the publication of the first and second editions of *Sense and Sensibility* in October 1811 and October 1813, Austen prepared for publication what had once been 'First Impressions'. The novel was retitled *Pride and Prejudice*, a phrase almost certainly borrowed from Burney's *Cecilia* (1782), in which it is used three times, and one which perhaps echoes the final title of Austen's first published novel. Austen Leigh's *Memoir* suggests that Austen reworked the novel alongside *Sense and Sensibility* during '[t]he first year of her residence at Chawton' in 1809–10.[21] During this period of revision, Austen seems to have made a number of fundamental changes to the prototype, dealing mainly with the size of the work and its internal chronology. *Pride and Prejudice* (nearly 122,000 words) is about one-fifth shorter than *Evelina* (just under 155,000 words), which would indicate a certain amount of cutting before publication. In January 1813, Austen herself told Cassandra that 'I have lopt & cropt so successfully ... that I imagine it must be rather shorter than S. & S. altogether' (*Letters*, p. 210) – in fact, her second novel is about the same length as the first, but it was printed more economically, spanning about thirty fewer pages. Fergus, drawing on J. F. Burrows's computer-based linguistic analysis, concludes that 'Austen's revisions consisted largely of cutting: condensing and refining a much longer original.'[22] Austen felt that the novel had perhaps been 'lopt & cropt' too enthusiastically, noting in the same letter that '[t]he 2d vol. is shorter than I cd wish – but the difference is not so much in reality as in look, there being a larger proportion of Narrative in that part.' Whether these deletions were made to the original 'First Impressions', to an intermediate manuscript (worked on anytime between 1799 and 1811) or

---

[21] Austen-Leigh, *Memoir*, p. 86.
[22] Fergus, *Literary Life*, p. 82, is referring to J. F. Burrows's *Computation into Criticism: A Study of Jane Austen's Novels and an Experiment in Method* (Oxford: Clarendon Press, 1987).

progressively through the years is a moot point, but, as R. W. Chapman has asserted, some changes were likely made in the 1810s because *Pride and Prejudice* employs an 1811–12 calendar.[23]

In a letter to Martha Lloyd written on 30 November 1812, Austen commented that 'P. &. P. is sold' (*Letters*, p. 205). Encouraged by the success of *Sense and Sensibility*, Egerton had decided to purchase the copyright to the novel, obviously hoping to benefit substantially from its sale. Austen was a little disappointed by the settlement, but still accepted his terms:

> Egerton gives £110 for it. – I would rather have had £150, but we could not both be pleased, & I am not at all surprised that he should not chuse to hazard so much. – Its' being sold will I hope be a great saving of Trouble to Henry, & therefore must be welcome to me. – The Money is to be paid at the end of the twelvemonth.

Although the £140 that Austen had made on *Sense and Sensibility* led her to hope for a similar amount, she nonetheless appreciated her vulnerable position as a female author and accepted Egerton's offer. The novel was published within two months of purchase, being first advertised in the *Morning Chronicle* on 28 January 1813, as by 'a Lady, the Author of *Sense and Sensibility*'. The size of the edition is not known, although one of 1,500 seems appropriate for a second-time, reasonably successful author; the retail price was 18s, slightly higher than the mean cost of a triple-decker during the 1810s.[24] In order to expedite publication – no doubt because he had a far greater investment than with *Sense and Sensibility* – Egerton divided up the printing of the three volumes. Charles Roworth of Temple Bar handled the first volume, while the last two were printed by George Sidney of the Strand (more carelessly, according to David Gilson).[25] By 29 January 1813, Austen had received copies of her 'own darling Child from London', which had been sent by Henry (*Letters*, p. 210). Having had a few days to peruse her copy, Austen noticed a few inconsistencies in the printed version which she found irritating: 'The greatest blunder in the Printing that I have met with is in Page 220 – Vol. 3. where two speeches are made into one' (*Letters*, p. 212). Interestingly, William Gifford – the editor of the *Quarterly Review*, who afterwards advised John Murray to accept *Emma* for publication and invited Walter Scott to write his famous review of the novel – later echoed Austen's own feelings about the poor quality of the edition: ''tis very good – wretchedly printed, and so pointed as to be almost unintelligible'.[26]

[23] Jane Austen, *Pride and Prejudice*, ed. R. W. Chapman (London: Oxford University Press, 1965), pp. 400–7. See Gilson, *Bibliography*, p. 24 for a fuller discussion of arguments by various scholars in favour of alternative chronologies of revision.

[24] See Mandal, *Austen and the Popular Novel*, p. 34.   [25] Gilson, *Bibliography*, p. 22.

[26] Samuel Smiles, *A Publisher and his Friends: Memoir and Correspondence of the Late John Murray*, 2nd edition, 2 vols. (London: John Murray, 1891), vol. I, p. 282.

In the same letter she makes her famous comment that '[t]he work is rather too light & bright & sparkling; – it wants shade; – it wants to be stretched out here & there with a long Chapter – of sense if it could be had, if not of solemn specious nonsense'. Nonetheless, as far as she was concerned, '[u]pon the whole however I am quite vain enough & well satisfied enough'. *Pride and Prejudice* was reviewed in three journals – the *British Critic*, *Critical Review* and *New Review* – all of which agreed that Elizabeth Bennet was perfectly executed, although Darcy appeared to some reviewers a little two-dimensional in his transformation from indifferent snob to passionate lover. All agreed that Mr Collins was excellent. The *British Critic* noted that the novel was 'very far superior to almost all the publications of the kind which have come before us ... the story is well told, the characters remarkably well drawn and supported, and written with great spirit as well as vigour'.[27] The *Critical Review* similarly observed that 'this performance ... rises very superior to any novel we have lately met with in a delineation of domestic scenes. Nor is there one character which appears flat, or obtrudes itself upon the notice of the reader with troublesome impertinence.'[28] The *New Review* simply offered a synopsis of the plot.[29] The critical acclaim and public taste for Austen's style of domestic comedy led Egerton to issue a second edition in October 1813, although specific details of the print run are not available.

In its new incarnation, *Pride and Prejudice* was once again circulated among the family circle, and Austen's letters between January and September 1813 refer to several instances of the novel being read aloud and copies being distributed to the various homes of Austen's siblings (*Letters*, pp. 205, 209, 214, 227, 230, 237). Le Faye notes that knowledge of Austen's authorship of her first two novels was restricted to her mother, siblings, eldest niece Fanny (eldest daughter of Edward) and a few close acquaintances.[30] Fanny, Edward's eldest daughter, recorded in her diary for 5 June 1813, that 'Aunt Jane spent the morning with me and read Pride and Prejudice to me as Papa and Aunt Louisa went out.'[31] It was not until their visit to Chawton in summer 1813 that the children of Austen's eldest brother, James, finally learnt the secret of their aunt's authorship. Once it was common family knowledge, however, James Edward admits the 'family conceit' that ranked Austen alongside luminaries like Burney or Edgeworth.[32] In wider circles, the issue of the author's identity remained uncertain for a while, with authorship

---

[27] *British Critic* 41 (February 1813), p. 189.
[28] *Critical Review*, 4th series, 3 (March 1813), p. 324.
[29] *New Review* 1 (April 1813), pp. 393–6. [30] Le Faye, *Family Record*, p. 187.
[31] Ibid., p. 202. [32] Austen-Leigh, *Memoir*, p. 105.

being ascribed to various figures, among them the aristocratic Lady Boringdon, later Countess of Morley (to whom Austen later sent a copy of *Emma*) and the sister of the novelist Charlotte Smith.[33] It was not long before the author's identity had become something of an open secret, as Austen's letter to Francis of 25 September 1813 reveals:

> the Secret has spread so far as to be scarcely the Shadow of a secret now – & that I beleive [*sic*] when the 3d appears, I shall not even attempt to tell Lies about it. – I shall rather try to make all the Money than all the Mystery I can of it. – People shall pay for their Knowledge if I can make them. – Henry heard P. & P. warmly praised in Scotland ... & what does he do in the warmth of his Brotherly vanity & Love, but immediately tell them who wrote it! – A Thing once set going in that way – one knows how it spreads! – and he, dear Creature, has set it going so much more than once.   (*Letters*, p. 241)

Austen's levity at this exposure can be contrasted with the anxiety of a contemporary female novelist, Mary Brunton, whose evangelical *Self-Control* (1811) was an unexpected best-seller. Her response to being revealed as a successful novelist is a fraught and painful one: 'if, before *Self-Control* went to press, I could have guessed it would be traced to me, I would certainly have put it in the fire. It is now universally believed to be mine; and this, in spite of its success, I shall always think my misfortune; but I am sure it is not my fault.'[34] Cheryl Turner observes that 'the emergence of women's professional writing was partly dependent upon the confirmation of more reductive notions of women's abilities'; while Lucy Newlyn notes that one consequence of this was that '[t]he rhetoric of modesty continued ... to pervade women's representations of themselves as writers, becoming increasingly difficult to decode as the reading public adjusted to their pervasive presence, and to the likelihood that self-deprecation camouflaged ambition'.[35] In such a context, Austen's almost defiant honesty – albeit within personal correspondence – is nevertheless a refreshing admission of authorial ambition.

Pride and Prejudice was the work that launched Austen's career, and it was for this novel that she was most esteemed by contemporaries. Other writers responded positively, with commentators such as Maria Edgeworth, Susan

[33] See William Jarvis, 'Jane Austen and the Countess of Morley', in *Jane Austen Society: Collected Reports 1986–1995* (Alton, Hampshire: Jane Austen Society, 1997), pp. 6–14; Gilson, *Bibliography*, p. 25.

[34] Quoted in Alexander Brunton, 'Memoir', in Mary Brunton's *Emmeline. With Some Other Pieces ... to Which Is Prefixed a Memoir of her Life* (Edinburgh: Manners & Miller, 1819), p. lxxi.

[35] Cheryl Turner, *Living by the Pen: Women Writers in the Eighteenth Century* (London and New York: Routledge, 1994), p. 58; Lucy Newlyn, *Reading, Writing, and Romanticism: The Anxiety of Reception* (Oxford University Press, 2000), p. 226.

Ferrier and Mary Russell Mitford voicing approbation. Walter Scott identified *Pride and Prejudice* as the novel which had 'attracted, with justice, an attention from the public far superior to what is granted to the ephemeral productions which supply the regular demand of watering-places and circulating libraries'.[36] Henry Austen's 'Memoir of Miss Austen', which accompanied Bentley's 1833 edition of *Sense and Sensibility*, emphasised how the speculation surrounding the novel's authorship ensured the author's lasting fame in the intervening decades: 'When *"Pride and Prejudice"* made its appearance, a gentleman, celebrated for his literary attainments, advised a friend of the authoress to read it, adding, with more point than gallantry, "I should like to know who is the author, for it is much too clever to have been written by a woman."'[37]

Conclusion

As Austen had sold the copyright to Egerton, it appears she had no further involvement with subsequent editions of *Pride and Prejudice*. This is corroborated by the fact that the error of the conflated speeches which she had complained of was not corrected in the second edition, and the emendations consist mainly of regularisations of spelling and corrections of misprints, rather than substantive changes. This edition, again published in three volumes and divided between Roworth and Sidney, did not sell as well as Egerton had hoped, as it was still being advertised as late as November 1815, alongside the second edition of *Sense and Sensibility*. A third edition was published, this printed in two volumes by Roworth for Egerton in 1817, again without any apparent intervention by Austen, and certainly with no mention of it in her surviving letters. As Gilson notes, it is not clear whether this edition was published posthumously or not, although a handwritten inscription on a surviving copy bears the date 'Sept. 6. 1817', two months after Austen's death.[38] The switch to the two-volume format reflects conventional publishing practices for issuing later editions once the initial commercial demand for the novel had diminished, as paper was the most expensive component of the process.

No further editions were issued until 1832, when Richard Bentley decided to include all of Austen's published novels in his Standard Novels. In July of that year, Henry and Cassandra received £210 for the copyrights of all the novels excepting *Pride and Prejudice*, the copyright of which still belonged to the now-deceased Egerton and was due to expire in 1841. Egerton's executors

---

[36] *Quarterly Review*, 14 (March 1816), p. 189. [37] Austen-Leigh, *Memoir*, p. 149.
[38] Gilson, *Bibliography*, pp. 41–2.

negotiated its sale to Bentley for £40, enabling *Pride and Prejudice* to be published in July 1833 as the last of Austen's six novels included in the Standard Novels, most likely issued in the series' typical print run of 4,000 copies.[39] Reprints of the Standard Novels appeared at regular intervals until 1854, as well as in a collected five-volume 'Novels of Miss Austen' set in 1833, 1856 and 1866. Amidst the male-dominated fiction market of the 1830s, it was in no small measure through her inclusion in Bentley's Standard Novels that Austen's works gained a secure purchase upon the literary canon for a new generation of readers. Southam notes that Bentley's editions 'gave the novels a new lease of life and aroused a certain amount of comment among readers who can fairly be classed as intellectual, or at least literary'.[40] The inclusion of Jane Austen in the Standard Novels ensured a continuous supply of cheap editions of her works, fixing *Pride and Prejudice* in the popular gaze throughout the nineteenth century, in anticipation of the phenomenal success that the novel would enjoy from the twentieth century to the present day.

[39] See Royal A. Gettmann, *A Victorian Publisher: A Study of the Bentley Papers* (Cambridge University Press, 1960), pp. 52–3.
[40] Brian Southam (ed.), *Jane Austen: The Critical Heritage* (London: Routledge, 1968), p. 22.

5

LINDA BREE

The literary context

Jane Austen's literary tastes were wide-ranging. According to her brother Henry '[h]er reading was very extensive in history and belles lettres' and her nephew James Edward Austen Leigh wrote that 'She was well acquainted with the old periodicals, from the "Spectator" downwards.'[1] Her letters refer to many hours spent in reading and discussing sermons and travel-writing, and books concerned with matters of contemporary religious and political interest. She read plays by Shakespeare and eighteenth-century dramatists (as well as visiting the theatre regularly during her visits to London); and she was familiar with the work of George Crabbe (1754–1832) and William Cowper (1731–1800) among poets, as well as other writers including the prominent figure whom she refers to on one occasion as 'my dear Dr Johnson'.[2]

But judging by the evidence of her letters most of her reading was in prose fiction, a form of literature disdained by some of her contemporaries but hugely popular in the Austen family. When in 1798 Austen accepted an invitation to subscribe to a local library she was scornful of the proprietor's claim that the library was to consist not only of novels, but of 'every kind of Literature &c &c': 'She might have spared this pretension to *our* family, who are great Novel-readers & not ashamed of being so.'[3]

Prose fiction in the second half of the eighteenth century was still dominated by the two towering literary figures of the 1740s and 1750s, Samuel Richardson (1689–1761) and Henry Fielding (1707–54). They were the first writers to take full advantage of the way in which fiction could explore how people lived and what they felt in a realistic contemporary world, and their hegemony lasted until Walter Scott took the novel in new directions from

---

[1] Henry Austen, 'Biographical Notice of the Author', 1817, reproduced in *P*, p. 330; James Edward Austen-Leigh, *A Memoir of Jane Austen* (1870), p. 109.
[2] Jane Austen to Cassandra Austen, 8–9 February 1807, reproduced in *Letters*, p. 126.
[3] Jane Austen to Cassandra Austen, 18–19 December, 1798, in *Letters*, p. 27.

1814, the year after *Pride and Prejudice* was published. When Henry Austen wanted to give an account of his sister's likes and dislikes in fiction he began with her response to Richardson and Fielding.

Fielding brought an unprecedented scale and scope to the novel, in terms both of subject matter and of narrative sweep. However, his broadmindedness in moral issues, subject of hostile criticism in his own time, created a stumbling-block to appreciation of his work, particularly for female readers, in the context of stricter late eighteenth-century codes of propriety. While acknowledging his sister's enjoyment of Fielding, Henry Austen concluded that for her '[n]either nature, wit, nor humour, could make her amends for so very low a scale of morals'.[4] Such a verdict may not tell the whole story, however. Jane Austen knew *Tom Jones* well enough in the mid 1790s to liken a friend's light coat to the colour of Tom's after he had been wounded.[5] Moreover, she must have learned much from Fielding's observant, idiosyncratic, often manipulative narrative voice, and his occasional innovative use of the indirect free style later so closely associated with her own work. And though she may not have known of *Shamela*, Fielding's witty and scurrilous parody of Richardson's first, massively successful novel, *Pamela* (1740–1), Austen, with her love of the burlesque, must have noticed the ebullient way in which Fielding's *Joseph Andrews* (1743) derived much of its energy and humour from sparking off Richardson's blockbuster.

Samuel Richardson was the acknowledged master of epistolary fiction, a narrative form which he used to trace, in an intense, even claustrophobic, way, the intricacies of lust, love and courtship among the English aristocracy and gentry. In *Pamela, Clarissa* (1747–8) and *Sir Charles Grandison* (1753–4) he offered, through a series of letters from the various participants, long, obsessive tales, in both tragic and comic modes. Austen, like many of her contemporaries, admired Richardson immensely, especially *Sir Charles Grandison*, now the least read of his novels. 'Her knowledge of Richardson's works was such as no one is likely again to acquire ... Every circumstance narrated in Sir Charles Grandison, all that was ever said or done in the cedar parlour, was familiar to her.'[6] Henry Austen wrote that his sister particularly enjoyed Richardson's 'power of creating, and preserving the consistency of his characters'. Alongside this, especially in *Sir Charles Grandison*, there are lively and entertaining scenes of conversation among groups of well-delineated individuals, in the cedar parlour and elsewhere, where subjects are wittily and rationally canvassed and relationships develop through social interaction.

[4] H. Austen, 'Biographical Notice', p. 330.
[5] Jane Austen to Cassandra Austen, 9–10 January 1796, in *Letters*, p. 2.
[6] Austen-Leigh, *Memoir*, pp. 109–10.

For decades after the deaths of Richardson and Fielding, though the number of novels published increased steadily, reflecting the ever-growing popularity of fiction as a literary form, no novelist achieved the same dominance among readers. In the second half of the century an increasing preoccupation with sensibility and sentiment led to fictions like Laurence Sterne's *A Sentimental Journey* (1768), with its suggestion that the chief concern of travel might be to provide an education in the emotions, and Henry Mackenzie's *Man of Feeling* (1771), which offered a protagonist whose sensitivities more or less preclude his taking any action at all. Meanwhile large numbers of other writers, often maintaining the epistolary form in order to privilege personal accounts of subjective experience, emulated Richardson's portrayal of wicked rakes and virtuous heroines without anything like Richardson's skill. In the 1780s, prose fiction was increasingly influenced by the threat of revolution in France and corresponding debates about liberty and equality in Britain, and these ideological tendencies hardened as revolutionary events took their course. Radical novelists presented aristocrats as rakes and parasites, and young women as either victimised or finding new independence in thought and action; conservatives, on the other hand, wrote about benevolent patriarchs, virtuously submissive heroines and wrongheadedly self-willed young women who needed to learn the error of their ways. More generally, the ever-popular seduction plot, given new intensity by fears of social and political violence, gathered into itself earlier features of romance, and flowered into the full-blown gothic fiction of novelists such as Ann Radcliffe, with outrageous events set in sublime locations. As revolutionary ideas receded, or were stifled, in Britain in the late 1790s, the interests of many novelists and their readers shifted again, turning from political allegory and high romance alike towards a less highly charged exploration of moral issues, emphasising the importance of establishing and maintaining a domestic stability which had come to seem metonymic of peace and security at a national level.

Austen read novels of all these kinds and more, often within weeks or months of their first publication. She read them attentively and frequently more than once: she often recalls characters or situations, even words or phrases, in her own writing. She owned a copy of *Hermsprong, or Man as He Is Not* (published in 1796, the year she began to write 'First Impressions', the first version of the tale that later became *Pride and Prejudice*), by the radical Robert Bage, a work that features a comparison between a mild and a lively heroine, a good deal of witty dialogue, a romance between the heroine and an enigmatic young man new to the area in which she lives, and an admittedly rather convoluted conjunction of the words 'pride' and 'prejudice', when the hero asks of the heroine, no 'sacrifice except of prejudice', and in return assumes she will 'not require of me the sacrifice of my integrity to pride'.[7] In general Austen seems not to have favoured either the extremely sentimental or the gothic modes of writing, except as an ever-fertile source of humour or ridicule. Some of her own earliest creative work takes the form of burlesques of the extreme situations presented in many contemporary novels, and this continued into her adult life: a spoof letter, ostensibly to be sent to the author of *Lady Maclairn, the Victim of Villany* (1806) mocking the over-sentimentality and verbosity of the novel, survives (*LM*, p. 213). Throughout her reading life she relished others' burlesques of overblown writing, from Charlotte Lennox's *The Female Quixote* (1752) – which in 1807 'makes our evening amusement; to me a very high one, as I find the work quite equal to what I remembered it' – to Eaton Stannard Barrett's *The Heroine*, which she read with pleasure in 1814: 'I have torn through the 3d vol ... It is a delightful burlesque, particularly on the Radcliffe style'.[8] A little later she wrote her own comic 'Plan of a Novel' which neatly satirises the most clichéd personalities and situations beloved of novel writers of her time: her heroine, for example, is 'often reduced to support herself & her Father by her Talents, & work for her Bread; – continually cheated & defrauded of her hire, worn down to a skeleton, & now & then starved to death' (*LM*, pp. 226–9).

Most of Austen's comments on contemporary novels are critical, and she reverts again and again to the same faults: lack of probability, shortage of realism or absence of sheer common sense. Egerton Brydges's *Fitz-Albini* (1798) has 'very little story, and what there is told in a strange, unconnected way'; Sarah Harriet Burney's *Clarentine* (1798) is 'full of unnatural conduct & forced difficulties'; Mrs Hawkins's *Rosanne* (1814) 'falls into many absurdities' with 'a thousand improbabilities in the story'.[9]

Perhaps her most pointed criticism was of Mary Brunton's *Self-Control*, which was published in 1811, the same year as *Sense and Sensibility*, and around the time that Austen was preparing to revise and shorten *Pride and Prejudice* for publication. Austen had looked forward with some trepidation to reading it, in case her own narrative would be pre-empted. Once she had taken a thorough look at it she was less concerned, and when she read it again late in 1813, with *Pride and Prejudice* safely in the public domain, 'my opinion is confirmed of its' being an excellently-meant, elegantly-written

[7] Robert Bage, *Hermsprong: Or, Man as He Is Not* (1796), ed. Peter Faulkner (Oxford University Press, 1985), p. 155. Jane Austen's copy, with her name signed on the flyleaf of each of the three volumes, is now held at the Huntington Library, California.
[8] Jane Austen to Cassandra Austen, 7–8 January 1807, 2–3 March 1814, in *Letters*, pp. 120, 267.
[9] Jane Austen to Cassandra Austen, 25 November 1798, 8–9 February 1807, Feb.–March 1815, in *Letters*, pp. 23, 126, 301.

Work, without anything of Nature or Probability in it. I declare,' she added, 'I do not know whether Laura's passage down the American River [in a barrel, in order to escape the man who has abducted her], is not the most natural, possible, every-day thing she ever does.'[10]

Austen's defence of the novel as a literary form – producing 'performances which have only genius, wit, and taste to recommend them' – in an early chapter of *Northanger Abbey* is justifiably famous:

> 'And what are you reading, Miss ——?' 'Oh! it is only a novel!' replies the young lady; while she lays down her book with affected indifference, or momentary shame. – 'It is only Cecilia, or Camilla, or Belinda;' or, in short, only some work in which the greatest powers of the mind are displayed, in which the most thorough knowledge of human nature, the happiest delineation of its varieties, the liveliest effusions of wit and humour are conveyed to the world in the best chosen language. (*NA*, p. 31)

The novels that Austen refers to here are *Cecilia* (1782) and *Camilla* (1796) by Frances Burney (the latter published under her married name of Madame d'Arblay), and *Belinda* (1801) by Maria Edgeworth. Although other novelists, including Charlotte Smith, Jane West and Elizabeth Hamilton, achieved considerable popularity around the turn of the century, Burney and Edgeworth were the two most prominent novelists of Austen's adult life, until the Walter Scott phenomenon began with *Waverley* (1814). Unlike some earlier female novelists these two women combined respectability (Burney spent time as a lady-in-waiting at court; Edgeworth was the daughter of an Irish landowner) with being successful producers of popular novels. Edgeworth wrote with a more overtly moral purpose, especially in her educational tales for children and young adults, but also in her novels, where she discussed serious issues such as the position of the gentry and peasantry in Ireland in *Castle Rackrent* (1800) and *The Absentee* (1811) or the ramifications of the prevailing system of patronage in her 1814 novel of that name.

Ironically in the light of Austen's praise of *Cecilia*, *Camilla* and *Belinda* as novels, none of the three works claim the term for themselves. Maria Edgeworth states in the preface to *Belinda* that 'The following work is offered to the public as a Moral Tale – the author not wishing to acknowledge a Novel', on the grounds that 'so much folly, errour, and vice are disseminated in books classed under this denomination, that it is hoped the wish to assume another title will be attributed to feelings that are laudable, and not fastidious'.[11] Burney simply sidesteps the term: the advertisement to *Cecilia* refers

---

[10] Jane Austen to Cassandra Austen, 11–12 October 1813, in *Letters*, p. 244.
[11] Maria Edgeworth, *Belinda* (1801), ed. Kathryn J. Kirkpatrick (Oxford University Press, 1994), p. 3. Page references hereafter in the text.

only to 'the following sheets'[12] while both the dedication and the advertisement to *Camilla* describe it – with spectacular inaccuracy, given its length (five
substantial volumes; more than 900 pages in a modern edition) – as 'this little
Work'.[13] Each of the three novels traces the experiences of a young heroine,
bereft of strong family (and specifically maternal) guidance, as she gains on
the one hand an increased level of emotional maturity, and on the other
fulfilment through marriage. All three work on a significantly larger scale
than Austen, in terms of the range of their characters and the subjects
addressed. Considering the action of *Pride and Prejudice* alongside *Cecilia*
(bankruptcy, suicide), *Camilla* (extortion, physical disability) and *Belinda*
(cancer, quack medicines) emphasises the way that Austen pared down the
actions and interests of the novelists she admired, and reinforces her claim to
'the little bit (two Inches wide) of Ivory on which I work with so fine a Brush,
as produces little effect after much labour'.[14]

Burney and Edgeworth both launch into their narratives with striking
openings, and *Camilla* and *Belinda* both begin with a generalisation. In fact
Camilla offers two: Book 1 volume 1 is introduced with a general paragraph –
'The historian of human life finds less of difficulty and of intricacy to develop,
in its accidents and adventures, than the investigator of the human heart in its
feelings and its changes' and so on (p. 7) – and then chapter 1 proper begins
with 'Repose is not more welcome to the worn and to the aged, to the sick and
to the unhappy, than danger, difficulty, and toil to the young and adventur-
ous' (pp. 7–8). Edgeworth begins in a very different register: 'Mrs Stanhope, a
well-bred woman, accomplished in that branch of knowledge, which is called
the art of rising in the world, had, with but a small fortune, contrived to live in
the highest company' (p. 7). In comparison with Burney's opening statements,
very much influenced by the example of Samuel Johnson (whom Burney knew
and admired), Austen's 'It is a truth universally acknowledged that a single
man in possession of a good fortune must be in want of a wife' seems
remarkably light on its feet, aligning itself with Edgeworth's witty satire at
the same time as it burlesques Burney's heavy declarations.

Burney was the leading new novelist of Austen's formative years, and a
shining example of the success that a woman could achieve with fiction. Her
first novel, *Evelina*, had taken the reading world by storm on its publication in
1778, when Burney herself had been just twenty-five. In her preface to that

[12] Fanny Burney, *Cecilia, Or Memoirs of an Heiress* (1782), ed. Peter Sabor and Margaret
Anne Doody (Oxford University Press, 1988), p. 3. Page references hereafter in the text.
[13] Fanny Burney, *Camilla, or A Picture of Youth* (1796), ed. Edward A. and Lillian D. Bloom
(Oxford University Press, 1972; Oxford World's Classics, 1983), p. 5. Page references
hereafter in the text.
[14] Jane Austen to James Edward Austen, 16–17 December 1816, in *Letters*, p. 337.

work Burney had staked her claim to a place in a tradition formed by a formidable range of (male) predecessors – 'enlightened by the knowledge of Johnson, charmed with the eloquence of Rousseau, softened by the pathetic powers of Richardson, and exhilarated by the wit of Fielding, and humour of Smollet' – and yet taking her own route, which was '[t]o draw characters from nature ... and to mark the manners of the times'.[15] Her claim to naturalism was somewhat exaggerated – years later Austen advised her niece, then writing a novel, to avoid having a lover speaking in the third person because it reminded her of Lord Orville, the hero of *Evelina*, '& I think is not natural'[16] – but her scenes of contemporary life among the English gentry, and her skilful deployment of groups of characters in social situations, marked an advance in the ability of the novel as a form to deal with the ordinary lives of genteel men and women. And in *Cecilia* and *Camilla*, her second and third novels, which replaced *Evelina*'s epistolary structure with an omniscient narrator, there was much for Austen to learn about the use of narrative voice.

Burney's style in *Cecilia* is an odd mixture of the overheated and the wittily observant. On the one hand there are many scenes of heightened emotion for the heroine, such as when her estranged lover finds her grieving for him, 'and the wild rambling of fancy with which she had incautiously indulged her sorrow, rushing suddenly upon her mind, she felt herself wholly overpowered by consciousness and shame, and sunk, almost fainting, upon a window-seat' (p. 547), where the narrator seems at one with the torments she is describing; on the other the narrator stands back from involvement with the characters and their feelings, as when she dryly observes of the profligate Mr and Mrs Harrel: 'in everything regarding expence, Mr. Harrel had no feeling, and his lady had no thought' (p. 127). There is occasionally a linguistic foreshadowing of Austen: it is hard to believe that the haughty patriarch Mr Delvile's message for Cecilia – 'that either *he,* or *you* must see his son never more' (p. 692) – was not in Austen's mind when she later had Mr Bennet outline to his daughter the equally unhappy alternative before her: 'From this day you must be a stranger to one of your parents. – Your mother will never see you again if you do *not* marry Mr Collins, and I will never see you again if you *do*' (*P&P*, p. 125). It is also worth noting that a mean and malignant minor character in the novel is a Miss Bennet – if Austen deliberately borrowed the name, it might have been as an in-joke of the kind she is known to have enjoyed within her family circle.

---

[15] Fanny Burney, *Evelina: or, The History of a Young Lady's Entrance into the World* (1778), ed. Edward A. Bloom (Oxford University Press, 1968; Oxford World's Classics, 1982), pp. 9, 7.
[16] Jane Austen to Anna Austen, ?mid-July 1814, in *Letters*, p. 278.

It has often been pointed out that the phrase 'pride and prejudice' appears towards the end of *Cecilia*: indeed, it is hard to miss the words, as they appear in capital letters, and as a central part of the moral of the tale: 'The whole of this unfortunate business', said Dr Lyster [referring to the problems experienced by the hero and heroine], 'has been the result of PRIDE and PREJUDICE ... Yet this, however, remember; if to PRIDE and PREJUDICE you owe your miseries, so wonderfully is good and evil balanced, that to PRIDE and PREJUDICE you will also owe their termination' (p. 930). And in fact the interplay between pride and prejudice is important both to plot and theme. Cecilia Beverley is a wealthy heiress who can marry as she wishes – with the one proviso that her husband must take her name. Mortimer Delvile is the son of one of Cecilia's guardians, an impoverished but haughty patriarch who requires his son to marry for money, but will not sacrifice the family name. Consideration of 'pride' and 'prejudice' in various forms plays an ongoing part in the development of the plot, but one episode seems particularly relevant to Austen's novel. Cecilia visits the Delvile family at their country estate. There she learns more about Mortimer: 'the adoration of every inhabitant ... had impressed her with the strongest belief in his general worthiness, and greatly, though imperceptibly, encreased her regard for him' (p. 480). There she consolidates her positive first impression of Mortimer's mother Mrs Delvile: 'though I waited upon her with a strong prejudice in her disfavour, I observed in her no pride that exceeded the bounds of propriety and native dignity' (p. 166). Tensions arise when Mrs Delvile, showing many of the qualities later prominent in Lady Catherine de Bourgh, opposes any possibility of a marriage between Cecilia and Mortimer, arguing in favour of the pride of the Delviles against the obscurity of Cecilia's family, and claiming that Mortimer is already promised in marriage to the suitably aristocratic Lady Honoria. Cecilia is convinced and crushed by these arguments, and relinquishes all pretension to Mortimer – an outcome that might well have provoked Austen into imagining how things might have turned out differently had the heroine shown more spirit and self-confidence.

If *Cecilia* may lie behind aspects of *Pride and Prejudice*, *Camilla* also has a particular significance for Austen's novel. *Camilla* was published by subscription in 1796, and one of the subscribers – at the substantial cost of one guinea – was the twenty-year-old Miss J. Austen of Steventon, Hampshire. She must have received her copy in July or August and there are three references to the novel in the letters she wrote to her sister Cassandra in September – it was therefore much in her mind in the weeks before she began to draft 'First Impressions' in October of the same year. Then and later, Austen must have been intrigued that the novel was set largely in Hampshire, and that places well known to her were featured (Camilla even stays overnight in Alton, the small town only a mile from Chawton, where the Austens lived from 1810).

To the modern reader *Camilla* is a frustrating novel, in which a series of overcontrived misunderstandings and misinterpretations, and the overcaution, refinement and sheer misogyny of the hero's male mentor, defer the coming together of two young lovers for a very long time. Austen clearly shared this frustration: she tartly advised Cassandra to tell one of their friends that 'I wish whenever she is attached to a young Man, some *respectable* Dr Marchmont may keep them apart for five Volumes', and she wrote on the bottom of the last page of her copy of the novel a tiny sequel: 'Since this work went to the Press a Circumstance of some Importance to the happiness of Camilla has taken place, namely that Dr Marchmont has at last [died]'.[17] During this very extended deferral of resolution, the inexperienced heroine repeatedly finds herself, consciously or unconsciously, on the brink of social and even moral disaster, while negotiating her way, largely unguided, among a wide-ranging and disparate group of other characters, including the comic extremes of vulgar 'cits' and aristocratic fops alongside members of the gentry represented in a relatively realistic manner.

Burney had a gift for the dramatic presentation of broad comedy which Austen relished: one of her nieces remembered that she read aloud the scenes of the awful Branghtons in *Evelina* 'and I thought it was like a play',[18] and the vulgar Mr Dubster in *Camilla* is one of the characters who gets a nod in Austen's letters to Cassandra. But however much she enjoyed it in her reading, neither this kind of class-based comedy, nor the comedy of extreme embarrassment, which is widespread in Burney's novels, reappears in Austen's. In this, as in other features of her work, Burney offered an example that Austen, rather than accepting, filtered through her own fictional interests. In producing scenes such as Elizabeth's embarrassment over the behaviour of her family at the Netherfield ball, Austen is writing against the more famous novelist in much the same way as her juvenile burlesques bounced off the sentimental novels then current, though with a different effect.

Burney tends to present rather ordinary activities of teenagers – flirting, taking a walk, attending a ball – in the highly stylised language of sentimental fiction, which in turn has a distant origin in chivalric romance. At regular intervals Camilla is 'in dismay unspeakable', 'almost petrified with amazement'

[17] Jane Austen to Cassandra Austen, 5 September 1796, in *Letters*, p. 9. Jane Austen's copy of *Camilla* is in the Bodleian Library. The comment was made in pencil and is now indecipherable by the naked eye, even with a magnifying glass. See Park Honan, *Jane Austen: Her Life* (1987; revised and updated, London: Phoenix, 1997), p. 120.

[18] Caroline Austen, 'My Aunt Jane Austen: A Memoir' (1867), reproduced in James Edward Austen-Leigh, *A Memoir of Jane Austen and Other Family Recollections*, ed. Kathryn Sutherland (Oxford University Press, 2002), p. 174.

(both p. 525) or full of 'imperious shame' (p. 641). When she realises she has inadvertently encouraged a young man, through ill-judged flirtation,

> she felt guilty to have involved herself in an intercourse so fertile of danger: she thought over, with severest repentance, her short, but unjustifiable deviation from that transparent openness, and undesigning plainness of conduct, which her disposition as much as her education ought to have rendered unchangeable. To that, alone, was owing all her actual difficulty[.]   (pp. 542–3)

We can only be relieved that Austen did not emulate Burney's language in passages like this. But while dismissing the terms within which Burney framed her heroine's thoughts, the presentation of the heroine reflecting on her conduct, working out what she has done wrong and how she can do right in future, feeds straight through to Elizabeth Bennet, as does the sense of the narrative being at least partly mediated through Camilla's consciousness (is it Camilla or the narrator who makes the final comment about the cause of her difficulty?).

In other respects too Burney offered a positive example. *Camilla* tells the story of a lively heroine, set off by several sisters, one of whom has the quiet poise and sweet disposition of Jane Bennet. Camilla herself, at seventeen, is significantly younger than Elizabeth and only occasionally shows sparks of her wit, but a minor character, Mrs Arlbery, has a neat turn for mockery, as when (with some justification) she calls the vacillating hero 'a pile of accumulated punctilios' (p. 484). And there are day-to-day situations familiar to the gentry of the time – local assemblies, country-house visits, being embarrassed by family members, courtship encounters between young men and women – presented in a less lofty way. When Major Cerwood, a soldier seeking a wealthy wife, discovers in the course of being rejected by Camilla that she is not in fact wealthy at all, the narrator skilfully accounts for his actions: 'Repulse was not new to the Major; who, in various country towns, had sought to retrieve his affairs by some prudent connection ... He bowed profoundly, called himself, without knowing what he said, the most unhappy of men; and, without risking one solicitation, or a moment for repentance, hastily took leave' (p. 534).

Edgeworth's novels appeared too late to affect 'First Impressions', which had been finished long enough before June 1799 for Austen to write to Cassandra, 'I would not let Martha read First Impressions again upon any account ... She is very cunning, but I see through her design; – she means to publish it from memory, & one more perusal must enable her to do it.'[19] And it is impossible now to reconstruct what kind of changes Austen may have made to her manuscript in order to prepare it for publication in 1813, beyond

[19] Jane Austen to Cassandra Austen, 11 June 1799, in *Letters*, p. 46.

the fact that she 'lopt & cropt' it.[20] But we know that by the time she was publishing her own novels she was watching out for other new work, 'always half afraid of finding a clever novel *too clever* – & of finding my own story & my own people all forestalled'.[21] And this was a much more likely possibility as fiction's interest in domestic concerns, and everyday realities, grew. *Belinda*, for example, contains some melodramatic incidents and characters, and includes traces of the romance form in its narrative tone – 'he listened not . . . [but] darted . . . a glance of mingled scorn and rage' (p. 352) – but such situations are often subject to the author's own mockery. The hero's very eighteenth-century idea of nurturing a beautiful, ignorant girl in seclusion to be his bride is neatly punctured – and the hero made to look not a little foolish – when he realises the likely disadvantages of having a companion in life who can neither read nor write. The main themes of the novel – Lady Delacour's fear that a wound in her breast has become cancerous, Belinda's unenviable situation as a young woman so promoted for marriage by her manoeuvring aunt as to be 'as well advertised, as Packwood's razor strops' (p. 25), a comment by the hero that Belinda herself overhears at a ball – are neither strained nor overheated. Edgeworth's aims, and her tone, are more overtly didactic than those of Austen, but her wit often comes much nearer Austen's than does Burney's broad humour or heavy commentary.

Many of the novels Austen read and enjoyed, or at least found entertainment in, lapsed into obscurity very shortly after publication – *Lady Maclairn*, for example, was never reprinted after 1806. It was evident to contemporaries that the two novelists of this period whose work would last were Edgeworth (who was publishing into the 1830s) and Burney (whose last novel, *The Wanderer*, came out in 1814). It is to Burney (as Madame d'Arblay) and Edgeworth that Austen is compared, by her brother in his 'Biographical Notice' of 1818, and by her nephew in the *Memoir* of 1870. In 1818 Henry Austen referred to her novels 'which by many have been placed on the same shelf as the works of a D'Arblay and an Edgeworth' and James Edward Austen Leigh acknowledged that if friends or neighbours had known that the family, 'in our secret thoughts, classed her with Madame D'Arblay or Miss Edgeworth . . . they would have considered it an amusing instance of family conceit'.[22] Austen's brother and nephew thought they were making great claims for their relative by the comparison. But by 1870, if not by 1818, Austen's reputation had entirely eclipsed that of those writers who may have been a major influence on her work.

<hr/>

20 Jane Austen to Cassandra Austen, 29 January 1813, in *Letters*, p. 210.
21 Jane Austen to Cassandra Austen, 30 April 1811, in *Letters*, p. 194.
22 H. Austen, 'Biographical Notice', p. 327; Austen-Leigh, *Memoir* (1870), p. 167.

6

BHARAT TANDON

The historical background

I do not wonder at your wanting to read *first impressions* again, so
seldom as you have gone through it, & that so long ago.
Jane Austen to Cassandra Austen, 8–9 January 1799
(*Letters*, p. 36)

It can be one of the great clichés of literary history to say of an author that she or
he lived in 'changing times'; after all, time is always changing, which is what
makes it time. However, when applied to certain writers, the phrase still has
some pertinence: to read Milton, Tennyson or Hardy, for example, illustrates
different ways in which transitions – from the largest national upheavals to the
most personal losses and gains – are worked into the texture of imaginative
writing. Austen, likewise, whether she wanted to be or not, was not only a
peerless documenter of the shifts in the status and functions of manners and
decorum in late eighteenth-century English society, but a writer whose writing
life witnessed some rapid shifts in fiction's form, style and popular reception.
Nowhere in her career is this illustrated with greater aptness than in the private
history of *Pride and Prejudice* itself – a novel originally conceived and drafted
in the 1790s, amid the literary and social culture of the Revolution decade, re-
thought over a period of more than a decade, and finally re-written to emerge as
the fashionable Regency novel of its day. In the process, this novel that
happened twice casts light, first on the world into which it failed to emerge,
then on the public world of literary reception in which 'THE AUTHOR OF "SENSE
AND SENSIBILITY"'[1] worked in 1812–13, despite her anonymity. At the same
time, placing the gestation of *Pride and Prejudice* back into the context of
Austen's larger artistic development challenges some critical notions of the very
idea of 'artistic development' – especially versions of history in which artists
only grow smoothly and progressively. *Pride and Prejudice* is a work of the
1790s that erupted suddenly back into the main trajectory of Austen's published career in the 1810s – one that is felicitously in tune with the way in which
elements from her early writings keep resurrecting themselves indecorously
even in her most 'mature' and 'accomplished' fictions.

---

[1] Title page of the first edition of *Pride and Prejudice* [1813], reproduced *P&P*,
p. lxxxi.

This emphasis is especially pertinent in the case of Austen, because the official version of her authorial history, and its relations to its times, tries to tell a rather different story. Henry Austen's 'Biographical Notice', appended to the edition of *Northanger Abbey* and *Persuasion* that John Murray published after Austen's death, confines itself to the most basic details of Austen's life and work – her brother's phrasing even seems intent on downplaying his late sister's creativity in favour of her unimpeachable piety:

> Short and easy will be the task of the mere biographer. A life of usefulness, literature, and religion, was not by any means a life of event. To those who lament their irreparable loss, it is consolatory to think that, as she never deserved disapprobation, so, in the circle of her family and friends, she never met reproof; that her wishes were not only reasonable, but gratified; and that to the little disappointments incidental to human life was never added, even for a moment, an abatement of good-will from any who knew her.[2]

Aside from the ironic fact that Henry Austen's phrasing could come from Mary Bennet in *Pride and Prejudice* ('Unhappy as the event must be for Lydia, we may draw from it this useful lesson; that loss of virtue in a female is irretrievable – that one false step involves her in endless ruin – that her reputation is no less brittle than it is beautiful, – and that she cannot be too much guarded in her behaviour towards the undeserving of the other sex' (*P&P*, p. 319), the 'Biographical Notice' has the more deadening effect of stressing at every possible opportunity that Austen's relations to her times were entirely conventional and inoffensive ('the cathedral church of Winchester ... does not contain the ashes of a brighter genius or a sincerer Christian' (*Memoir*, p. 138)). This version of Austen became a signal part of many Victorian images of her as the faithful chronicler of a distant, gentler world, as did Henry Austen's account of her reading habits. 'Her favourite moral writers', he observed, 'were Johnson in prose, and Cowper in verse ... She did not rank any work of Fielding quite so high' (*Memoir*, p. 144). The cumulative effect was, at the very least, to play down the importance to Austen's style of less 'proper' models such as *Tom Jones* and *Joseph Andrews*, not to mention the works of Tobias Smollett and Laurence Sterne.

A rather different mode of historical myth-making came with the publication of James Edward Austen Leigh's *A Memoir of Jane Austen* in 1870.

---

[2] Henry Austen, 'Biographical Notice of the Author' [1818], in James Edward Austen-Leigh, *A Memoir of Jane Austen and Other Family Recollections*, ed. Kathryn Sutherland (Oxford University Press, 2002), p. 137. Hereafter *Memoir*.

While it still has much merit today, not least as the only full-length reminiscence of Austen by someone who knew her in life (even if only as a child), the *Memoir* has also contributed to a simplified version of Austen's creative development that divides it cleanly into phases. Most influential in this regard is Austen Leigh's picture of a 'Steventon phase' of the fiction ('There some of her most successful writing was composed at such an early age' (*Memoir*, p. 43)), followed by a mysterious creative hiatus in Bath and Southampton between 1801 and 1809, and then a massively fertile period at Chawton, in which 'the last five years of her life produced the same number of novels with those that had been written in her early youth' (*Memoir*, p. 81). The problem with this version of her career, as Kathryn Sutherland has cogently argued, is not just that it ignores interstitial works such as 'The Watsons' (1804) and the fair-copy version of 'Lady Susan' (1805), but that it downplays the extent to which the late Chawton phase may be a 'culmination' rather than a sudden revival. Looking again at Austen Leigh's chronological divisions, Sutherland observes: '[o]ne advantage of refusing the bi-partite division of Austen's career is that it brings into focus and creative association the full range of the non-published writings. For there is a further chronology to take into account: that of the fiction which remained in manuscript.'[3] Another advantage of taking this view is that it takes seriously the continuities, as well as the differences, between the literary and cultural environments of 'First Impressions' in 1796–7 and *Pride and Prejudice* in 1811–12. A reader needs to take into account both the distance between the two moments of *Pride and Prejudice*, and the often strange filiations that Austen's writing creates between the 1790s and the 1810s, in order to appreciate how her literary history sets its own challenges to literary historiography.

There remains an important caveat in any discussion of the early compositional history of *Pride and Prejudice* – namely, the fact that we have only conjecture to go on, in the absence of any extant manuscript evidence. However, there are enough circumstantial facts and contexts that a reader can bring to bear – such as Austen's revelation on 29 January 1813 that 'First Impressions' had to be 'lopt & cropt' significantly in its final revisions (*Letters*, p. 202) – to enable some kind of contextual reconstruction. We also have the evidence of Austen's surviving manuscript works from the 1790s – a body of work that offers a rather more badly behaved atmosphere in which to set the growth of Austen's greatest comedy of manners. Put what we do know together, and a plausible relief-image of 'First Impressions' emerges, of a story at once out of time and ahead of its time.

[3] Kathryn Sutherland, 'Chronology of Composition and Publication', in *Context*, p. 13.

Even in the 1810s, Austen's earliest published works were met with little notice, and that little notice often damned them with faint praise, as when the *Critical Review* noted of *Pride and Prejudice* in 1813 that '[t]he sentiments, which are dispersed over the work, do great credit to the *sense* and *sensibility* of the authoress'.[4] That said, one only has to look at some of the notable fictional publications from the latter half of the 1790s to get a sense of the even more alienating climate of readerly expectation with which 'First Impressions' would have had to contend, had Thomas Cadell not declined to view the manuscript that the Revd Austen wished to send him. This was the age of Mrs Radcliffe (*The Mysteries of Udolpho* was published in 1794, and *The Italian* followed in 1797), of Matthew Lewis (whose notoriously salacious *The Monk* appeared in 1796) and of the 'horrid' novels which fire Catherine Morland's imagination in *Northanger Abbey* (and help to date the novel's original composition): Peter Teuthold's *The Necromancer; or The Tale of the Black Forest* (1794), Mrs Parsons's *The Mysterious Warning* (1796), Peter Will's *Horrid Mysteries* (1796) and Francis Lathom's *The Midnight Bell* (1798). Not all of these novels go as far as *The Monk*, which features torture, bleeding nuns, decomposing babies and a final cameo from the Devil himself ('Are you not safe from the Inquisition – safe from all but me? Fool that you were to confide yourself to a Devil!'[5]), but they do play to a taste somewhat removed from the late Augustan literary context in which Mr Austen's application to Cadell placed 'First Impressions' ('I have in my possession a manuscript novel, comprising 3 vols, about the length of Miss Burney's "Evelina"' (*Memoir*, p. 105)),[6] which may go some way towards explaining the publisher's lack of interest. The particular mode of social romance which Fanny Burney represented was certainly somewhat out of fashion by the mid 1790s. Whether or not one subscribes to the direct causal link that the Marquis de Sade drew between historical events and the rise of

---

[4] Review of *Pride and Prejudice*, *Critical Review* (March 1813); reprinted in *Jane Austen: The Critical Heritage*, ed. B. C. Southam, 2 vols. (London: Routledge and Kegan Paul, 1968–87), vol. I, p. 46.

[5] Matthew Lewis, *The Monk* [1793], ed. Howard Anderson (Oxford University Press, 1973; repr. 2008), p. 441.

[6] Janet Todd has recently raised the question of the precise identity of this 'manuscript novel', suggesting that it may in fact have been 'Elinor and Marianne', rather than 'First Impressions': 'I do not know whether George Austen *was* proposing to send out "Elinor and Marianne" or not; if he was, it would illuminate another question: why did Jane Austen choose to prepare and then to submit for publication *Sense and Sensibility* rather than (to a modern taste) the more immediately appealing *Pride and Prejudice* as her first book, since both were in manuscript and early form when she moved to Chawton and (we assume) began to think seriously of publication?' ('A Tentative Query on Jane Austen', *Notes and Queries* 59.1 (March 2012), pp. 105–6).

gothic shocks in fiction ('le fruit indispensable des secousses révolutionnaires, dont l'Europe entière se ressentait' [the unavoidable result of the revolutionary shocks which all of Europe was suffering]),[7] it is clear that there was at least some correlation between a larger political climate of fear in the mid 1790s, and an aesthetic taste for having those fears both raised and palliated.

For British novel readers in 1797, a large part of this anxiety derived from the threats posed, whether directly or indirectly, by events across the Channel following the French Revolution in 1789, and particularly after the official declaration of war between the two nations in February 1793. In *Pride and Prejudice*, Austen finds a brilliant and ingenious way of making this feeling of threat perennially manifest, without needing to spell it out loudly to a readership that would hardly require reminding, by making the militia so significant a presence throughout the novel. The county militias had long been an important home-front supplement to the standing army, especially after they were modernised by the Militia Act of 1757; but they were freshly embodied and mobilised in 1792, even before the official outbreak of hostilities, out of the pervasive fear of an imminent French invasion.[8] The novel may paint an accurate picture of a world in which the life of militia officers can largely be one of socialising and intriguing, as in Lydia Bennet's surreal, visionary daydream about Brighton:

> In Lydia's imagination, a visit to Brighton comprised every possibility of earthly happiness. She saw with the creative eye of fancy, the streets of that gay bathing place covered with officers. She saw herself the object of attention, to tens and to scores of them presently unknown. She saw all the glories of the camp; its tents stretched forth in beautiful uniformity of lines, crowded with the young and the gay, and dazzling with scarlet; and to complete the view, she saw herself seated beneath a tent, tenderly flirting with at least six officers at once. (*P&P*, p. 258)

Nevertheless, the 'scarlet' of the officers' uniforms works not only to attract the women of Meryton and Brighton, but also subliminally to alert Austen's contemporary readers to the more distant threat that prompts the militia's presence in the first place. If we are to conjecture that the original 'First Impressions' also featured the militia in some capacity (and since the novel was 'lopt and cropt' rather than filled out, this is not unlikely), then the references would have carried an extra urgency, since there had been another

---

[7] D. A. F. de Sade, 'Idée sur les romans', in *Les Crimes de l'amour* [1800] (Paris: Le Livre de Poche, 1987), p. 42.
[8] See J. R. Western, *The English Militia in the Eighteenth Century: The Story of a Political Issue, 1660–1802* (London: Routledge & Kegan Paul, and Toronto: University of Toronto Press, 1965).

heightened fear of a French invasion in 1796, which would have occupied the militiamen at England's coastal resorts in a rather more serious manner than anything we see in the novel, even as Austen's sailor brothers Frank and Charles were more directly engaged in the defence of the realm. In addition, by the end of 1797, Britain had been left as the only major opponent of the revolutionary forces, increasing the feeling of geographical and tactical isolation, and rendering the exposed coastal edges of the nation that much more vulnerable.

I mentioned earlier how the history of *Pride and Prejudice* demonstrates the ability of Austen's writing to measure both continuities and cultural distances, and the role of the militia is a signal example of this. If it meant one thing in its 1790s context, it would have carried a whole new set of connotations for its 1813 readers once Austen had transposed the novel's chronology to fit the timespan of 1811 to 1812. Take the account of Wickham's plans for married life, as related in Mr Gardiner's letter:

> The principal purport of his letter was to inform them, that Mr. Wickham had resolved on quitting the Militia.
>
> 'It was greatly my wish that he should do so,' he added, 'as soon as his marriage was fixed on. And I think you will agree with me, in considering a removal from that corps as highly advisable, both on his account and my niece's. It is Mr. Wickham's intention to go into the regulars, and, among his former friends, there are still some who are able and willing to assist him in the army. He has the promise of an ensigncy in General – – 's regiment, now quartered in the North. It is an advantage to have it so far from this part of the kingdom'. (*P&P*, p. 345)

There is a lot going on in this short passage, both in terms of direct statement, and in terms of the kind of glancing implication that constitutes Austen's truest and subtlest engagement with her historical circumstances. Wickham's decision (albeit one enabled by powerful sponsors) implicitly recognises the impropriety of his conduct with Lydia, and the social stigma that it carries, even when rectified by marriage ('an advantage to have it so far from this part of the kingdom'); in addition, a charitable interpretation of his entering the 'regulars' at the lowly rank of ensign might see in it some desire to atone through honest service – although, of course, it may also simply be the best he can manage under the conditions he has created for himself, or the highest rank that Darcy is willing to shell out for. Over and above this, though, for a character to be quitting the militia for the regular army would have carried an extra resonance for readers coming to the novel eighteen years after the beginning of hostilities with revolutionary France, and at a significant phase in the land-manoeuvres of the Napoleonic Wars. While Wickham's action does not have the same fatalistic resignation as that of the speaker in Tennyson's *Maud*, heading off to the Crimea ('I have felt with my native land, I am one with my kind, / I embrace the purpose of God, and the doom assigned'),[9] it would not have been lost on an 1813 reader that joining the regulars would expose Wickham to what the final chapter of *Persuasion* describes so finely as 'the tax of quick alarm' (*P*, p. 275) – the risk of being suddenly (and, potentially, irreversibly) drawn into the main theatre of war on the European mainland, even as *Pride and Prejudice*'s final chapter counterfactually imagines a speculative future 'restoration of peace' (*P&P*, p. 429). Thus, while the novel's overt punishment for Lydia and Wickham is a life of ennui and mutual forbearance ('His affection for her soon sunk into indifference, her's lasted a little longer' (ibid.)), Austen's little historical references strike sparks off her readers' shared knowledge of the background against which the events take place. And if those references would have struck one set of sparks had 'First Impressions' appeared in 1798, Austen deftly re-tools them to strike new ones in the changed political and military conditions of 1812–13.

Another unavoidable presence in the background to both versions of *Pride and Prejudice*, and one which also exercised different pressures in the novel's two historical moments (not least on Austen herself), is that of monetary demand. As in *Sense and Sensibility* before it, money plays such a prominent part in determining both the social climate of the novel and the permissible 'moves' of the plot that it could almost be considered as a character in itself – a powerful and largely invisible off-stage presence that nevertheless exerts an extraordinary force on everyone and everything on-stage. There are overt references in the narrative to the importance of income and financial 'competence', such as the famous joke that Austen stages about Darcy's income at the Netherfield ball:

> Mr. Bingley was good looking and gentlemanlike; he had a pleasant counten-
> ance, and easy, unaffected manners. His sisters were fine women, with an air of
> decided fashion. His brother-in-law, Mr. Hurst, merely looked the gentleman;
> but his friend Mr. Darcy soon drew the attention of the room by his fine, tall
> person, handsome features, noble mien; and the report which was in general
> circulation within five minutes after his entrance, of his having ten thousand a
> year. (*P&P*, p. 10)

Austen's gag presupposes an absurdly precise, and inverse, arithmetical relation between the size of Darcy's income and the speed at which the 'report'

---

[9] Alfred Tennyson, 'Maud: A Monodrama' [1855], in *Selected Poems*, ed. Christopher Ricks (London: Penguin, 2007), p. 266.

gets around the room; then again, the joke would not work if it did not touch on a fundamental truth about the economic basis of *Pride and Prejudice*'s social world: the fact that, as Edward Copeland has remarked, 'money in Jane Austen's first three novels exists for the most part as a set of restrictive anxieties attached to the romance plot by the narrowest definition of domestic economy – fear of debt'.[10]

Those 'restrictive anxieties' were ones that the Austen women were only too familiar with from their own experience (especially after the death of Mr Austen in 1805, and the concomitant loss of income) and which must have had some influence on the basic plot-motif of female disinheritance which moves *Sense and Sensibility*'s action in its revised version, and is re-deployed by Austen to such effect in her next book. It is, perhaps, a measure of the tongue-in-cheek quality that Austen habitually affects in her correspondence with her sister, that one of the earliest surviving letters, from 14–15 January 1796, claims that 'I write only for Fame, and without any view to pecuniary Emolument' (*Letters*, p. 3); much closer to the real truth of the situation is the story she tells Cassandra from the Bull and George at Dartford, a tale whose disastrous possibilities are only partly offset by the happy ending and the comic tone:

> I should have begun my letter soon after our arrival but for a little adventure which prevented me. After we had been here a quarter of an hour it was discovered that my writing and dressing boxes had been by accident put into a chaise which was just packing off as we came in, and were driven away towards Gravesend in their way to the West Indies. No part of my property could have been such a prize before, for in my writing-box was all my worldly wealth, 7*l*., and my dear Harry's deputation. (*Letters*, p. 15)

From the comfortable position of hindsight, there may be a certain pre-post-colonial irony in the fact of money's being spirited away from England to the West Indies, when the usual direction of capital-flow was the other way round; however, for someone in Austen's position, there would have been nothing remotely funny about losing £7 for good. Nor was this awareness of potentially straitened circumstances unique to the Austens: by the time Jane drafted 'First Impressions', the state of the wartime British economy was worsening, and some of the economic anxieties depicted in the final version of *Pride and Prejudice* had become even more pressing in the interim. For example, the decision to suspend the public's ability to exchange paper money for gold in 1797 led to fears that banknotes (by definition, already at one

---

[10] Edward Copeland, 'Money', in *The Cambridge Companion to Jane Austen*, ed. Edward Copeland and Juliet McMaster (Cambridge University Press, 1997), p. 138.

metaphorical remove from what they stood for) might become completely detached, and thus tools of speculation; the ethical dimensions of the paper/gold connection are caught well in James Gillray's famous contemporary cartoon 'Political Ravishment', in which the Old Lady of Threadneedle Street (the Bank of England) rebuffs William Pitt's advances with a cry of 'Murder! – murder! Rape! – murder! – O you Villain! – what have I kept my Honor untainted so long, to have it broke up by you at last?'. Indeed, the late eighteenth-century displacement of paper from gold bequeathed to nineteenth-century imaginative writing (from the Brontës, through Dickens, to George Gissing) a sense for money as what one might call, in post-structuralist terms, a dangerously and promiscuously 'free-floating signifier'.[11] One can see throughout Austen's first published novels the impact of the various economic shifts that took place across the Revolution decade, even if that impact often registers in oblique but resonant fashions – as when Mrs Dashwood, in *Sense and Sensibility*, checks her speculative alterations to Barton Cottage with 'I shall see how much I am before-hand with the world in the spring, and we will plan our improvements accordingly' (*S&S*, p. 35), or when the narrator offers a little, concessive pun amid her sarcastic summary of Mrs Bennet's character at the end of *Pride and Prejudice*'s first chapter: 'The business of her life was to get her daughters married; its solace was visiting and news' (*P&P*, p. 5). Any reader, now or then, would be expected to 'get' the first layer of narratorial irony, but readers in 1813 might more readily have sensed the way in which the irony also pulls in the other direction, acknowledging, even as Mrs Bennet is exposed as the shallow creature she undoubtedly is, that for a woman in her financial position (having to make do within Mr Bennet's £2,000-a-year income, itself entailed away from the female line), dealing with five unmarried daughters would indeed merit the title of a serious 'business'.

Nevertheless, it may also be the case that the very economic conditions that worried the central plots of *Sense and Sensibility* and *Pride and Prejudice* into being eventually contributed to an atmosphere in which the revised version of 'First Impressions' could find a commercial audience. As so often, there is not one single causal explanation for these changes in the climate of literary production and reception. One factor has to be the increasing popularity, through the first decade of the nineteenth century, of various kinds of social fiction by women that did not owe so much to the example of 'Miss Burney's *Evelina*'. Often of a subtly or unsubtly didactic stamp, the works of Hannah More (notably *Coelebs in Search of a Wife* (1809), which Austen knew well),

---

[11] For more on this issue, see Simon J. James, *Unsettled Accounts: Money and Narrative in the Novels of George Gissing* (London: Anthem Press, 2003).

Maria Edgeworth (including *Belinda* (1801) and *Tales of Fashionable Life* (1809–12)), and lesser writers like Mary Brunton (whose 1811 novel *Self-Control* amused and irked Austen in equal measure) helped to establish a popular taste that was more receptive to works such as the revised *Sense and Sensibility* and *Pride and Prejudice* than the sensation-craving ambience of the late 1790s might have been to the original 'Elinor and Marianne' and 'First Impressions'. The influence of Edgeworth is of particular importance in this regard, since, in Marilyn Butler's terms, she had established a framework for 'the "feminine" novel – domestic comedy, centring on a heroine, in which the critical action is an inward progress towards judgement':[12] the very shape that Austen's mature romances came to inhabit, albeit with some significant twists of their own.

As I have been discussing, though, these broad changes in readerly taste (never the easiest factors to plot causally) cannot be cleanly separated from the influence of the economic hardships that intensified in the late 1790s, hardships that, as is so often the case in Austen's career, offered her unexpected advantages as well as unavoidable constraints. In the case of fiction, the rise of direct and indirect taxation meant that by the beginning of the nineteenth century, book ownership on a large scale was increasingly something that only the rich could afford; in *Pride and Prejudice*, for instance, Darcy's protest about book-buying ('I cannot comprehend the neglect of a family library in such days as these' (*P&P*, p. 41)) might have struck a contemporary reader less as a proof of his aesthetic taste than as a sign of his (perhaps alluring) economic freedom from the cares of most of the other characters in the novel. For Austen, as for any aspiring novelist, the hike in book prices at the turn of the century had one overarching consequence: an increase in the power and influence of the circulating libraries, which became the main buyers for editions of new novels at a time when many private consumers were priced out of ownership.[13] (Thomas Egerton sold the first edition of *Pride and Prejudice* at 18 shillings, almost half the cost of a whole year's individual subscription to the average circulating library.) Of course, with the opportunities that this form of publication offered, there also came a whole set of potentially trammelling expectations – not least the automatic equation of circulating-library fiction with triviality or, worse, immorality, as amply illustrated by Mr Collins:

---

[12] Marilyn Butler, *Jane Austen and the War of Ideas* (Oxford: Clarendon Press, 1975; 2nd edn, 1987), p. 145.
[13] See Lee Erickson, *The Economy of Literary Form: English Literature and the Industrialization of Publishing, 1800–1850* (Baltimore: Johns Hopkins University Press, 1996).

Mr. Collins readily assented, and a book was produced; but on beholding it (for every thing announced it to be from a circulating library,) he started back, and begging pardon, protested that he never read novels. (*P&P*, p. 76)

Then again, one of the defining characteristics of Austen's career is her ability to turn constraints into possibilities, refusing to be defined by what confines her; and, if the conditions of the literary marketplace in the early 1810s made her, to some extent, the prisoner of a set of generic expectations, they also afforded her a chance to commit her own refined version of aesthetic 'entry-ism', using the structures of the romance plot and the three-volume circulating-library novel as means of reviving some of the darker energies of her 1790s work in a more genteel context.

Key to this is the quality of continuity and ongoing revision across Austen's *œuvre* on which Sutherland insists, in opposition to James Edward Austen Leigh's clean historical divisions. At the level of form, critics have noted echoes of older forms of writing still at work in *Sense and Sensibility* and *Pride and Prejudice*, including a structural emphasis on the scene or tableau that harks back both to eighteenth-century theatre and to the detached components of epistolary fiction.[14] It is a recognition that also underpins Austen's own comic 'review' of the novel for Cassandra: that 'a "said he" or a "said she" would sometimes make the Dialogue more immediately clear' (*Letters*, p. 210) suggests the novelist's awareness of her story's original debts to forms that did not feature external, third-person narration. More important than these formal marks of the novel's pre-history, though, are the ways in which even the revised *Pride and Prejudice* still remembers the company which its first version kept, among the often indecorous manuscript work which Austen created in the 1790s.

One of the strongest impressions left by a reading of the juvenilia (*c.*1787–93), and of transitional manuscript works like 'Lady Susan' (probably drafted in 1795 and possibly revised in 1805), is of an anarchic world that decorous late-Augustan literary form is only barely and transiently able to keep in tolerable order, a world summed up in the great line from 'Henry and Eliza': 'she began to find herself rather hungry, and had reason to think, by their biting off two of her fingers, that her Children were in much the same situation' (*Juvenilia*, p. 43). And if we place *Pride and Prejudice* back into the point in Austen's creative history at which it was first conceived, other debts and crossovers come into focus. Lady Catherine de Bourgh feels like a relation of Lady Susan, especially in the way in which both stories

---

[14] See, for example, Paula Byrne, *Jane Austen and the Theatre* (London and New York: Hambledon and London, 2002), and Richard Jenkyns, *A Fine Brush on Ivory* (Oxford University Press, 2004).

retain a fundamental ambivalence towards these dangerously powerful females; likewise, the paradox that Mr Bennet sets up after Collins's proposal ('Your mother will never see you again if you do *not* marry Mr. Collins, and I will never see you again if you *do*' (*P&P*, p. 125)) borrows directly from 'Jack and Alice' ('Lady Williams ... declared that she would never forgive her if she did not, and that she should never survive it if she did' (*Juvenilia*, p. 27)); and the plot-logic of early tales like 'The Generous Curate' – in which Williams's eldest son goes to Newfoundland, 'where his promising & able Disposition had procured him many friends among the Natives, and from whence he regularly sent home a large Newfoundland Dog every Month to his family' (*Juvenilia*, p. 94) – is always threatening to revive itself amid the later novel's more decorous treatments of chance and design. *Pride and Prejudice* may be a 'comedy of manners', but its memories of its own pasts, the ghosts of the novel it might have become in the 1790s, open up a conduit from a less well-mannered phase of Austen's writing, one which stays open for the rest of her published career, and which, indeed, rises to even greater prominence in *Persuasion* and 'Sanditon'. Among her published works, it is *Pride and Prejudice*, with its manifold historical memories, that defines the ongoing contention between decorum and chaos that is at once her mature subject, and the essence of her mature style.

7

ROBERT MARKLEY

The economic context

When he first walks into the assembly in *Pride and Prejudice*, Darcy claims 'the attention of the room' with his 'fine, tall person, handsome features, [and] noble mien' (*P&P*, p. 10), a fascination enhanced as reports circulate 'within five minutes' that he is worth £10,000 a year. When he quickly offends the company with his pride and arrogance, the implied voices we hear and the judgments of Darcy with which we identify, are, to a large extent, those of the women in the room. After he dismisses Bingley's suggestion that he dance with Elizabeth, who is merely, he declares, 'tolerable; but not handsome enough to tempt *me*' (*P&P*, p. 12), no first-time reader of the novel can possibly find Darcy sympathetic. To a great extent, much of the sheer fun in reading *Pride and Prejudice* is that we, along with Elizabeth, must learn to interpret Darcy's reserve and understand the basis of his pride; we, too, have to chart our own responses to his transformation from a seemingly arrogant prig to a romantic hero. While many critics have suggested that this transformation occurs as much in Elizabeth's mind as it does in his manners, her view of Darcy changes only when she realises how being master of Pemberley, his large Derbyshire estate, shapes his character. In the twenty-first century, we are accustomed to thinking of individuals possessing land and earning incomes, but in Jane Austen's world, it is as illuminating to think of her characters being possessed by their estates, social positions and inherited responsibilities and obligations; this is, after all, the hard-won lesson that Emma Woodhouse learns from Mr Knightley after she has thoughtlessly insulted Miss Bates at Box Hill. For the last century or so, those of us living in Western, capitalist countries have been trained to think of our possessions – houses, cars, stock portfolios, livestock or crops that we might grow – as alienable; that is, we can dispose of our property in whatever ways we choose: selling it, donating it to charity, leaving it to our relatives or friends in our wills. *Pride and Prejudice*, however, asks us to consider the complicated situations in which upper-class men and women find themselves when property comes with legal restrictions and ethical obligations, and when their incomes from their estates or investments come with all sorts of strings attached.

In this chapter, then, I want to situate both Darcy's income and his psychological investments in his estate in their historical contexts. While almost every edition of, and guide to, Austen's novels makes some effort to convert sums like Darcy's £10,000 a year or Mr Bennet's £2,000 from his entailed estate into terms that modern readers can understand, they often rely on overly simple formulas, outdated economic histories and very scant data to try to convert 1813 monetary values into 2013 sums.[1] Not only do many of these efforts get the maths wrong, they also discourage us from paying attention to the nuances about incomes, inheritances, legal instruments (like the entail) and the nature of money made in 'trade' that many of Austen's readers in the early nineteenth century would have recognised intuitively. As much as modern readers delight in the social world of *Pride and Prejudice*, the characters themselves view that world through the prisms of money, inheritance law, and the values and obligations imposed on gentlemen and gentlewomen by their estates.

During Austen's lifetime, the gap in wealth between the propertied and unpropertied classes in England grew much wider; and, as significantly, income gaps *within* the upper classes – within the ranks of gentlemen – increased as well. A century before Austen was born, 'the relationship of staple food prices and rents to the overall cost of living differed sharply across [social] classes'; the lower one's income, the higher the percentage of it that had to go to paying for necessities, and, as a result, the more vulnerable one was to fluctuations in food and commodity prices.[2] The cost of living also differed for men and women; even upper-class women had comparatively few opportunities to increase their incomes by selling assets or changing how their money was invested, and women writers, as Austen well knew, were paid less than their male counterparts.[3] These changes in income distribution resulted,

---

[1] For a typical effort, see James Heldman, 'How Wealthy Is Mr. Darcy – Really? Pounds and Dollars in the World of *Pride and Prejudice*', *Persuasions* 16 (1990), pp. 38–49, and, for a useful corrective, see J. A. Downie, 'Who Says She's a Bourgeois Writer? Reconsidering the Social and Political Contexts of Jane Austen's Novels', *Eighteenth-Century Studies* 40 (2006), pp. 69–84.

[2] Peter H. Lindert, 'When Did Inequality Rise in Britain and America?', *Journal of Income Distribution* 9 (2000), p. 12.

[3] See Edward Copeland, *Women Writing About Money: Women's Fiction in England, 1790–1820* (Cambridge University Press, 1995), Susan Staves, *Married Women's Separate Property in England, 1660–1833* (Cambridge, MA: Harvard University Press, 1990) and Betty Schellenberg, *The Professionalization of Women Writers in Eighteenth-Century Britain* (Cambridge University Press, 2005).

in part, from what economic historian Peter Lindert calls the 'severe relative price movements' of commodities (grain, tobacco, tea and sugar) brought on by Britain's overseas wars with France, disruptions in international trade and unfavourable weather that affected crop yields.[4] In simple terms, the purchasing power of the incomes that the gentry derived from their tenants' rents began to erode as prices for imported goods rose, and those for agricultural commodities (wheat, livestock, wool, timber and so on) fluctuated, often significantly. While rents were generally stable over the short term, the price of commodities grown by tenant farmers varied widely, as did prices for the natural resources – timber and coal, in particular – that estate owners could convert into cash for improvements, renovations or managing their debts. Even as Austen's novels capture brilliantly the sense of entitlement that many members of the upper classes felt, they also give us a good sense of the underlying concerns about how extravagantly the gentry could afford to live, how much their estates and investments generated and how far their incomes went in maintaining their lifestyles.[5] Although the annual incomes of Darcy, Bingley (£4,000–5,000) and Mr Bennet (£2,000) and the independent fortunes of Caroline Bingley (£20,000), Georgiana Darcy (£30,000) and Mrs Bennet (£5,000) seem to be rock-solid markers of wealth and status, they invite readers to examine what these large sums of money meant to them, their (potential) marriage partners and their families.

In an age when Britain instituted an income tax in 1799 to fund its wars against France, and increased excise taxes on numerous items, the task of assessing the values of estates and inheritances was not an exact science. In recalculating the demographic estimates of income made by the Scots jurist Patrick Colquhoun for 1801–3, Lindert and Jeffrey Williamson suggest that per capita income – *not* family income – for Britain's 9 million people averaged about £22 a year. If anything, this figure only hints at the vast disparities in wealth between the aristocracy, the gentry and the wealthier merchant and banking classes on the one hand, and the 60 per cent of the population who survived on less than £30 per year on the other.[6] Family size, dowries and obligations to unmarried women matter significantly in Austen's novels because typically the households of the gentry had far more mouths to feed and bodies to clothe (of extended family members and servants) than did those of artisans, labourers and tenant farmers. Responsible for five daughters and a wife, several servants and a carriage, Mr Bennet's £2,000 income

---

[4] Lindert, 'When Did Inequality Rise in Britain and America?', pp. 12–17.
[5] The standard study is John Habakkuk, *Marriage, Debt, and the Estates System: English Landownership 1650–1950* (Oxford: Clarendon Press, 1994).
[6] Peter H. Lindert and Jeffrey G. Williamson, 'Revising England's Social Tables, 1688–1812', *Explorations in Economic History* 19 (1982), pp. 385–408.

from his estate is (particularly on a per capita basis) sizeable but not extravagant; once he learns that Lydia is indeed going to marry Wickham and wants only a £100 yearly allowance, Mr Bennet calculates that having her at home costs him £90 a year, 'what with her board and pocket allowance, and the continual presents in money, which passed to her, through her mother's hand' (*P&P*, p. 341). Her buying a bonnet she does not even like illustrates, in telling detail, the kinds of small expenditures that could eat away at a seemingly substantial income. In this respect, one of Darcy's advantages is that, except for his sister, who has her own fortune, he is not surrounded by the dependants, relatives and in-laws that typically constituted the extended households of the aristocracy. While his £10,000 a year would make him among the richest commoners in England, his income comparatively is even larger because he can devote it to maintaining Pemberley rather than supporting a large family.

Given his expenses and the entail on his estate, Mr Bennet's £2,000 a year delivers less than the same income seems to promise in the reveries of romantic heroines. In Austen's first novel, *Sense and Sensibility* (1811), the Dashwood sisters discuss how much money each would need to support their 'external comfort[s]' as the daughters of a gentleman. For Marianne, a suitable, 'very moderate income' would be 'about eighteen hundred or two thousand a-year; not more than that'. Although Elinor laughingly chides her by responding that, '*One* [thousand a year] is my wealth', her sister insists that 'A family cannot well be maintained on a smaller [income]. I am sure I am not extravagant in my demands. A proper establishment of servants, a carriage, perhaps two, and hunters, cannot be supported on less' (*S&S*, p. 106).[7] Marianne ultimately gets her £2,000 a year by marrying Colonel Brandon at the end of the novel, but her assumptions about what that income might buy are, to say the least, optimistic. If the Bennets are any indication, a family – with sons to educate, daughters to provide for through dowries or bequests, servants to feed and maintain – can encumber a seemingly generous income with a host of costs and obligations that stretch into the future. Marianne's vision of carriages, hunters and 'a proper establishment of servants' (including perhaps a cook, gardener, lady's maid, butler, scullery maid, upstairs maid and game-keeper) suggests that her desires for a 'very moderate' life outstrip her understanding of the value of money, particularly for a daughter who effectively has been disinherited by her half-brother and sister-in-law. The difference between Marianne and Elinor, or the greater gulf in understanding between Lydia and Elizabeth,

---

[7] See Downie's discussion of this passage, 'Who Says She's a Bourgeois Writer?', pp. 69–70.

testifies to the ways in which questions of money, social status and value subtly but insistently inform the worldviews of Austen's characters.

For many readers, including more than a few critics, questions of money, inheritance and the entail of Mr Bennet's estate to his nearest male relation, Mr Collins, create some uncertainty about the status of the Bennet family. The Bennets have been described as somehow representative (before the fact) of an emerging, 'bourgeois', upper-middle class; as a minor branch of a social elite; or as members of the 'pseudo gentry', or what we might call the aspirational gentry (those trying either to cling to their social status as their fortunes dwindle, or to improve their lot by marrying into families of greater social prestige or wealth).[8] Trying to place the Bennets, or the Gardiners, or Bingley too precisely within a rigid hierarchy of rank and wealth is to risk echoing the socio-economic prejudices of characters like Lady Catherine de Bourgh and Caroline Bingley, whose assertions of social superiority mark them as wealthy and prickly snobs. The Bennets, like the Dashwood sisters in *Sense and Sensibility*, illustrate one of Austen's favourite themes: how nuanced, complicated and uncertain the relationships between social status and money can be.

The characters in *Pride and Prejudice*, as in all of Austen's novels, have a double focus when it comes to the relationship between money and social status: on the one hand they are very conscious of their own relative positions within an elaborate social hierarchy, but on the other they often act – comically or almost heroically – to broaden understandings of what constitutes the status of 'gentlemen', their wives and their daughters. For every Mr Collins, fawning obsequiously over Lady Catherine de Bourgh (even though he is a reasonably well-off clergyman, and destined to become richer when he inherits Mr Bennet's estate), there is a Mr Elton in *Emma*, whose over-reaching social ambition in proposing to the heroine draws her disbelieving scorn. But Austen warns readers off both extremes – the cringing subservience that Lady Catherine (the daughter of an Earl) demands, and the over-reaching impudence that Wickham exhibits by trying to marry his way into the gentry, first with Georgiana and then Miss King. Instead, *Pride and Prejudice* seems to endorse an expansive rather than hierarchical view of upper-class social relations. Elizabeth asserts that if she were to marry Darcy, she would not be 'quit[ting] that sphere in which [she has] been brought up', as Lady Catherine charges, but marrying within her proper station: 'He is a gentleman; I am a gentleman's daughter; so far we are equal' (*P&P*, p. 395).

---

[8] See David Spring, 'Interpreters of Jane Austen's Social World: Literary Critics and Historians', in *Jane Austen: New Perspectives*, ed. Janet Todd (New York: Holmes & Meier, 1983), pp. 56–7; Edward Copeland, 'Money', in *The Cambridge Companion to Jane Austen*, ed. Copeland (Cambridge University Press, 1995), pp. 131–47, and Copeland, 'Money', in *Context*, pp. 317–26.

Elizabeth's implied definition of a 'gentleman' is inclusive rather than exclus-ive, and it is this larger sense of accommodations among the gentry, nobility and well-bred merchant classes that the narrator ultimately endorses.[9]

Although every reader of *Pride and Prejudice* remembers Darcy's first pro-posal to Elizabeth – his arrogance in telling her he had to struggle to overcome his 'sense of her inferiority – of [a marriage to her] being a degradation – of the family obstacles which [his] judgment had always opposed to [his] inclination' (*P&P*, p. 211), he is ventriloquising the pride that is part of his inheritance and that we hear, satirically exaggerated, from his aunt, Lady Catherine. At the end of the novel, after Elizabeth has accepted his second proposal, Darcy admits, 'I have been a selfish being all my life, in practice, though not in principle . . . I was given good principles [by his parents], but left to follow them in pride and conceit' (p. 409). While Darcy's 'principles' motivate him to act generously to his servants and tenants, his 'practice' exhibits the kind of snobbery, social and economic, that Lady Catherine voices. It is significant that, except for his cousin Colonel Fitzwilliam, who shares with him the guardianship of his sister, Bingley seems to be his only friend. Pemberley isolates as well as enriches him. His rejection of his inbred 'pride and conceit' is both the precondition and the result of his recognition that he and Elizabeth can be suitable marriage partners only if they are 'equal', only if Darcy learns to embrace a more tolerant and inclusive view of the relationships among money, inheritance and social status. He can be a gentleman, and a romantic hero, only when he accepts Elizabeth as a gentleman's daughter.

Elizabeth's status is in question only because her father's estate is entailed to Mr Collins, severely limiting what she can expect as a dowry or as independent settlement. In English common law, an entail restricted the heirs to whom property could be transmitted, usually with formulations that provided estates would descend to eldest or only sons, or, if the deceased had no living sons, to his closest male relative. Although many critics have treated the entail of the Bennet estate as characteristic of a rigid patriarchalism, Sandra Macpherson argues persuasively that the entail system involved a fundamental contradiction: it granted an absolute legal authority to an original donor, who could dictate the future ownership of his estate long after he had died, but it made his heirs – both living and yet to be born – merely presumptive; that is, they could inherit land and wealth only because the entail curtailed their rights to dispose of their inherited estates as they might wish.[10] For these heirs, an entailed estate

---

[9] On self-definitions of 'polite' and 'genteel' women in the late eighteenth-century provinces, see Amanda Vickery, *The Gentleman's Daughter: Women's Lives in Georgian England* (New Haven, CT: Yale University Press, 1998), p. 13.

[10] Sandra Macpherson, 'Rent to Own; or, What's Entailed in *Pride and Prejudice*', *Representations* 82 (2003), pp. 1–23.

produces income and secures a particular social status, but paradoxically guarantees no financial freedom, no ability (for example) to raise money by renting it or selling off some of its land or assets. An entail obligates the land-owner asymmetrically: he must take care of a property that his immediate descendants may not inherit. In this regard, the entail on Mr Bennet's estate serves a crucial double function in the novel: the Longbourn estate defines Elizabeth and Jane as a gentleman's daughters, and therefore deserving partners for wealthy men like Bingley and Darcy; and yet because it will pass out of his immediate family after their father's death, it also symbolises the temporal and generational instability of inherited wealth and, as significantly, the precarious position of women in a contractual society when all the contracts are written by men. Entails, then, are not just legal instruments to preserve male lines of descent, but a means to impose restrictions on the property, incomes and indeed social status of future generations.

Macpherson reminds us that, because of the entail put in place by one of his ancestors, 'Mr. Bennet has only a life interest in [his] estate'; otherwise he could sell the 'feehold' (the legal ownership of his house and grounds) and thereby disinherit Mr Collins while securing a large sum of money for himself and his daughters. We learn, fairly late in the novel, that, had Mr Bennet produced a male heir, he and his son, as the narrator tells us, could 'join in cutting off the entail, as soon as [the son] should be of age' (*P&P*, p. 340). By initiating a legal action to ensure that full ownership (in legal terms, a 'fee simple') passed to Mr Bennet's son and his male heirs rather than to Mr Collins, the Bennets could keep the Longbourn estate in the immediate family.[11] One of the novel's ironies is that Mrs Bennet, the daughter of an attorney, has no understanding of the complications that entails routinely created, nor of the logic behind them: in the eighteenth century, entails were frequently crafted to ensure that profligate sons (like Tom Bertram in *Mansfield Park*) did not ruin or mortgage estates that previous generations had inherited, improved or, in many cases, purchased with wealth accumu-lated through trade or manufacturing.

In another sense, the entail reveals the ways in which eighteenth-century property law placed structural obligations on landowning families that, as Macpherson suggests, had the effect of subordinating ideas of individual will to a logic of obligation. It is not only that Darcy has inherited Pemberley but that Pemberley has inherited him. As Macpherson puts it, 'Darcy's sense of responsibility comes from the logic of entailment' – abstract, future-oriented and, 'in important ways, involuntary'[12] – so that he feels a sense of obligation to the very idea of inheritance, of perpetuating all that Pemberley represents.

[11] Macpherson, 'Rent to Own', p. 10.   [12] Ibid., p. 16.

The logic of the entail – the subordination of individual will to the legal demands of inheritance – structures the relationship between the estate and its owners over many generations. Inheritance law ensures the continuity of property and prestige for noble, or, as in Darcy's case, near-noble families by placing restrictions on their ability to sell, rent, mortgage or subdivide the estate. Moreover, ownership demands that the estate be maintained, even improved, from generation to generation. While Pemberley secures Darcy's income, it also commits him to the vast expenses of caring for his estate (the Park alone, the gardener tells Elizabeth and her aunt and uncle, is 'ten mile around' (*P&P*, p. 280)) and to dealing with his tenants and servants in a manner that serves Pemberley's interest as much as it does his own.

For a twenty-first-century reader, Austen's descriptions of Pemberley may seem filtered by the cinematic vistas of manicured countryside that have become a staple of film adaptations of her novels.[13] What these carefully selected sites cannot show, however, are the vast maintenance costs – figured in labour, money and resources – that a large estate required. Evidently, Darcy is an ideal landowner, worthy of his idyllic estate. Mrs Reynolds, Pemberley's housekeeper, declares that he 'is the best landlord, and the best master ... that ever lived ... There is not one of his tenants or servants but what will give him a good name' (*P&P*, p. 276). Her praise of her master is cast in terms of his socio-economic roles rather than his intrinsic qualities; even her descriptions of him as a child, 'always the sweetest tempered, most generous-hearted boy in the world' (p. 275), define his character in relation both to his role as a property-owner and as the inheritor of his father's virtues; as Mrs Reynolds assures Elizabeth and the Gardiners: Darcy 'will be just like [his father] – just as affable to the poor' (p. 275). His generosity to his servants and tenants testifies to his benevolence more than his wealth; but this generosity is enhanced if we realise the significance of his seemingly small gifts and allowances: to 'the poor' (those earning less than, say, £20 a year), a suit of second-hand clothes, a barrel of apples or a side of mutton could make a dramatic contribution to the household economy. These virtues are expressions of a character that is formed by and through his management of the estate. Put another way, the estate obligates the owner to behave in a manner that ensures its beauty, elegance and endurance.

The fact that Bingley rents Netherfield, and is in no hurry to purchase an estate of his own, is a measure of the distance he maintains from the responsibilities that characterise Darcy as the inheritor of Pemberley. Macpherson defines Bingley's good nature as, in part, a function of his 'preference for

---

[13] See Linda V. Troost, 'Filming Tourism, Portraying Pemberley', *Eighteenth-Century Fiction* 18 (2006), pp. 477–98.

short- over long-term commitment', his impulsiveness in renting and later abruptly leaving Netherfield.[14] As a gentleman without an estate, Bingley enjoys life without the obligations that characterised landownership in the late eighteenth and early nineteenth centuries; but, despite his fine manners and good nature, his character is unformed by the rigours and responsibilities of being the master of an estate. At the very beginning of the novel, Mrs Bennet asks her husband if he has heard that 'Netherfield Park is let at last' (*P&P*, p. 3) to Bingley by Mr Morris, either the agent for the owner of the estate or perhaps the landowner himself. Her modifier 'at last' implies that this substantial estate has been on the discreet, word-of-mouth rental market for some time. While Mr Morris or his employer has found the ideal tenant in Bingley, an unmarried man with a 'large fortune; four or five thousand a year' (p. 4), what Austen leaves implicit are the circumstances that forced Netherfield to be let in the first place. In her last published novel, *Persuasion* (1818), the profligate Sir Walter Elliot has to be pressured into leasing his estate, Kellynch Hall, to Admiral Croft and taking up residence in Bath in order to reduce his extravagant expenses and substantial debts. It is not as if he has abandoned Kellynch Hall; Kellynch Hall has dispossessed him. Behind the letting of Netherfield to Bingley lies an untold tale of an estate that has gone from being a source of stability for its owner to a sinkhole of debt.

In an important sense, Darcy and Bingley's relationships to their estates – inherited Pemberley and rented Netherfield – help define different versions of masculine social responsibility and even romantic desirability. It is significant that Darcy is literally a different man at Pemberley than he is at Netherfield or at Rosings. Elizabeth is aghast as she listens to Mrs Reynolds's praise of her master's sweet temper and generous behaviour because this description contradicts everything that the heroine has observed and come to believe about him. Even stranger, in a way, is Darcy's confession to Elizabeth that as a youth he was full of 'pride and conceit', qualities that somehow escaped Mrs Reynolds's notice. At Pemberley, Darcy embodies the virtues identified with ideals of the English countryside; away from his estate, his pride has no context, no referent: it is as though his moral character has been cut off from the source that sustains it. When he returns to Netherfield with Bingley before he proposes for a second time, Elizabeth still is unsure of how to interpret his behaviour, although she is profoundly thankful for his efforts to save Lydia's reputation. Because Darcy's responsibilities to his sister and to the memory of Wickham's father prevented him from warning the inhabitants of Longbourn about his former childhood companion, he atones

[14] Macpherson, 'Rent to Own', p. 9.

for his previous silence by inducing Wickham to marry Lydia, however reluctantly, by paying off his debts and by purchasing a commission for him in the army. Darcy's motivations – his love for Elizabeth and his duty to rectify the wrongs done by a former family dependant – are mutually reinforcing. He becomes worthy of her love precisely when he is acting as the 'best master ... that ever lived', taking responsibility for Wickham's debts – moral as well as financial.

In contrast, Bingley's lack of deliberation and his openness and amiability seem functions of a fortune that has been inherited but not defined by the values of estate ownership. Within the upper-class society of the early nineteenth century, Bingley is a comparatively free agent, encumbered only by an unmarried sister, whose £20,000 all but assures her of a socially suitable marriage, and the company of a married sister and brother-in-law, the 'gentleman-like' but otherwise undistinguished Mr Hurst, the owner of a house in the fashionable West End of London. We learn from Darcy's letter to Elizabeth that, before he met Jane, Bingley was 'often ... in love' (*P&P*, p. 219) with pretty women, implying the kind of carefree existence we might expect from a man of wealth, sensibility and fashion, but with no responsibilities to an estate and its tenants. It is worth noting, in this regard, that when Mrs Bennet imagines Jane's marrying Bingley, she assumes that he will be buying Netherfield. Although Mr Bingley's father 'had intended to purchase an estate but did not live to do it', and, for his part, Bingley 'intended it likewise, ... he was now [by renting Netherfield] provided with a good house' (pp. 16–17) and hunting privileges. These requirements satisfied, 'it was doubtful to many of those who best knew the easiness of his temper, whether he might not spend the remainder of his days at Netherfield, and leave the next generation to purchase' (p. 17). Bingley's diffidence about buying an estate suggests why he is not an ideal romantic hero; he lacks the inherent sense of the responsibilities of owning an estate that help to form Darcy's character as master of Pemberley. He can be swayed by Darcy into dropping Jane, and then later proposing to her; he eventually, at the novel's end, buys an estate within thirty miles of Pemberley. For the most part, Bingley conceives of Netherfield as a site of his pleasures, hunting on its grounds and hosting balls. He has no second thoughts about offering his carriage to take Jane and Elizabeth back to Longbourn because his horses, unlike Mr Bennet's, will never be needed on the farm.

In contrast to his friend, who falls in love easily even before he meets Jane Bennet, Darcy, who is twenty-eight by the novel's end, has no romantic past that we know of, Caroline Bingley's best efforts notwithstanding. Like Mr Knightley in *Emma*, Darcy seems to invest his erotic energy as well as ethical judgment in the management of his estate – Pemberley not only reveals his impeccable taste, kindness to his servants and generosity to his tenants, but suggests that these virtues, to the manor bred and cultivated, enhance his sexual desirability. Elizabeth laughingly tells Jane that she began to fall in love with him when she 'first [saw] his beautiful grounds at Pemberley' (*P&P*, p. 414). Her wit is cleverly and characteristically double-edged. Darcy's estate is indeed part of his erotic appeal: his love for Elizabeth and her love for him ultimately cannot be distinguished from the generosity and sweet temper that are the consequences of his life at Pemberley.

In contrast to Darcy's sense of responsibility and Bingley's impetuousness, Mr Bennet's entailed estate produces a different relationship between land ownership and masculine sexuality. From the first page of *Pride and Prejudice* on, Mr Bennet exercises his wit at the expense of his wife and his daughters, 'all silly and ignorant like other girls' (*P&P*, p. 5), except Elizabeth. Mrs Bennet, he tells her, is 'as handsome as any of them' (p. 4), and this wry comment suggests why he was initially attracted to a woman of 'weak understanding and illiberal mind' (p. 262). 'Captivated by her youth and beauty, and that appearance of good humour, which youth and beauty generally give' (p. 262), he married her because his sexual and property-driven desires apparently converged; of all the men in the novel, Mr Bennet is the one most compelled by the demands of primogeniture: he must produce a male heir to ensure the future of his family and estate. Although 'very early in their marriage' he loses 'respect, esteem, and confidence' for his wife, 'her ignorance and folly' (p. 262) apparently do not hamper their sex life. Even as he mocks her, 'exposing [her] to the contempt of her own children' (p. 263), he is still trying to father a male heir: 'Five daughters successively entered the world, but yet the son was to come; and Mrs. Bennet, for many years after Lydia's birth, had been certain that he would' (p. 340). Since Austen's own mother had given birth to her youngest son, Charles, when she was forty (and the novelist herself was born when her mother was thirty-six), the implication seems to be that the Bennets have been trying, until some time in the recent past, to produce a son.[15] In Mr Bennet's case, the entailed estate allows Austen to draw a psychologically astute portrait of a gentleman-for-life, a man whose daughters' fortunes, in some measure, are bound to his mortality. Without a son to 'cut off the entail', Mr Bennet retreats into his study, and to the irony and satire that disturb Elizabeth. While he lives within his £2,000 a year income, he has little incentive, unlike Darcy, to invest in the future of his estate, or even in the future of his own family. Mr Bennet's life – sexual intimacies with a woman he habitually mocks – alienates him from the

---

[15] Deirdre Le Faye, *Jane Austen: A Family Record*, 2nd edn (Cambridge University Press, 2004), p. 41.

structures of obligation that bind Darcy to both individuals and the ideals of propriety, duty and responsibility that attend the ownership of an estate.

No reader of *Pride and Prejudice* likes Bingley's sisters. Although their father's and brother's fortune, and their own dowries, come from trade, they mock Jane's uncles, Mr Phillips, an attorney in Meryton, and Mr Gardiner, 'who lives somewhere near Cheapside' (*P&P*, p. 40). The Gardiners' house, however, is actually in Gracechurch Street, not in Cheapside, a commercial area of second-tier bankers, stockbrokers and insurance agents. The sisters' joke about Cheapside, 'That is capital' (p. 40), points to the social tensions within the communities of merchants, bankers and lawyers who made up a significant and growing percentage of the upper echelons of British society, those families and professions with average incomes of more than £100 per capita.[16] 'Capital' implies that Mr Gardiner is involved with ungentlemanly forms of moneymaking; and the narrator tells us that they 'would have had difficulty in believing that a man who lived by trade, and within view of his own warehouses, could have been so well bred and agreeable' (p. 158). The warehouses that one could see from Gracechurch Street in the early nineteenth century belonged to the East India Company, headquartered on Leadenhall Street, a short walk from the Gardiners' fictional residence. The East India Company was a controversial, though essential, part of Britain's worldwide commercial empire.[17]

Most readers in 1813 would probably assume that Mr Gardiner is making his fortune in the lucrative East India trade. The Company imported commodities from the East – tea, porcelain, silks and spices – that long had been staples of upper-class life in Britain and were rapidly becoming fixtures in the homes of artisans, clergymen, shopkeepers and even labourers throughout Britain.[18] Although there is no mention of his role in the East India Company, Elizabeth's uncle is thus identified with the most fashionable aspects of British overseas commercial ventures; rather than the ungentlemanly money-grubbing that Bingley's sisters sneer at, he is apparently involved in Asian trading ventures that were increasingly perceived as a source of much-needed income for the gentry, aristocracy and the nation as a whole. That Mr Gardiner

[16] Lindert, 'When Did Inequality Arise', pp. 15–16.
[17] On the East India Company during this period, see John Keay, *The Honourable Company: A History of the English East India Company* (New York: Macmillan, 1991), pp. 297–335. Jane Austen's elder brother Frank had been in the Far East as early as the 1780s (1788–93) as a midshipman and then lieutenant in the Navy, protecting East India Company conveys. After being promoted, he was given command of HMS *St. Albans* in 1807 in order to protect Britain's sea routes to and from China. See Le Faye, *Family Record*, pp. 65, 161.
[18] See David Porter, *The Chinese Taste in Eighteenth-Century England* (Cambridge University Press, 2010).

is 'well-bred' suggests that he is as much a gentleman as Bingley or Mr Hurst. Because he is in trade, earning money from the shares that he holds in specific cargoes, the narrator does not label him with a precise annual income. But Elizabeth's assumption that he, not Darcy, discharged Wickham's debts, suggests that his wealth ranks him among the upper echelon of merchants; as a group, their per capita income was, on average, only slightly lower than that of the hereditary nobility. Because he can leave his money to his children, he is, in many ways, better off than his brother-in-law, Mr Bennet.

The Bingley sisters' laughter at their pun on 'capital' also betrays a nervousness about the source of their own wealth. There were several ways that Bingley's father might have accumulated £100,000 in trade, although since the family is from the north of England, and the town of Bingley in West Yorkshire was home to several woollen mills in Austen's lifetime, the name itself suggests a connection to the wool industry. In an important sense, Mr Gardiner can be seen as a version of Bingley's father, a merchant who has acquired impeccable manners as well as a sizeable fortune, though as yet not an estate, to pass on to his children. It is precisely because Mr Gardiner's fortune, like their brother's, is unentailed, that he poses a threat to the Bingley sisters. He threatens their efforts to complete the erasure of remaining distinctions between their wealth and Darcy's. Unlike Sir William, who shrivels into silence before Lady Catherine at Rosings, Mr Gardiner is unawed by the trappings of wealth and status when he visits Pemberley, although appreciative of its natural beauty and architectural elegance. In the last sentence of *Pride and Prejudice*, Austen emphasises that the Gardiners, frequent visitors to Pemberley, remain 'on the most intimate terms' with Darcy and Elizabeth, and that 'Darcy, as well as Elizabeth, really loved them' (*P&P*, p. 431). Those who make their fortunes in the East India trade thus are encompassed within the realm of Pemberley and its values.

Although money, estates and questions of inheritance are everywhere in *Pride and Prejudice*, they are yet mentioned openly only by impolitic, ill-bred women, like Mrs Bennet and Lady Catherine, or unscrupulous males, like Wickham. Restraint in discussing these questions, particularly between the sexes, is a mark of good breeding. Midway through the novel, when she is staying with Charlotte and her new husband near Rosings, Elizabeth and Colonel Fitzwilliam, Darcy's cousin, seem drawn to each other. At a time among the aristocracy when long walks, frequent visits and several dances were acknowledged as signs of courtship, the Colonel's attentions to Elizabeth seem to be nudging the two towards a marriage proposal. But this possibility is forestalled by Colonel Fitzwilliam's polite but unmistakable indication that he is a dependent younger son who must limit his choices in marriage to eligible heiresses with generous dowries and large fortunes. The ideals of succession, propriety, duty and responsibility that define Darcy's character weigh very differently on his cousin.

Colonel Fitzwilliam, the younger son of an Earl, describes this sense of obligation and dependence by gently indicating to Elizabeth why, despite his attraction to her, he cannot act on it by proposing marriage: 'A younger son, you know, must be inured to self-denial and dependence ... Younger sons cannot marry where they like' (*P&P*, p. 160). As an officer with a purchased commission, Colonel Fitzwilliam has a comfortable but not extravagant income (likely well under £1,000 a year) and possibly some form of an allowance from his father. And he is acutely conscious of the gap between his aristocratic desires and the current state of his finances: 'our habits of expence make us too dependant, and there are not many in my rank of life who can afford to marry without some attention to money' (p. 206). His comments to Elizabeth call to mind more than a century of stage comedies and novels (many still popular in Austen's time) that dramatised the dilemmas of younger sons who were born with the spending habits of gentlemen but not the income. Younger sons exist in a kind of perpetual adolescence that, like Edward Bertram in *Mansfield Park*, limits or, in less genial characters, frustrates their ambitions. As a younger son, Colonel Fitzwilliam's future is uncertain, an inverted image of what awaits Mr Collins. As long as he outlives Mr Bennet, Collins inherits the estate in Longbourn; Colonel Fitzwilliam could spend his career in the army and retire as an untitled member of the gentry, or he could outlive his elder brother(s) and eventually inherit his father's title, estate and fortune.[19] If he and his brother were both to die without male heirs, Darcy himself (or his son) might be next in line to inherit the title, a plot device that Elizabeth Inchbald used in her 1791 novel, *A Simple Story*. As he explains his situation to Elizabeth, Colonel Fitzwilliam is still waiting for his future to arrive.

Elizabeth, blushing after deducing that Colonel Fitzwilliam's remark may be meant for her, asks in her 'lively' manner, the 'usual price of an Earl's younger son?', and answers her own question by suggesting 'you would not ask above fifty thousand pounds' (*P&P*, p. 206). Her playful comment reveals some of the ironies and tensions within a system of patrilineal descent. In theory passing down estates, titles and inheritances from father to eldest son tended to conserve the wealth of propertied families, but typically at the expense of younger sons and daughters who could have their choices of potential husbands limited or their preferences denied, or (as in Samuel Richardson's 1748 novel, *Clarissa*) be pressured into marriages based on

---

[19] See Tim Fulford, 'Sighing for a Soldier: Jane Austen and Military Pride and Prejudice', *Nineteenth-Century Literature* 57 (2002), pp. 153–78.

their family's desire for money, power or land. Ironically, Colonel Fitzwilliam, despite his birth, is not his own man. While Darcy easily resists Lady Catherine's desire that he marry her daughter, Anne, the Colonel has fewer resources to fend off his father's apparent wishes that he marry for money. Elizabeth, with her comparatively modest inheritance ('one thousand pounds in the 4 per cents' (*P&P*, p. 119), as Mr Collins says), has far more options in *Pride and Prejudice* than does a younger son of the nobility.

Although *Pride and Prejudice* is usually read as a romantic love story, it also lets readers see how limited the choices of suitable husbands are for an attractive and intelligent woman like Elizabeth or her beautiful and generous sister Jane. In the class-stratified world of the gentry, suitable marriage partners for young men and women of the upper classes were comparatively few, as Austen herself knew only too well. One does not have to be a statistician to calculate from Lindert and Williamson's demographic table that the younger son of an Earl, if shopping for a wife with a fortune of £50,000, would be choosing from a handful of marriageable women in all of Britain – from dozens rather than hundreds or thousands. If his family were to lower its sights and settle for a wife with a fortune the size of Caroline Bingley's £20,000, Colonel Fitzwilliam would still find himself choosing from a very small group. The socio-economic realities of the early nineteenth century put even greater pressure on women of the upper classes, given their limited property rights in inheritance and marriage law. When Mr Collins blunders into the novel, obsequiously and condescendingly seeking to marry one of Mr Bennet's daughters, he quickly becomes the butt of Mr Bennet's jokes (and the reader's laughter). After his unintentionally hilarious proposal to Elizabeth, Mr Bennet responds to his wife's insistence on the match by telling his daughter that

> An unhappy alternative is before you, Elizabeth. From this day you must be a stranger to one of your parents. – Your mother will never see you again if you do *not* marry Mr. Collins, and I will never see you again if you *do*. (*P&P*, p. 125)

As foolish as Mr Collins appears, however, his proposals need to be taken almost as seriously by the reader as they are by Charlotte Lucas: suitable opportunities for Jane or Elizabeth, no matter what their personal qualities, are not likely to be terribly frequent. Their prospective husbands would have to be either rich aristocrats who do not have to worry about money or status (like Darcy); well-off merchants or attorneys willing to use marriage to buy their way into the gentry (like Bingley); or clergymen or army officers willing to marry without the prospect of being made rich by their wives (like Mr Price in *Mansfield Park*). Elizabeth's lack of a sizeable dowry explains, in part, her initial fascination with George Wickham.

Before Wickham is revealed as a gambler, liar and opportunistic seducer of women, his flirtation with Elizabeth is treated with some seriousness as a plot device. As a junior officer in the militia, a reserve force that did not pay as well as the regular army, Wickham earns a meagre salary, probably less than £100 a year. Having squandered his godfather's bequest of £1,000 and renounced his right to the living he was promised had he been ordained as a clergyman, he is propertyless. Yet he makes a first impression on Elizabeth that is matched by that of no other male character: 'Elizabeth went away [from the Philips' party] with her head full of him. She could think of nothing but of Mr. Wickham, and of what he had told her, all the way home' (*P&P*, p. 94). Elizabeth knows that Wickham is penniless, yet his comparative poverty does not necessarily disqual-ify him as a potential mate or, even after he has redirected his attentions to another woman, cast him beyond the pale of polite society. In a much-cited scene after Wickham has shifted his attention to Miss King, 'a very good kind of girl' with an inheritance of £10,000, Elizabeth defends the man she still con-siders a friend from Mrs Gardiner's questions about his motivations:

'But, my dear Elizabeth,' she added, 'what sort of girl is Miss King? I should be sorry to think our friend mercenary.'

'Pray, my dear aunt, what is the difference in matrimonial affairs between the mercenary and the prudent motive? Where does discretion end, and avarice begin? Last Christmas you were afraid of his marrying me, because it would be imprudent; and now, because he is trying to get a girl with only ten thousand pounds, you want to find out that he is mercenary.'

. . .

'But he paid her not the smallest attention, till her grandfather's death made her mistress of this fortune.'

'No – why should he? If it was not allowable for him to gain *my* affections, because I had no money, what occasion could there be for making love to a girl whom he did not care about, and who was equally poor?'

'But there seems indelicacy in directing his attentions towards her, so soon after this event.'

'A man in distressed circumstances has not time for all those elegant decorums which other people may observe. If *she* does not object to it, why should *we*?'   (*P&P*, pp. 173–4)

In one respect, Elizabeth seems to empathise with Wickham; his 'distressed circumstances' justify dispensing with 'elegant decorums'; what appear 'mer-cenary' motives from the perspective of the well-off Mrs Gardiner seem like 'prudent' self-interest to a young woman, as the heroine describes herself, with 'no money'. Elizabeth's interesting turn of phrase, 'if it was not allowable for him to gain *my* affections, because I had no money', implies that it would have been 'allowable' – that is, socially understandable and even morally forgivable – for him to pursue her if she indeed had a substantial fortune. It is not until Darcy's letter reveals that Wickham had tried to elope with Georgiana and her £30,000 that Elizabeth recognises his motives as 'solely and hatefully mercenary'; she even takes what she now terms 'the mediocrity of [Miss King's] fortune' as evidence of Wickham's desperation in 'grasp[ing] at any thing' (*P&P*, p. 229). She has gone from empathising with his position – a man with the manners but not the money of a gentleman – to seeing him as a predator, motivated by 'avarice' rather than self-interest.

Yet in many ways, Wickham, as much as Darcy, seems a product of his upbringing at Pemberley. Wickham's father, Darcy writes to Elizabeth, managed the business affairs of 'all the Pemberley estates', including the extensive holdings farmed by tenants that generate Darcy's £10,000 a year. Yet although he was entrusted with this responsibility, the elder Mr Wickham nonetheless remained 'always poor from the extravagance of his wife' (p. 222) – too poor even to educate his son without assistance. If Darcy embodies the virtues of Pemberley itself, Wickham, like his father, is alienated from the social and moral economy that yokes inheritance and responsibility, ownership and duty. For both father and son, social appearance is at odds with personal failures: an honest and efficient steward unable to manage his family's finances; a man with a 'gentleman's education' (p. 222) but no principles beyond self-interest. Because everything Wickham receives from Mr Darcy (father and son) is either a gift, a severance payment or a bribe, he has no true stake in the values that Pemberley represents. He is the novel's most extreme example of a man alienated from the values and obligations that define a true gentleman. With neither Colonel Fitzwilliam's deference to his family nor Mr Bennet's ironic take on his status as the lifetime owner of an entailed estate, Wickham takes to seducing women (Georgiana, Miss King and Lydia) as a way to seek a kind of existential revenge on men of property. Although Mrs Gardiner proves correct in her concerns about Wickham's character, Elizabeth, as the daughter of a country gentleman with an entailed estate, recognises in him a twisted version of the kind of self-interest that leads Charlotte Lucas to marry Mr Collins.

With the exception of Emma, all of Austen's heroines face the prospect of being banished from the estates to which they have been born (or, in Fanny's case in *Mansfield Park*, bred). Suitable marriages – financially, socially and romantically – are essential for them to *be* heroines rather than becoming objects of our comic (Mary Bennet) or satiric (Caroline Bingley) laughter. Elizabeth Bennet and her sisters thus face both challenges and opportunities: without significant dowries, they must secure husbands to support them in a socio-economic world rife with the social expectations and psychological pressures that many of Austen's original readers apparently found true to life. The first review of *Pride and Prejudice* in February 1813 in the *British Critic* praised particularly its 'characters remarkably well drawn and supported'; a month later the *Critical Review* declared, 'There is not one person in the drama with whom we could readily dispense; – they have all their proper places ... [no] one character ... appears flat, or obtrudes itself upon the notice of the reader with troublesome impertinence.'[20] This praise suggests that readers recognised the ways in which the characters' dilemmas offered them images of many of their own lives hemmed in by the dictates of property and marriage. And they appreciated as well the kind of wish fulfilment that Elizabeth's marriage to Darcy, or Jane's to Bingley, represents. In a letter to her sister Cassandra in February 1813, Austen declared that she was 'quite vain enough & well satisfied enough' with *Pride and Prejudice*, although, in retrospect, she found that it 'is rather too light & bright & sparkling; – it wants shade'.[21] In one sense, it is precisely the 'shade', provided by the prospect of a heroine's disinheritance, that figures in the novel that she was then writing, *Mansfield Park*. For the 1813 readers of *Pride and Prejudice*, the Bennet sisters' happy endings meant that they had to find the estates as well as the husbands they deserved.

---

[20] Quoted in Le Faye, *Family Record*, pp. 195, 196.   [21] Quoted ibid., p. 195.

8

JUDITH W. PAGE

Estates

On 12 January 1848, Charlotte Brontë wrote to G. H. Lewes that in *Pride and Prejudice* she found 'a carefully-fenced, highly cultivated garden with neat borders and delicate flowers – but no glance of a bright vivid physiognomy – no open country – no fresh air – no blue hill – no bonny beck'.[1] Perhaps Austen's landscapes appear overly delicate and cultivated in contrast to the wild moors of Brontë's native Yorkshire, but Brontë overlooks the diversity and subtlety of Austen's topography and its role in her novels. As Alistair Duckworth has argued, the 'logic of the metonym' influences the presentation of estates and landscapes, so that gardens and houses 'play a variety of coded roles in the English novel'.[2] In *Pride and Prejudice*, crucial insights into character and the meanings attributed to class are linked to landscapes. In this chapter, I shall chart the development of the main characters by the ways they relate to and respond to the houses, estates and grounds that they encounter. Through these dynamic relationships between characters and places, Austen explores the aesthetic, emotional and moral dimensions of cultivated gardens and of open country. We follow Elizabeth and Darcy, in particular, through various natural and cultivated landscapes – Netherfield, Rosings-Hunsford, Pemberley, Longbourn – as they discover both themselves and each other. In following their journeys through these distinctive places and landscapes, the reader, too, comes to understand the values and meanings attached to them.

In *Pride and Prejudice*, Austen adapts elements of the picturesque aesthetic as a lens through which to view the physical and moral world associated with key locations. Although some early readers of Austen assumed

---

[1] Margaret Smith (ed.), *The Letters of Charlotte Brontë*, 2 vols. (Oxford: Clarendon Press, 2000), vol. II, p. 10.

[2] Alistair Duckworth, 'Gardens, Houses, and the Rhetoric of Description in the English Novel', in *The Fashioning and Functioning of the British Country House*, ed. Gervase Jackson-Stops et al., Studies in the History of Art 25, National Gallery of Art, Washington (Washington, DC: National Gallery of Art, distributed by the University Press of New England, 1989), p. 396.

that she is merely critical of the picturesque, the more recent consensus holds that she distinguishes between the 'surface' and 'moral' picturesque and between picturesque improvement and picturesque aesthetics.[3] As an aesthetic that valued the rough, the wild, the playful, the surprising, the intricate, the ruined or the incomplete, the picturesque eschewed the extremes of Edmund Burke's binary of the sublime and the beautiful. Furthermore, the picturesque framed the landscape aesthetically: travellers viewed new landscapes as if they were viewing paintings, while designers and property owners modified or 'improved' their ground to adhere to the new aesthetic.

According to Ann Bermingham and other theorists, the picturesque arose as a movement just as the land was changing for ever, with wealthy landowners enclosing the common or public areas for private, often ornamental, use. The picturesque enacts the processes of 'loss and of imaginative recovery' as landscapers and tourists come to value the very open spaces that had once been the products of nature rather than of art or preservation.[4] They seek ruins or the evidence of time's hand in the landscape, often fabricating ruins or follies that made such spaces more rustic. But in treasuring the charmingly run-down cottage or the exotic ruin, adherents of the picturesque often failed to recognise that 'the aesthetic and moral may conflict', as Ruskin later put it. Hungry children might live in that visually charming cottage. In *Pride and Prejudice*, however, Austen is more interested in the ability of the picturesque to capture what Martin Price calls 'the growing interest in the way the mind creates its world' than in the extended social or political ramifications of this aesthetic view.[5] As Jill Heydt [Stevenson] has claimed more recently, Austen prefers in *Pride and Prejudice* the epistemological process of the 'true' picturesque, which is based on experience, to the predetermined rule-bound 'false' picturesque.[6] Part of our interest in Elizabeth and Darcy develops from the way they begin to correct their prejudices and misapprehensions about each other through an immediate apprehension and observation of the world.

---

[3] See A. Walton Litz, 'The Picturesque in *Pride and Prejudice*', *Persuasions* 1 (1979) (www.jasna.org/persuasions/printed/number1/litz/htm) 10/19/2010, on the first distinction and Jill Heydt-Stevenson, 'Liberty, Connection, and Tyranny: The Novels of Jane Austen and the Aesthetic Movement of the Picturesque', in *Lessons of Romanticism: A Critical Companion*, ed. Thomas Pfau and Robert F. Gleckner (Durham, NC: Duke University Press, 1998), pp. 261–79, p. 262, on the latter distinction.

[4] Ann Bermingham, *Landscape and Ideology: The English Rustic Tradition, 1740–1860* (Berkeley: University of California Press, 1986), p. 9.

[5] Martin Price, 'The Picturesque Moment', in *From Sensibility to Romanticism*, ed. Frederick W. Hilles and Harold Bloom (Oxford University Press, 1965), pp. 263, 271.

[6] Jill Heydt [Stevenson], '"First Impressions" and Later Recollections: The 'Place' of the Picturesque in *Pride and Prejudice*', *Studies in the Humanities* 12.2 (December 1985), pp. 115–24, pp. 123–4.

In addition to her engagement with the picturesque, Austen was interested in what we might call a Romantic vision of nature, in relation both to the development of character and to the expression of emotion. Moments of deep emotion and revelation often take place out of doors, revealing a conception of nature that focuses on the emotional tenor of the scene rather than on the visual elements for their own sake. As Rosemarie Bodenheimer has commented,

> Austen's landscape writing is related to romantic narrative and poetic technique in the sense that it points inward, consistently pulling the emphasis away from pictorial description itself to the vision of feeling of the viewer. Her artful uses of descriptions as projections of a character's sense of self or view of others reveal her sensitivity to the subject–object entanglements implicit in poetical responses to nature, and her ability to put them in the service of her wit.[7]

The outdoor space offers freedom but paradoxically also privacy that would be impossible in the drawing room, and, consequently, an emotional outlet for the characters. When characters go for a 'stroll' in the drawing room – as Elinor Dashwood does with Lucy Steele in *Sense and Sensibility* or Elizabeth Bennet does with Caroline Bingley in *Pride and Prejudice*, they are on display and the content of their conversation is either overheard or queried by the others. However, the shrubbery, which gives some solace to Fanny Price in *Mansfield Park*, often affords more intimate moments, as when Emma Woodhouse hurries into the shrubbery overwhelmed by the revelation of her love for Mr Knightley: 'Never had the exquisite sight, smell, sensation of nature, tranquil, warm, and brilliant after a storm, been more attractive to her' (*E*, p. 462). In this case, the sensory warmth is an objective correlative of Emma's awakened passion, and the narrative functions to impart this 'vision of feeling', to borrow a phrase from Bodenheimer, to the reader. The shrubbery and the beauty of the afternoon after a storm afford the perfect setting for Emma's rendezvous with Mr Knightley at the garden gate – and for the resolution of the various emotional conflicts and misunderstandings that have prevented the union of the lovers.

It is not so far from the shrubberies of Hartfield or grounds of Pemberley to the green hues of Tintern Abbey, where the 'wild secluded scene' impresses 'thoughts of more deep seclusion'[8] on the meditative imagination of the speaker. And it is no coincidence that this process of observation and increasing emotional depth occurs most fully as linked to particular places and

[7] Rosemarie Bodenheimer, 'Looking at the Landscape in Jane Austen', *SEL Studies in English Literature, 1500–1900* 21 (Autumn 1981), pp. 605–23, p. 622.
[8] 'Lines Written a Few Miles above Tintern Abbey', in *William Wordsworth: The Major Works*, ed. Stephen Gill (Oxford University Press, 2000), p. 131.

landscapes, to Pemberley, of course, or to walkways and shrubberies around Longbourn, as we shall see in the following pages. Furthermore, on the tour that Elizabeth takes with the Gardiners, the narrator abdicates the descriptive function and tells us that 'It is not the object of this work to give a description of Derbyshire, nor of any of the remarkable places through which their route thither lay; Oxford, Blenheim, Warwick, Kenilworth, Birmingham, &c. are sufficiently known' (*P&P*, p. 266). Unlike a popular tour guide such as Gilpin's *Observations*, Austen's narrative focuses on the emotional qualities, character development, and values that various places represent and not on description from the first words of the novel.

We are introduced to Netherfield Park in the very first lines, as Mrs Bennet informs her bored husband that 'Netherfield Park is let at last' by the rich young man Mr Bingley. Netherfield Park is significant not so much for the description of the house and grounds as for the circumstances surrounding it. We learn that Mr Bingley has rented Netherfield because he does not have an estate of his own, not for lack of money but because his father's fortune had been made in trade and he was not a member of the landed elite. Of the Bingley sisters, the narrator shrewdly states that 'They were of a respectable family in the north of England; a circumstance more deeply impressed on their memories than that their brother's fortune and their own had been acquired by trade' (*P&P*, p. 16). This insight into the Bingley family and their class background sets the stage for the various responses surrounding Elizabeth Bennet's three-mile trek across the autumn fields to Netherfield to visit her ailing sister Jane, who falls sick while visiting the Bingleys.

The Bingleys have established themselves in their rented house in the high fashion consistent with the sisters' aspirations. Elizabeth's actions reveal a very different sensibility, especially when she is shown into the elegant breakfast parlour. For, after walking part of the way with her own sisters, Elizabeth has

> continued her walk alone, crossing field after field at a quick pace, jumping over stiles and springing over puddles with impatient activity, and finding herself at last within view of the house, with weary ancles [*sic*], dirty stockings, and a face glowing with the warmth of exercise. (*P&P*, p. 36)

Contrary to Brontë's complaint, there is plenty of fresh air and open country here, and there are real puddles and country dirt. In the next chapter, jealous Miss Bingley takes great pains to critique Elizabeth's 'almost wild' appearance, concluding that Elizabeth's actions 'shew an abominable sort of conceited independence, a most country town indifference to decorum' (p. 39). Her verbal assaults on Elizabeth, with expressions like 'Her hair so untidy, so blowsy!' (p. 39), however, have the opposite of her intended effect.

Elizabeth's warmth, wildness and independent spirit pique Darcy's interest and arouse his passion. Like the picturesque landscape itself, Elizabeth defies Miss Bingley's stiff sense of decorum and form,[9] and she embodies instead imperfections that have their own appeal. Not bound by the false proprieties of a social climber like Miss Bingley, Elizabeth acts out of genuine concern.

The landscape surrounding Netherfield is never described in detail, but we infer things about the surroundings from the description of Elizabeth's activity – such as the stiles that she must jump over, indicating that there are many enclosures and fences along the way. She has obviously chosen to get to Netherfield on a footpath, which means 'field after field', rather than along the road or path that a carriage might have taken. More than mere topography, this description gives us a sense of Elizabeth's energy and character. Several important events will take place out of doors or inside looking out, and this early scene establishes Elizabeth as a young woman just as comfortable out of doors as in the drawing room. Elizabeth's affinity with walking and the natural landscape is crucial to the narrative: the various outside places provide alternately the privacy to meditate and the opportunity to talk privately to another person. This possibility will of course become very important when Elizabeth and Darcy are once again thrust together at Hunsford and Rosings.

Austen structures Elizabeth Bennet's visit to the newlywed Collinses at the Parsonage in Hunsford in Kent as a journey (from March to early May). The journey is broken each way with a stop at the Gardiners' home on Gracechurch Street in London. As in most parts of the novel, we experience this journey mostly through Elizabeth's perspective and her consciousness, and since 'everything was new and interesting' (*P&P*, p. 176), we get many interesting observations that help us to understand her responses to the scene.

Mr Collins of course takes advantage of this visit to show Elizabeth everything that she has missed out on in not becoming Mrs Collins; he is especially proud of the well-equipped and neat Parsonage and the surrounding garden, 'which was large and well laid out' (p. 177). As is appropriate for a parsonage and not an estate such as Netherfield Park, the garden is immediately adjacent to the house. Although we are not privy to what Mr Collins grows, we do know that he cultivates the garden himself, an occupation that he deems most respectable and that his wife encourages heartily, since it keeps him out of doors and out of her hair. We also learn that she has wisely chosen a room in the back of the parsonage, less attractive to her husband and also hidden from

[9] Jill Heydt [Stevenson], '"First Impressions"', p. 117. For a more recent suggestion that the Bingley sisters associate Elizabeth 'with profligate women, such as gypsies and prostitutes', see Heydt-Stevenson's *Austen's Unbecoming Conjunctions: Subversive Laughter, Embodied History* (New York: Palgrave Macmillan, 2005), p. 73.

the constant view of his gardening. Although Austen typically values gardens for their usefulness as places of exercise or meditation and for the promotion of various forms of sociability, including private conversations, the main use of this garden seems to be keeping Mr Collins busy.

Mr Collins's mind is prosaic, his characteristic stance is fawning and obsequious, and his garden is a perfect emblem of these qualities. As Collins takes Elizabeth around the garden, he points everything out 'with a minuteness which left beauty entirely behind. He could number the fields in every direction, and could tell how many trees there were in the most distant clump' (*P&P*, p. 177). Like Wordsworth's superstitious narrator in 'The Thorn', who obsessively measures the pond (''Tis three feet long, and two feet wide', lines 32–3),[10] Mr Collins sees nature and the garden as something to be weighed and measured. For him it all comes down to status: how much money, what kind of plate at meals, how many trees in Lady Catherine's park: place is a mark of social status rather than true character, measurement rather than emotional connection. One of the jokes here is that Mr Collins exults in these measured things with the pride of ownership when he possesses them only through Lady Catherine's 'condescension'. In contrast to Collins, Elizabeth has a curious and observant mind. On the morning after rejecting Darcy she goes for a walk and through her consciousness we are aware of the coming of spring: 'The five weeks which she had now passed in Kent, had made a great difference in the country, and every day was adding to the verdure of the early trees' (*P&P*, p. 217). Elizabeth's direct apprehension of the fresh beauty of spring growth is a far cry from the quasi-scientific calculations of Mr Collins.

It is no coincidence that we have our first description of Rosings, Lady Catherine's estate, through Mr Collins and his garden: 'of all the views which his garden, or which the county, or the kingdom could boast, none were to be compared with the prospect of Rosings, afforded by an opening in the trees that bordered the park nearly opposite the front of his house' (*P&P*, pp. 177–8). So, Mr Collins's main view or prospect is of Rosings, the 'handsome modern building' on 'rising ground' (p. 178) that he practically worships as the height of everything to which he aspires. In the glimpse that we get of the sweep of the landscape, furthermore, there is a hint that Rosings has been landscaped according to Capability Brown's improving aesthetic, with 'clumps of trees' rather than the noble avenues that Fanny Price admires at Sotherton, or the picturesque and variegated terrain of Pemberley. We know, too, from comments in other novels that Austen actually recognises the old-fashioned value of houses nestled in little dips and valleys, which are less

---

[10] 'The Thorn', in *Wordsworth*, ed. Gill, p. 60.

vulnerable to unfavourable winds and the vagaries of the weather. As the relentless improver and developer Mr Parker explains in 'Sanditon', 'Our ancestors, you know, always built in a hole. – Here were we, pent down in this little contracted nook, without air or view, only one mile and three quarters from the noblest expanse of ocean between the South Foreland and the Land's End, and without the smallest advantage from it' (*LM*, p. 156). When his wife looks with nostalgia back at the ancestral home, Mr Parker assures her that modern attention to elevation and prospect outweigh any such attachments.

In terms of the plot, of course, the significance of Elizabeth's visit to Hunsford is the proximity to Rosings, where she will meet Lady Catherine and once again be thrust into Darcy's company. Furthermore, Austen is careful to let us know that Elizabeth's favourite occupation while staying at the Parsonage is walking freely when the others are visiting Rosings: 'Her favourite walk, and where she frequently went while the others were calling on Lady Catherine, was along the open grove which edged that side of the park, where there was a nice sheltered path, which no one seemed to value but herself, and where she felt beyond the reach of Lady Catherine's curiosity' (*P&P*, p. 191). Of course Darcy soon learns her secret and is drawn to her during these once-solitary walks – and Elizabeth absurdly sees his action as 'wilful ill-nature' or 'voluntary penance' (p. 204) rather than a sign of his deepening attraction to her. Although Darcy's ill-fated first proposal takes place indoors, in the Parsonage, he finds her the next morning walking out of doors and hands her his letter. She in turn can read the letter privately because she is 'Pursuing her way along the lane' (p. 218) alone.

The journey to Hunsford and Rosings marks the mid-point in the novel and a turning point in the action, but it is not the only significant journey that Elizabeth takes. In contemplating a tour of Derbyshire and the Lakes with the Gardiners, Elizabeth becomes something of a picturesque tourist 'in pursuit of novelty and amusement' (*P&P*, p. 266), although not one completely bound by the letter of the picturesque law. It turns out that their tour is cut short in any event: Mr Gardiner's business obligations prevent an extended tour of the Lakes, so the trio will focus on Derbyshire (home of Pemberley) in high summer. As several readers have observed, Austen had certainly read Gilpin's popular *Observations*, as Elizabeth's recitation of the itinerary and 'the celebrated beauties of Matlock, Chatsworth, Dovedale, or the Peak' (p. 265) reveals. Furthermore, whereas the journey to Kent was to visit her friend, the Derbyshire trip is to see the natural and architectural wonders of that county.

As members of the rising commercial classes with the means and the leisure time for travel, the Gardiners were prime candidates for the picturesque tour. Travellers were especially interested in grand estates, such as Pemberley, set in a gorgeous park and forming a little world of its own. More important, Pemberley intensifies the shift in Elizabeth's way of seeing and understanding Darcy, a process begun on the lanes of Rosings. It is equally important for Darcy, who sees the intelligence, tact and good humour of the Gardiners, despite their association with trade and their address near Cheapside. Whereas Miss Bingley mocked the Cheapside relatives in order to injure Elizabeth's prospects, Darcy's own experience of them contradicts the class anxiety that she promulgates. Their presence does not pollute the shades of Pemberley: rather, Pemberley sets their good manners and fine characters in relief.

Volume three opens with Elizabeth and the Gardiners entering Pemberley, with Elizabeth's 'spirits' in 'high flutter' (*P&P*, p. 271). From the first, the narrator describes the park as containing 'great variety of ground' (p. 271), a hallmark of the picturesque aesthetic and an indication of a park that has not been altered or 'improved' by smoothing out this variety. This is not to say that art has not been at the service of nature, but even the natural stream, which has been 'swelled' into great importance, does not appear artificial. The familiar aesthetic language of the paragraph makes the most of the paradoxical relationship between nature and art, or taste: 'She had never seen a place for which nature had done more, or where natural beauty had been so little counteracted by an awkward taste' (p. 271). As Alistair Duckworth has commented, 'There is a kind of scenic *mediocritas* about the estate, a mean between the extremes of the improver's art and uncultivated nature.'[11] We see from the various descriptions that the house and grounds are metonyms of their owner and his masculine attraction: Pemberley is 'a large, handsome, stone building, standing well on rising ground' (*P&P*, p. 271), and the reader assumes that Elizabeth's spirits are even more aflutter on seeing the house.

Some readers have seen Elizabeth as mercenary for falling in love with Darcy (so it seems) at the moment she sees the grandeur of Pemberley, but that interpretation neglects the aesthetic shorthand of the novel. Whereas at Netherfield or Rosings Elizabeth registered Darcy's pride and arrogance, at Pemberley she sees him at home with his status and in the elegance of his estate. The whole package – the 'natural' beauty of the park and the tasteful elegance of the house – reinforces for Elizabeth that she is seeing Darcy in a new way – not in terms of the awkward arrogance of her early encounters with him but in the context of his own home and environment and his true character, where he is revered by the housekeeper ('none so handsome', *P&P*, p. 274; 'I have never had a cross word from him in my life, and I have known

---

[11] Alistair Duckworth, *The Improvement of the Estate: A Study of Jane Austen's Novels* (1971; Baltimore: Johns Hopkins University Press, 1994), p. 123.

him ever since he was four years old', p. 275). Pemberley teaches Elizabeth how to read Darcy: it gives her both the language and the context for understanding him and his origins. He not only possesses impeccable taste in home and landscape, but he is, according to the housekeeper Mrs Reynolds, 'the best landlord and the best master' (p. 276), indicating that he fulfils his social responsibilities. Mrs Reynolds paints a very different picture of Darcy: her instruction culminates in the guests actually viewing his portrait in the gallery, a visual emblem of Elizabeth's re-imagination of him. And, as Alistair Duckworth has helpfully added, Darcy actually looks at Elizabeth in this scene, fixing his eyes on her from the portrait and thus helping her to imagine how *he* reads *her*.[12] Significantly, when in the house under Mrs Reynolds's guidance, Elizabeth is once again drawn to the outside and to new ways of seeing:

> she went to a window to enjoy the prospect. The hill, crowned with wood, from which they had descended, receiving increased abruptness from the distance, was a beautiful object. Every disposition of the ground was good; and she looked on the whole scene, the river, the trees scattered on its banks, the winding of the valley, as far as she could trace it, with delight. As they passed into other rooms, these objects were taking different positions; but from every window there were beauties to be seen. (*P&P*, p. 272)

As several readers have noted, this description fits very well with the notion of a picturesque landscape – scattered trees, serpentine lines – but the main point, I think, is that Elizabeth looks out of the windows and truly *sees*: she recognises that from different windows the objects in the landscape look different, so that her window-viewing is related to new ways of seeing Darcy too. Of course the plentiful windows also reinforce for us the elegance and scale of the house and the means of its inhabitants, who can afford to enjoy such prospects from every window.

All this is preparation for the appearance of Darcy at Pemberley, for now Elizabeth and we readers understand him more fully. He appears abruptly: as the tourists look back at the house from the lawn 'the owner of it [Pemberley] suddenly came forward from the road' (*P&P*, p. 278). Darcy at this moment emerges as a kind of Blakean manifestation of Elizabeth's desire. Austen's realism does not prevent us from seeing the subtle dynamics of desire and of the close relationship between the characters and the landscapes that they inhabit.

In fact the remainder of the Pemberley episode, the reconnection of Elizabeth and Darcy, takes place as the party walks in the grounds and

---

[12] Duckworth, *Improvement of the Estate*, p. 123.

further admires the picturesque beauty. For Elizabeth, this experience is something like the mirror image of her view from within the house. Now that she knows he is at Pemberley, Elizabeth can see nothing but him:

> They had now entered a beautiful walk by the side of the water, and every step was bringing forward a nobler fall of ground, or a finer reach of woods to which they were approaching: but it was some time before Elizabeth was sensible of any of it; and, though she answered mechanically to the repeated appeals of her uncle and aunt, and seemed to direct her eyes to such objects as they pointed out, she distinguished no part of the scene. Her thoughts were all fixed on that one spot of Pemberley House, whichever it might be, where Darcy was then. She longed to know what at that moment was passing in his mind; in what manner he thought of her, and whether, in defiance of everything, she was still dear to him. (pp. 279–80)

Now on the outside looking in, Elizabeth can only think of Darcy in the house – the most exquisite landscape (already beautifully delineated) simply falls away because it has awakened her spirits and her feelings for Darcy, who fixes her thoughts. Darcy does return and join the group on their walk, showing the utmost civility to Elizabeth's relatives. The long walk affords the couple the opportunity to talk more openly and to give Darcy the courage to begin to believe that Elizabeth's feelings have changed. Hence, the almost magical meeting at Pemberley serves as the stage for bringing the two together, just before the news of Lydia's elopement puts an end to the tour and sets up the hurried and painful return home to Longbourn.

Technically, of course, the novel begins with the Bennet parents having a conversation at Longbourn, but it is the return home after the tour that reveals to us the importance of Longbourn and its grounds. It is here where several key scenes take place outside that lead to the denouement and also help further to define Elizabeth in relation to her family. Longbourn is claustrophobic to Elizabeth, especially when she returns after Lydia's elopement – her father is gone, her mother has taken to bed, and anxiety reigns. Elizabeth takes refuge in the out of doors in order to escape this deadening atmosphere. As in other episodes, such as when Elizabeth is staying at the Parsonage in Hunsford, she seeks the outdoors both for emotional release and for the privacy of thought. Although not on the scale of Pemberley, Longbourn has ample walks and grounds for this purpose.

But the two important scenes at Longbourn involve encounters with others, first Lady Catherine de Bourgh and then Darcy. When Lady Catherine makes a surprise visit to Longbourn, she chooses the 'prettyish kind of little wilderness' (*P&P*, p. 391) or ornamentally planted area beside the lawn for their private conversation. Given what we know of Elizabeth's outdoor sensibility and her familiarity with the grounds of her own home, we readers are confident that she will triumph over her noble visitor, who attempts to brow-beat her into swearing that she will never marry Darcy. The scene not only involves no actual description of the grounds, but it also sets up Mrs Bennet's reference to her 'hermitage' (p. 391), a small structure popular to picturesque 'improvement' but insignificant both in terms of Lady Catherine's scorn and Elizabeth's deeper engagement with the picturesque landscape.

Once again, the crucial scenes occur out of doors: Darcy renews his proposal as they are walking near Longbourn, having left with Jane and Bingley but outstripping them and walking for miles. Austen offers no exact description of the walk, but the reader understands the freedom that the lovers enjoy while walking in the fresh air. Austen focuses on this emotional quality rather than any description of the natural world. In fact, it seems that the lack of description reflects the way the lovers experience the moment: 'They walked on, without knowing in what direction. There was too much to be thought, and felt, and said, for attention to any other objects' (*P&P*, p. 407). When Elizabeth and Darcy return to the house they must hide all of the emotion and joy they feel. On the next day, when Mrs Bennet unwittingly sends them out to see the prospect from Oakham Mount to which 'Mr. Darcy expressed a great curiosity', the lovers have an opportunity to talk again (p. 416). Of course Mr Darcy is not a curious picturesque tourist. At this point he has no interest in the view: the walk to Oakham Mount simply assures that the two have a chance to plan the next steps in seeking consent and moving forward. As before, the narrator gives us no description of this view, which serves as background and occasion for the intimate conversation. But the fact that the conversation takes place outside – perhaps could only happen outside – reveals the real significance of Oakham Mount for the narrative.

Although the conflicts are resolved at Longbourn, the focus of the novel after the reconciliation of Elizabeth and Darcy is on Pemberley – not directly, but in the repeated allusions to Pemberley as the site of their future happiness. The final vision is (mostly) inclusive: although Wickham will never be welcome and Mrs Bennet is not mentioned, Lady Catherine will eventually relent and visit the 'polluted' woods. Pemberley serves as the focal point for this warm circle of friends to which the final pages allude; even Bingley, after remaining a year at Netherfield, will buy an estate in a neighbouring county to Derbyshire so that he and Jane can live within the circumference of Pemberley. In the concluding pages, then, we no longer see Pemberley so much in aesthetic or even visual terms, but as the metonym for the personal and communal values that the novel and its main characters have come to embrace.

This conclusion endorses the position that Austen was interested in the aesthetic appreciation of the natural world up to a certain point. Like her

Romantic contemporaries, she could celebrate the beauties of nature. But, like Wordsworth, for instance, she finally valued the emotional and moral insights associated with nature, the way that landscape could reveal character – not so much the Tintern landscape as the thoughts and memories that it impressed on the mind; not so much the view from Oakham Mount as the opportunity that a long walk provided for connection and communication. This full appreciation of the natural world is the very thing that the rank-obsessed Collins cannot experience as he counts and measures every bit of ground. Collins and his views are mere foils for the depth that characters such as Elizabeth find both in the landscape and within themselves, and for the depth that Austen continues to impart to her readers.

9

ANDREW ELFENBEIN

Austen's minimalism

Early in *Pride and Prejudice*, Elizabeth Bennet, having noticed the attachment between Bingley and her sister Jane,

> considered with pleasure that it was not likely to be discovered by the world in general, since Jane united, with great strength of feeling, a composure of temper and a uniform cheerfulness of manner, which would guard her from the suspicions of the impertinent. She mentioned this to her friend Miss Lucas.
>
> 'It may perhaps be pleasant,' replied Charlotte, 'to be able to impose on the public in such a case; but it is sometimes a disadvantage to be so very guarded.' (*P&P*, p. 23)

This is a strange passage. Elizabeth pivots from an interior monologue to a chat with Charlotte as if Charlotte materialises out of nowhere, in response to her mind. Even after Charlotte's voice appears, her body does not: the ensuing conversation takes place in a vacuum. Although this incident is ordinary, the description is not. No later writer would describe it in the same way because Jane Austen leaves out most of what other writers would consider essential. Just where are Elizabeth and Charlotte? How have they come together? What is their physical relation to each other? What are they doing during this conversation?

This seeming indifference to setting is not unusual in Austen. A long tradition of reading Austen as a master realist has masked her weird, experimental minimalism. This masking may have arisen because earlier critics used words like 'minimalism' to denigrate Austen as a small-scale writer limiting herself to a feminine, domestic world. Austen criticism of the past four decades has demolished this view by showing how deeply her novels engage Georgian culture. If earlier Austen criticism made her reach too narrow, contemporary criticism has turned her into a British encyclopedia, an authoritative commentator on everything from politics and economics to religion and medicine, from gender and colonialism to cognition and the environment.

Without resurrecting the condescension of earlier Austen criticism, I want to analyse why she hardly mentions what for other writers would be central information. Although when earlier critics described Austen's minimalism, they meant her focus on supposedly small things, I use it instead to describe her skilled, odd omissions. For example, after an important conversation between Jane and Elizabeth, she notes, 'The two young ladies were summoned from the shrubbery where this conversation had passed' (*P&P*, p. 96) as a sketchy afterthought. While it may not be surprising that she delays describing the setting of one particular conversation, in the novel she can hardly bear to part with far more important information. Not until Chapter 3 does she let us know, buried in the middle of a paragraph, that the Bennets live at Longbourn; not until Chapter 16, that the novel is set in Hertfordshire. Who else but Austen would hold back until almost the novel's end that Longbourn has an interesting architectural feature, a 'hermitage' (p. 391), that any other novelist would have exploited earlier?

The more one knows about Austen's culture, the stranger her minimalism seems. Eighteenth-century Britain loved the kind of detail that she omits. Scientific empiricism, stemming from the work of John Locke, claimed that all knowledge arose from the senses, so understanding the world needed precise descriptions of external experience. Travel writers produced particularised accounts of landscape, flora, fauna and civilisations. Burgeoning commerce needed exact records of goods, trade routes and monetary exchanges. Perhaps most important for literature, Britons favoured the picturesque, an aesthetic style that became one of the most durable contributions of eighteenth-century Britain to world culture. Judging landscapes as if they were pictures, picturesque theorists developed a precise vocabulary for evaluating the environment as a pleasing variety that alternated light with shade, clumps with open areas, hills with valleys, all in a comfortable frame.[1]

---

[1] For useful treatments of the picturesque in Austen, see the works by Heydt-Stevenson and Knox-Shaw in the Guide to further reading; in addition, Pat Rogers's endnotes in the Cambridge edition of *Pride and Prejudice* make many references to William Gilpin's writings on the picturesque, especially in relation to Pemberley.

In the 1790s, novels, especially Ann Radcliffe's gothic, eagerly adapted the picturesque. In her influential novelisation of its vocabulary, Radcliffe used landscape to mirror the interiors of her characters, so that outside reflected inside. When the heroine of *The Italian* (1797) reaches the convent of the Santa della Pietà, for example, Radcliffe describes the wise leadership of its virtuous abbess. The convent's surroundings testify to her character:

> These extensive domains included olive-grounds, vineyards, and some corn-land; a considerable tract was devoted to the pleasures of the garden, whose groves supplied walnuts, almonds, oranges, and citrons, in abundance, and almost every kind of fruit and flower, which this luxurious climate nurtured. These gardens hung upon the slope of a hill, about a mile within the shore, and afforded extensive views of the country round Naples, and of the gulf. But from the terraces, which extended along a semicircular range of rocks, that rose over the convent, and formed a part of the domain, the prospects were infinitely finer.[2]

Far from being the restrictive, prison-like atmosphere of convents in many gothic novels (including *The Italian*), this one, because of its abbess, opens out onto 'extensive domains' and 'finer' prospects. The Edenic fullness of its 'walnuts, almonds, oranges, and citrons' reveals that, even though its nuns may be celibate, they are metaphorically fertile through the land around them. Its picturesqueness gauges their inner worth.

Given all the developments in eighteenth-century culture, from empiricism to the picturesque, Austen ought to have crammed *Pride and Prejudice* with detail. We should read minute descriptions of faces, dresses, houses, gardens, landscapes and prospects, all understood as metaphors for their owners. Instead, with a few exceptions, the novel reads as if an overzealous editor had outlawed such information. This strange lack of detail marks Austen's allegiance to an older aesthetic style, long predating the eighteenth century, that had received new currency through its forceful expression in Samuel Johnson's best-selling *Rasselas* (1759). For Imlac, the (imperfect) wise man of the story, a good poet

> does not number the streaks of the tulip, or describe the different shades of the verdure of the forest. He is to exhibit in his portraits of nature such prominent

---

[2] Ann Radcliffe, *The Italian; Or, The Confessional of the Black Penitents*, ed. Frederick Garber (Oxford University Press, 1968), p. 301.

and striking features, as recall the original to every mind; and must neglect the minuter discriminations, which one may have remarked and another have neglected, for those characteristics which are alike obvious to vigilance and carelessness.[3]

For Imlac, little things are for little people: only inferior minds bother with 'minuter discriminations' that distinguish one shade of 'verdure' from another. A writer who insists on minuteness merely displays his or her limited vision, rather than creating one accessible 'to every mind'. From Imlac's point of view, overly detailed description is bad art.

Whether or not Imlac represents Johnson, Austen took his advice seriously. She criticised a manuscript novel by her niece Anna in Johnsonian terms by noting, 'You describe a sweet place, but your descriptions are often more minute than will be liked.'[4] Although picturesque enthusiasts may have liked 'more minute' descriptions of 'sweet' places, *Pride and Prejudice* criticises Mr Collins for showing off his verdant particularities:

> Here, leading the way through every walk and cross walk, and scarcely allowing them an interval to utter the praises he asked for, every view was pointed out with a minuteness which left beauty entirely behind. He could number the fields in every direction, and could tell how many trees there were in the most distant clump. (*P&P*, p. 177)

Johnson insists that great poetry must neglect 'minuter discriminations', while Collins indulges a beauty-killing 'minuteness'; Johnson tells the poet not to 'number the streaks of the tulip', while Collins 'could number the fields in every direction'. Yet even as Austen echoes Johnson, her criticism of minuteness differs from his. For Johnson, it closes off art from 'every mind'; for Austen, Mr Collins's specificity kills off 'beauty', which remains tantalisingly abstract. Johnson claims that too much detail makes scenic description inaccessible, while, for Austen, beauty should speak for itself. She lets her concept of 'beauty' emerge by not modifying it ('which left beauty entirely behind'), as if doing so would make it less beautiful, too subject to Collins-like fussiness.

<hr />

[3] Johnson, *The History of Rasselas, Prince of Abyssinia*, in *Samuel Johnson: Selected Poetry and Prose*, ed. Frank Brady and W. K. Wimsatt (Berkeley: University of California Press, 1977), p. 90.
[4] To Anna Austen, Friday 9–Sunday 19 September 1814, in *Jane Austen's Letters*, ed. Deirdre Le Faye, 3rd edn (Oxford University Press, 1995), p. 275.

Austen's revision of Imlac's aesthetic philosophy requires that when Elizabeth and the Gardiners tour England, what they see is present as absence. Elizabeth determines, when she believes that she will visit the Lake District, that she will rise above other picturesque travellers, unable 'to give one accurate idea of any thing' (*P&P*, p. 174). Her criticism leads us to expect that she will fulfil her promise by accurately describing what she sees, even if it turns out to be Derbyshire instead of the Lakes. Yet, when the moment arrives, the narrator announces, 'It is not the object of this work to give a description of Derbyshire, nor of any of the remarkable places through which their route thither lay' (p. 266). The announcement has a comic mock-solemnity ('remarkable places' can go without remark); by this point in the novel, despite Elizabeth's earlier announcement, it should be clear that *Pride and Prejudice* is not about picturesque description. Nevertheless, Austen insists that picturesque tours are one thing, and novels like *Pride and Prejudice* are something else. Later in the novel, Elizabeth finds the pictur-esque useful not to demonstrate taste, accuracy or feeling, but to muddle through a stiff moment with Darcy: 'At last she recollected that she had been travelling, and they talked of Matlock and Dove Dale with great persever-ance' (p. 284). Austen's 'with great perseverance' turns the picturesque into a language so stylised that it allows a simulacrum of conversation without any real interchange.

Johnson adhered to the aesthetic voiced by Imlac in *Rasselas* by writing a didactic fable rather than a fiction set in contemporary England: his work had no claim to verisimilitude. He could write what would be recognised by everybody in an 'Oriental' setting recognised by nobody.[5] Johnson's choice allowed the general to trump the specific: a good writer should create uni-versal experiences by avoiding too detailed a setting. Even as Austen echoes Johnson's aesthetics when she makes fun of Mr Collins, she seems to ignore his advice by writing novels whose time, place and action invite specificity. Far from setting *Pride and Prejudice* in a *Rasselas*-like mythic location, she places it squarely in contemporary England. As such, she resembles many domestic novelists of her day, such as Frances Burney or Maria Edgeworth. Yet these novelists stake a claim to realistic representation on the precise accumulation of detail in novels like Burney's *Evelina* (1778) or Edgeworth's *Belinda* (1801). Austen, however, though often praised as a master of realism,

---

[5] Although it begins in a mythic space, *Rasselas* draws on contemporary travel writing and is sensitive to political relations between Europe and the Middle East, though these feature less prominently in the narrative than its universalising pronouncements.

does without one of traditional realism's hallmarks, the pile-up of verisimilar particularities. *Pride and Prejudice* instead develops a counter-aesthetics that locates realism not in the pile-up of sensory detail but in an awareness of how human perception makes the same space look different to different observers.

As Nancy Armstrong has noted, the detail favoured by picturesque writers assumed, with Locke, that human responses to sensory stimuli were universal: everyone would react to the same scene in the same way.[6] Austen treats this assumption as a serious mistake. *Pride and Prejudice*'s most telling conversation about perception occurs when Darcy and Elizabeth argue about Charlotte's marriage. Although Darcy considers the fifty miles between Lucas Lodge and Hunsford 'a *very* easy distance', Elizabeth disagrees, resenting his lofty blindness to the expense and trouble of such a trip for Charlotte. When he condescendingly assumes that she thereby merely proves her 'attachment to Hertfordshire', she fires back, 'The far and the near must be relative, and depend on many varying circumstances' (*P&P*, p. 201). For Elizabeth, distance comes from 'varying circumstances', not the yardstick.

While Elizabeth's comment is only one moment in a verbal duel with Darcy, it acquires larger significance in the context of the novel as a whole. If the 'far and near' are relative, then the aesthetics of the picturesque, which judges scenes with fixed, normative criteria, cannot account for them. Moreover, the eighteenth-century cult of detail turned perceptions like those of distance into a matter of fact: a quantifiable number of feet or inches. Austen, however, suggests that such quantification misses intricacies of 'circumstances', which can make distances different to different people. The detail of much eighteenth-century writing presents only a pseudo-truth because it ignores who is perceiving the details, and how. At issue is not only whether distances are near or far, but also whether a space is crowded or empty, hostile or friendly, beautiful or ugly. Austen refuses to give conventional descriptions because, from her perspective, they are fundamentally wrong. They endow places with a fixed, external appearance, rather than the shifting, flexible perceptions arising from multiple interactions and feelings.

Austen's resulting minimalism appears vividly in her treatment of the key space in *Pride and Prejudice*: the room. In Austen, a room is not floor, ceiling,

---

[6] Nancy Armstrong, *Fiction in the Age of Photography: The Legacy of British Realism* (Cambridge, MA: Harvard University Press, 1999), p. 34.

walls or furniture. When Bingley 'soon felt acquainted with all the room' (*P&P*, p. 18), Austen means not just that he felt acquainted with all the people in a particular space but that the room is a key social category. She cares about the room not as a collection of objects, but as an interweaving of place and action. The physical room may be static, but the social room is not; its identity rapidly alternates between public and private, homosocial and heterosocial, convivial and threatening. The ballroom at Netherfield can be a site of boredom for Darcy or of dawning love for Jane; a room at Rosings can be a site of ecstasy for Mr Collins, of awe-inspiring grandeur for Sir William and of teeth-gritting irritation for Elizabeth.

Instead of giving us detailed images of the contents of a room, Austen makes us aware of how the room cordons off inner and outer spaces to be entered and exited: 'he left the room' (*P&P*, p. 8); 'as she entered the room' (p. 13); 'as soon as she was out of the room' (p. 38); 'when she came into the room' (p. 39); 'Elizabeth soon afterwards left the room' (p. 43); 'in quitting the room' (pp. 82–3); 'walked into the room' (p. 85); 'followed them into the room' (p. 85); 'the three gentlemen entered the room' (p. 192); 'Mr. Darcy, and Mr. Darcy only, entered the room' (p. 199); 'on his entering the room' (p. 296); 'as he quitted the room' (p. 307); 'till he entered the room' (p. 309). A different novelist would have been content only with subjects and verbs ('he entered', 'she left'), but Austen always includes the direct object ('the room'), as if it were not obvious. This repetition underscores that 'the room' for Austen means more than just a physical space: it is the indispensable ground for human relationships. While other writers might explore marriage, society and love in the abstract, what counts in Austen is what happens in a room, as a concrete structure, a boundary for action and the frame for what counts as near and far.

Entering the room immediately plunges characters into shifting social tides simply by how they put their bodies forward or retire. For the most part, the better that two characters get along, the more invisible their bodies; when bodies become too visible, alarms go off. Yet the same physical action can lead to widely different perceptions, depending on who performs it and how it relates to the room. At the Netherfield ball, Darcy commits the unpardonable offence of spending the evening 'walking about the room' (*P&P*, p. 11), or, as Mrs Bennet notes, 'He walked here, and he walked there, fancying himself so very great!' (p. 14). For Darcy, not stationing himself signals his disdain for the room, whose inhabitants do not merit so much as a pause for conversation. When Miss Bingley repeats the same action at Netherfield, it works differently: 'Miss Bingley ... got up and walked about the room. Her figure was elegant, and she walked well; – but Darcy, at whom it was all aimed, was still inflexibly studious' (p. 61). While Darcy walks about the room because he cares for no one, Miss Bingley does so because she cares too much for one person. The narrator notes that Miss Bingley has an 'elegant' figure and walks 'well', as if walking were an accomplishment for which a woman (unlike a man) could expect to be admired, but Miss Bingley has badly misjudged her room: Darcy's studiousness removes him from it. Austen's novels discriminate the signals whereby a seemingly neutral action like walking about the room can acquire widely different social meanings. They ask us to understand space not as picturesque detail or an empty void but as the precondition for social legibility.

Miss Bingley's room failure contrasts with Elizabeth's mastery. After discussing Darcy's eavesdropping with Charlotte, for example, she calls his bluff as much through her physical placement in the room as through her language:

> On his approaching them soon afterwards, though without seeming to have any intention of speaking, Miss Lucas defied her friend to mention such a subject to him, which immediately provoking Elizabeth to do it, she turned to him and said:
> 'Did you not think, Mr. Darcy, that I expressed myself uncommonly well just now, when I was teazing Colonel Forster to give us a ball at Meryton?' (P&P, p. 26)

Elizabeth and Charlotte must have seen enough of Darcy to know that he was approaching and that he did not want to talk, yet by the time he reaches them, Elizabeth has angled her body enough that she can meaningfully 'turn' from Charlotte to him. The unusual knottiness of Austen's syntax raises unanswered questions: How exactly do Charlotte and Elizabeth know that Darcy seems not to want to speak? Has Darcy seen them notice him and then turn away from him? Does Elizabeth want Darcy to respond to her 'turn' as a spontaneous gesture or as a strategically planned intrusion? For Austen, bodies are as open to interpretation as sentences. Yet well-recognised conventions bring clarity. When Elizabeth is ready to stop conversation, she reverses her first move: she looks 'archly' and turns 'away' from Darcy back to Charlotte. Though we do not know what the physical room looks like or what Elizabeth and Charlotte are wearing, we know what matters about the social room. Elizabeth connects body and room so tightly that she functions almost like a living door, opening and closing on Darcy.

In some ways, Austen treats the outside much as she does the inside, not as picturesque landscape but as a space constantly shifting with entrances, exits, walking about, turning to and turning from. Yet even as the outdoors draws on protocols governing the indoors, it also expands them: new relationships to space become possible.[7] Austen signals this novelty early on in Elizabeth's headlong dash from Longbourn to Netherfield: she 'continued her walk alone, crossing field after field at a quick pace, jumping over stiles and springing over puddles with impatient activity' (*P&P*, p. 36). Plurals like 'stiles' and 'puddles' invite the reader to imagine that the actions described by the participles ('crossing', 'jumping', 'springing') have happened many times during Elizabeth's walk. Not only are the actions peculiar to the outdoors, but so is the possibility of doing them often. Just as important, Elizabeth outside (unlike Elizabeth inside) travels by herself, and, though she is never again quite so energetic as in this power workout, she keeps up her solitary walks: 'she rambled about' (p. 58); she takes a 'ramble within the Park' (p. 204): she spends time 'wandering along the lane' (p. 231). What provides freedom for Elizabeth is not a picturesque landscape, but the opportunity that the outdoors offers for exercise and reflection. For Austen, this freedom is bound up with an authorial freedom from description: whereas rooms require close monitoring, the outside needs only a minimal sketch.

This freedom becomes central to the bumpy relationship between Elizabeth and Darcy. Their 'far' moments happen inside rooms; the 'near' ones, outside, as if they can converse authentically only when they have left the room. While Darcy's regrettable first proposal to Elizabeth occurs inside, he gives her his autobiographical letter outside because he can dispense with indoor niceties. Instead, he can just disappear: 'With a slight bow', he 'turned again into the plantation, and was soon out of sight' (*P&P*, p. 218). Austen means that Darcy walks away from Elizabeth into a wooded area, but his retreat into nature seems more definitive: it is as if the natural world has reabsorbed him.

If, at this moment, the natural world allows Darcy a quick escape, Austen revises it later when Elizabeth and Darcy are reconciled. They come together during a long walk when they proceed 'without knowing in what direction' (p. 407). Earlier, Darcy knew too well how to escape from Elizabeth, and Elizabeth moved confidently through space as she jumped over stiles and dashed across fields, but their union depends on a more tentative, exploratory sense of space. When Jane later asks where they have been, Elizabeth 'had only to say in reply, that they had wandered about, till she was beyond her

---

[7] For more on this topic, see Judith W. Page's essay in this volume.

own knowledge' (p. 413). Austen's language here disrupts the picturesque's fixed beauties. Her sentence allows the simplest meaning of 'beyond her own knowledge' (of geographic location) to unfold into all the possible ways that love has led Elizabeth into new, unfamiliar places. If the Johnsonian tradition insisted on avoiding minute description, Austen turns the prohibition into possibility: by not defining too exactly where 'beyond her own knowledge' might be, she allows the phrase to ripple outward in meaning, as if only through such indirection could she capture a character in the act of rediscovering herself.

The dynamic quality of Austenian space extends beyond rooms to the houses that anchor the action: Longbourn, Netherfield, Hunsford, Rosings and Pemberley. In Radcliffe and even more in Austen's best-selling contemporary Walter Scott, places come to be associated with sets of values. In making such connections, Radcliffe and Scott joined a broader trend in eighteenth-century architectural writing, which emphasised that homes should mirror their owners. *Pride and Prejudice*, however, rejects this trend. Longbourn stands for no single set of values: it produces Jane, the conduct book archetype; Elizabeth, the convention-breaking heroine; and Lydia, the shameless flirt. Netherfield houses both the amiable Bingley and his scheming sister. Charlotte has organised space at Hunsford to separate herself from her husband; while Mr Collins spends his time 'looking out of window in his own book room' (*P&P*, p. 189), Charlotte forgoes the more comfortable dining parlour for a 'backwards' (p. 189) room permitting a life-saving distance from her husband.

More prominently, Austen sets us up to hate Rosings. The more we learn about Lady Catherine, the more Austen prepares for a fine satire of domestic architecture and landscape gone awry. Yet when Elizabeth at last visits Rosings, Austen holds back from equating place and inhabitants, scorching as she is about the latter. Instead, she notes simply, 'Every park has its beauty and its prospects; and Elizabeth saw much to be pleased with, though she could not be in such raptures as Mr. Collins expected the scene to inspire' (p. 182). Mr Collins is ridiculous, but the landscape around Rosings is not; while it has no distinctive beauty, it has no distinctive ugliness either, and Elizabeth even finds a 'favourite walk' (p. 191) there. As for Rosings's interior, Mr. Collins's rhapsodies on its 'fine proportion and finished ornaments' (p. 183) allow him to make a fool of himself without suggesting that the house indeed lacks fine proportion or finished ornaments.

The exception to Austen's de-allegorisation of landscape seems to be the famous description of Pemberley that opens Volume 3. Elizabeth and the Gardiners are touring Derbyshire, and Pemberley is the highlight:

> It was a large, handsome, stone building, standing well on rising ground, and backed by a ridge of high woody hills; – and in front, a stream of some natural importance was swelled into greater, but without any artificial appearance. Its banks were neither formal, nor falsely adorned. Elizabeth was delighted. She had never seen a place for which nature had done more, or where natural beauty had been so little counteracted by an awkward taste. They were all of them warm in their admiration; and at that moment she felt, that to be mistress of Pemberley might be something! *(P&P*, p. 271)

For Austen's contemporaries, such attention to setting would be unremarkable, but for an author as strict as Austen about avoiding description, this paucity looks almost dithyrambic. Admittedly, Austen stresses most Pemberley's absences: it is 'without any artificial appearance'; is 'neither formal nor falsely adorned'; and nature there is not 'counteracted by an awkward taste'.

As the chapter progresses, we learn more positives about Pemberley's grounds, including its 'beautiful oaks and Spanish chestnuts' (*P&P*, p. 295): Pemberley even has the obligatory trace of picturesque foreignness anchoring English beauty. The more we learn about Pemberley, the better it seems. Only at Pemberley does Austen allow Elizabeth a retrospective swipe at Rosings: the furniture has 'less of splendor, and more real elegance, than the furniture of Rosings' (p. 272). Even better, Pemberley's grounds have a 'beautiful walk' (p. 279), 'a nobler fall of ground, or a finer reach of woods' (p. 279) and 'charming views of the valley' (p. 280). Although presumably at least some of Pemberley is the work of previous generations, Elizabeth attributes its beauty all to Darcy: the furniture reflects 'his taste' (p. 272), and he has refurbished the 'pretty sitting-room ... to give pleasure to Miss Darcy' (p. 276). Moreover, the housekeeper Mrs Reynolds, a beneficent *genius loci*, has nothing but praise for him: 'He is the best landlord, and the best master ... that ever lived' (p. 276). Pemberley, at last, looks like the estate that all the other houses in the novel have not been, a paradise mirroring the good values of its owner.

Many critics of *Pride and Prejudice* have consequently fastened on to Pemberley as a refuge from Austenian irony, a solid core of good values that rises above imperfections found elsewhere. Yet Pemberley's beauty is less definitive than it is often taken to be: as always in Austen, no single impression is definitive. Elizabeth's initial impression is not a carefully reasoned deduction but a temporary emotion: 'at that moment she felt'. Even more telling is Austen's concluding phrase, 'to be mistress of Pemberley might be something!' A lesser writer would have concluded with a conventional adjective: 'magnificent', 'splendid', 'wonderful'. Austen's pronoun, 'something', is a triumph of her minimalism because it leaves tantalisingly vague just what 'something' is and spurs the imagination to grasp what it might be. Yet even as Austen's wording crowds the mind with possibilities, 'something' is a stubbornly humdrum word, ending the paragraph somewhere between a liftoff and a thud. Rhapsodic, but not too rhapsodic, Austen's minimalism staves off more sublime rhetoric.

Within the larger context of the novel, Pemberley's perfection becomes ever more questionable. Elizabeth visits knowing that it hides some secrets; when Mrs Reynolds notes that 'Miss Darcy is always down for the summer months', Elizabeth thinks, 'Except ... when she goes to Ramsgate' (P&P, p. 274), a catty allusion to Wickham's attempted seduction. The most serious condemnation of Pemberley comes from Darcy himself. Although Mrs Reynolds remembers him as 'the sweetest tempered, most generous-hearted, boy in the world' (p. 275), Darcy has quite a different view: 'I was spoilt by my parents, who though good themselves ... allowed, encouraged, almost taught me to be selfish and overbearing, to care for none beyond my own family circle, to think meanly of all the rest of the world, to *wish* at least to think meanly of their sense and worth compared with my own' (pp. 409–10). Much as Austen values Pemberley's beauty, she also sees the estate as a trap, an island that encourages its inhabitants to imagine themselves separate from and superior to everyone else. Given Darcy's upbringing, it is surprising that Pemberley is so tasteful; it ought to be as haughty as Rosings.

These twists in Austen's presentation of Pemberley thicken a critical moment of dialogue late in the novel, when Jane asks Elizabeth how long she has loved Darcy. Elizabeth answers, 'I believe I must date it from my first seeing his beautiful grounds at Pemberley' (P&P, p. 414). At first, we might be tempted to take her comment at face value because of how deeply impressed she is with Pemberley. Yet Austen sustains this impression only for a paragraph break because the next paragraph begins, 'Another intreaty that she would be serious, however, produced the desired effect' (p. 415). Jane, at least, takes Elizabeth's comment about Pemberley as a joke, and Elizabeth complies as if her first comment were indeed a throwaway. Yet, though Jane characterises Elizabeth as not being serious, Austen arranges the dialogue so as to make us uncertain of just how serious Elizabeth is or is not. In retrospect, it may be possible to detect an ironic mock-solemnity in her 'I must date it', yet this claim alone does not erase the sense that, whatever Jane thinks, the grounds of Pemberley have indeed mattered to Elizabeth. Just as earlier Elizabeth argued that the distance of Charlotte from her family cannot be fixed as a simple near or far, so Austen leaves open just how near or far from Elizabeth's heart Pemberley may be.

After Austen, nineteenth-century novels became famous, or infamous, for lengthy, detailed descriptions. These give loud clues about places and characters, in ways that Austen pointedly avoids and that have made her experiments in description hard to recognise. Refuting Darcy's comment that a 'country neighbourhood' presents 'a very confined and unvarying society', Elizabeth comments, 'But people themselves alter so much, that there is something new to be observed in them for ever' (p. 47). What counts for Elizabeth is what can be observed 'in' people, rather than 'on' them. For Austen, human relations weave themselves into the perception of setting in ways that require not floods of detail, but only a few hints about position to let us know how everyone stands.

10

GILLIAN DOW

Translations

Orgullo y prejuicio y zombies (2009), *Orgueil et préjugés et zombies* (2009), *Stolz und Vorurteil und Zombies* (2010), not to mention the Japanese 'Koman to Henken to Zombie' (2010): that publishers have been prepared to market Seth Grahame-Smith's *Pride and Prejudice and Zombies* (2009) in translation across the globe speaks volumes about the current brand recognition of Austen's novel. Thanks to the research of Austen scholars in recent decades, the story of her comparative neglect in Britain in the nineteenth century is now a familiar one. The transition to an author with broad appeal in Anglo-American circles moves through polite interest within her own lifetime to the early control of the author's literary reputation by her brothers' descendants, to increasing and discerning enthusiasm through the early and mid twentieth century, to a veritable explosion of interest in 'popular culture' from the mid 1990s, an interest that shows no sign of abating.

In some ways, Austen's global presence through translations can be mapped on to this narrative of increasing popularity and exposure. Indeed Austen's current omnipresence in translation can be said to be a predominantly late twentieth-century and twenty-first-century phenomenon, mirroring the Anglo-American cult of Austen. And it is only in the late twentieth century that the dominance of Austen's second novel, against other works, becomes established in translations into other languages.

This is not to say that the nineteenth century did not engage with Austen by providing translations of her novels for those unable to read the original English. On the contrary: there were French translations of selected passages from *Pride and Prejudice* in 1813, full versions of *Sense and Sensibility*, *Emma* and *Mansfield Park* were published within Austen's own lifetime, and all six novels were fully translated into French by 1824, with a November 1821 version *Orgueil et préventions* (dated 1822), and a rival *Orgueil et préjugé* published in March 1822. Other European languages translated Austen after her death: the nineteenth century saw German translations of *Persuasion* (1822) and *Pride and Prejudice* (*Stolz und Vorurteil*, 1830), Swedish translations of *Persuasion* (1836) and *Emma* (1857–8) and a Danish translation of *Sense and Sensibility* in 1855–6, which was not a translation of Austen's novel at all, but rather a translation of the celebrated Isabelle de Montolieu's *Raison et sensibilité, ou les deux manières d'aimer* of 1815.[1] On the surface, then, *Persuasion* – with translations into three languages – would appear to be the most popular of the novels in the nineteenth century, followed by *Sense and Sensibility*, *Pride and Prejudice* and *Emma* (two languages each). It is, however, notable that *Pride and Prejudice* has the distinction of being both the first novel to be translated into another language, French (and that in the same year of its publication in English), and that there were two rival French translations of the novel published in the decade after Austen's death.

The first translation of *Pride and Prejudice* was published in abridged and serial form in French in 1813, in four successive issues of the Genevan periodical the *Bibliothèque Britannique*. This periodical, published between 1795 and 1815, and edited by the brothers Marc-Auguste and Charles Pictet, had an enormous influence on the reading habits of Continental Europe, and was tremendously popular: Maria Edgeworth, in a letter dated 15 October 1802 from Brussels, writes that 'every public library' and 'every école centrale' takes a copy. Eighteen years later in a letter dated August 1820, her stepsister Harriet Edgeworth observed that the periodical was 'the most popular of any' of the volumes taken from the library in Geneva.[2] Since the *Bibliothèque Britannique* had, by then, not been published for five years, Harriet Edgeworth's comments remind us that serialised fiction in the nineteenth century had an influence beyond its immediate publication. Indeed, the publication of *Pride and Prejudice* in this compilation of anglophile accounts of popular science and moralising literature from across the Channel explains much about the translators' and editors' choices of how to translate Austen's novel. The extracts from *Pride and Prejudice* selected were carefully chosen to

[1] See Anthony Mandal and Brian Southam (eds.), *The Reception of Jane Austen in Europe* (London: Continuum, 2007). I have made extensive use of the careful scholarship in this volume in preparing this chapter; it will henceforth be shortened to *JA in Europe*. For comments on post-2005 translations of *Pride and Prejudice* (which the Mandal and Southam volume does not cover), I am grateful to my colleagues on the European-funded COST Action Women Writers in History – Toward a New Understanding of European Literary Culture. For a research residency that enabled me to consult copies of many early and mid-twentieth-century translations in person, I am grateful to Goucher College Library and Special Collections, Baltimore, Maryland.

[2] C. Colvin (ed.), *Maria Edgeworth in France and Switzerland: Selections from the Edgeworth Family Letters* (Oxford: Clarendon Press, 1979), pp. 7 and 203.

make Austen as 'English' an author as possible, whilst simultaneously striving to make the plot and narrative style fit the conventions of the sentimental Franco-Swiss prose fiction popular in the period.

Is it possible to translate Austen's characters from their spatial and temporal locations in late eighteenth-century and early nineteenth-century England? Should one even try? There is an additional complicating layer of interpretative material for foreign readers and translators of Austen to navigate that seems to apply less to translations of other English authors. Her presumed inability to travel into other languages is felt to be because of her inherent Englishness, and seems to be linked to biographical certainties about the author herself. The portrait of the quiet Hampshire-loving spinster who never left the southern counties of England in life, or in her fiction, and who never spoke other languages than her own, has had a lasting legacy: as T. E. Kebbel put it in 1885, 'Miss Austen could hardly be appreciated by anyone not thoroughly English.'[3] The question of how best to handle the 'Englishness' of the author has been a continually vexed one when *Pride and Prejudice* is translated.

In terms of translation theory, this has major implications. Here, the twenty-first-century scholar of Austen holds a different viewpoint from her nineteenth-century predecessors. Translation theorists now tend to view the purpose of translation as to provide a guide to the original, by which I mean an accurate sense of the 'foreignness' of the source text. The 'foreignizing translation' ethics of the influential scholar Lawrence Venuti insists on a model of translation that preserves the 'strangeness' of the source language: to adopt any other model, Venuti argues, is to commit ethnocentric violence.[4] Nineteenth-century practitioners – the first translators of *Pride and Prejudice* – saw things somewhat differently. All early translations adopted the domesticating model of translation, in which the source text is made to fit the horizon of expectations of the reader in the target language. Through this translation model, Austen's characters become less English, and more like characters who would be known to readers in the literatures of their own countries. The best-known expression of this practice for the Anglo-American reader is Dryden's famous assertion, in his *Dedication of the Aeneis* (1697), that he has 'endeavoured to make Virgil speak such English as he would himself have spoken, if he had been born in England, and in this present age'.[5] Similarly, the

---

[3] T. E. Kebbel, 'Jane Austen at Home', *Fortnightly Review* 43 (1885), pp. 262–70.
[4] Lawrence Venuti's translation ethics are set out in the polemical *The Translator's Invisibility: A History of Translation* (London: Routledge, 1995) and in the subsequent *The Scandals of Translation: Towards an Ethics of Difference* (London: Routledge, 1998).
[5] Quoted in *Translation – Theory and Practice: A Historical Reader*, ed. Daniel Weissbort and Astradur Eysteinsson (Oxford University Press, 2006), p. 150.

anonymous Franco-Swiss translators in the *Bibliothèque Britannique* made Austen speak such French as she would have spoken had she been born in Geneva in the early nineteenth century. This naturally affects Austen's language and style – it is a rare nineteenth-century translator who is able to deal effectively with Austen's irony. It also affects her characterisation, giving us an Elizabeth and a Darcy who are quite unlike their English originals.

Germaine de Staël's response to her reading of *Pride and Prejudice* in English (recommended to her by her friend Sir James Mackintosh during her stay in London in 1813) was untypically laconic: 'vulgaire'. On the surface, this may seem a surprising response to Austen's genteel comedy of manners. And yet an explanation may be found by examining the literary marketplace on the Continent. Franco-Swiss novels, including Staël's own, were peopled with aristocratic heroes and heroines, and never included frank discussions of money and the marriage market. Such references are omitted entirely from the first French translation of *Pride and Prejudice*. Yet in many ways, the characters are made more English – or rather, become little more than caricatures of Englishness. Where, as Valérie Cossy has pointed out, Austen's Darcy already fitted neatly in a line-up of English heroes of Franco-Swiss invention, including Bomston in Rousseau's *Julie, où la nouvelle Héloïse* (1761) and Oswald in Staël's own *Corinne* (1809), he is further anglicised in his appearance when he appears in the *Bibliothèque Britannique*.[6] In the translation of the scene in *P&P*, p. 278 (in which Darcy returns to Pemberley, and stands 'within twenty yards' of Elizabeth and the Gardiners), he is in 'bottes', and with 'un fouët à la main' (in boots, and with a whip in his hand) – a stereotypical representation of the British sports-loving hero viewed through Genevan eyes. Elizabeth Bennet – an original heroine for even the British fiction of her age – simply had no equivalent in the Continental fiction of the early nineteenth century. The response of these first Genevan translators was to make her a more orthodox and respectable heroine: she speaks less, and with a less forthright manner.

That Jane Austen does not travel well stands as a truism in studies of translations of her novels. We must be careful, however, of staking claims for the 'exceptional' nature of early translations of Austen when we draw attention to their omissions and errors, their idiosyncrasies and inaccuracies. The fact is that most of Austen's contemporaries and predecessors suffered the same fate on the Continent, as did their Continental counterparts in Britain. Very little foreign fiction travelled well in the long eighteenth and nineteenth centuries, if by 'travelling well', we mean travelling accurately.

---

[6] Valérie Cossy, *Jane Austen in Switzerland: A Study of the Early French Translations* (Geneva: Slatkine, 2006), p. 124.

Indeed, the first full-length translation by Eloïse Perks, *Orgueil et prévention*, published in Paris in late 1821 (dated 1822), seems to have been inspired more by Isabelle de Montolieu's translation of *Sense and Sensibility* than by Austen's own celebrity, or indeed her narrative style: Perks includes a glowing reference to Montolieu's 'plume élégante', but no reference to Austen herself. The anonymous rival version *Orgueil et préjugé*, published in Geneva in March 1822, adopts similar forms of censorship to those found in the *Bibliothèque Britannique*'s selections in the previous decade. The reasons behind Charlotte Lucas's acceptance of Collins's marriage proposal are omitted, and, by the end of the novel, the Swiss translator shows considerable signs of fatigue, frequently cutting out whole paragraphs, even when the modern reader would consider them essential to the development of Elizabeth's character. Similarly, the first German translation of *Pride and Prejudice*, *Stolz und Vorurteil* (1830) by the translator and editor of a newspaper for women, Louise Marezoll, advertises clearly that it is a 'free' translation. Like the Genevan translators, Marezoll heightens the sentiment: what results is, Annika Bautz has argued, 'a novel that lacks the painstaking structure of Austen's original and its nuanced tones'.[7] All of these translations would be better called adaptations; all are attempts to make *Pride and Prejudice* a more Swiss, French or German novel.

This domesticating model of translating *Pride and Prejudice* survives well into the twentieth century. Ellen Valle claims that early twentieth-century Finnish translators of Austen tend to domesticate her fiction by transposing the setting of the landed gentry to their nearest Finnish equivalent, the lower rural classes or the middle classes: the first Finnish translation of *Pride and Prejudice*, *Ylpes ja ennakkoluulo* (1922), contains 'numerous mistranslations owing to a misunderstanding of the source text'.[8] Marie Nedregotten Sørbø reveals a similar pattern when investigating the first Norwegian translation of *Pride and Prejudice* (1930). Here the translator, Alf Harbitz, wants to be 'free in letter, but faithful to the spirit' of the original, 'feeling that this freedom gave him a better chance to render Austen in a modern Norwegian context'.[9] Going on to document the omissions and inaccuracies in Harbitz's translation, Sørbø's conclusion is that he fails to be 'faithful' in any meaningful way. Ebba Brusendorff, the translator of the first Danish *Pride and Prejudice*, *Stolthed og fordom* (1928–30), attempts a faithful rendering, but, like the

---

[7] Annika Bautz, 'The Reception of Jane Austen in Germany', in *JA in Europe*, pp. 93–116 (p. 95).
[8] Ellen Valle, 'The Reception of Jane Austen in Finland', in *JA in Europe*, pp. 169–87 (p. 173).
[9] Marie Nedregotten Sørbø, 'Jane Austen and Norway: Sharing the Long Road to Recognition', in *JA in Europe*, pp. 132–51 (p. 134).

Swiss translation over a century earlier, she cannot resist 'improvement' through cuts, and she seems frustrated with Austen's attention to minutiae, to 'things which must necessarily be told, but which are not in themselves very interesting'.[10] Anthony Mandal and Brian Southam's comprehensive edited volume *The Reception of Jane Austen in Europe* offers countless examples of the failures of the early twentieth-century translations of *Pride and Prejudice*. Taken together, they form an inadequate collection that seems almost designed to ensure Austen's obscurity on the Continent.

That *Pride and Prejudice* survived such indignities is worth reflecting on. This brings us to an important point about dominant languages and cultures in different historical periods, and a related point about hegemonic English-language nations. For in the 200 years that Austen's *Pride and Prejudice* has been translated into other languages, there has been a significant sea change. When her novels were first published, French was the dominant language and culture within Europe. It served throughout the nineteenth century as both the educated *lingua franca*, and as the mediating language between the literatures of other European nations: English novels travelled into Spain via French translation in the early nineteenth century, and in nineteenth-century Russia, both English and German novels were read almost exclusively in French. Catharine Nepomnyashchy has argued persuasively that Aleksandr Pushkin's *Eugene Onegin* (1823–31) (which shares many striking parallels with *Pride and Prejudice*) could indeed have been influenced by Austen's novel, despite the fact that it was not published in Russian translation until 1967, and it is unlikely that Pushkin knew the original English text. Fluent in French from an early age, Pushkin may well have had access to either the *Bibliothèque Britannique* serialisation of 1813, or one of the two French translations of the 1820s, or indeed all three.[11] The influence of French translations continues beyond the nineteenth century: the first Romanian translation was entitled *Surorile Bennet* (1943; The Bennet Sisters), and seems to have been informed by the 1932 French translation that was circulating in Romania in the 1940s. And yet by this time, the novel in English was steadily replacing the French novel in the collective global consciousness, as both nineteenth- and twentieth-century British novelists took Europe and America by storm.

In many ways, this increasing enthusiasm for English fiction can be traced through translations of *Pride and Prejudice*, which seems frequently to have been translated in the twentieth century because editors wanted more English

[10] Peter Mortensen, 'Unconditional Surrender: Jane Austen's Reception in Denmark', in *JA in Europe*, pp. 117–31 (p. 122).
[11] Catharine Nepomnyashchy, 'The Reception of Jane Austen in Russia', in *JA in Europe*, pp. 334–49 (p. 338).

'classics' to translate, and turned to Anglo-American publishers, editors and critics to define what these 'classics' were. The first Spanish translation of *Pride and Prejudice* appeared in 1922, and there have been at least seventy editions since then; Giulio Caprin's 1932 translation of the novel into Italian introduced Austen to that country for the first time. The first Brazilian Portuguese *Pride and Prejudice* appeared in 1941, followed rapidly by a European Portuguese translation in 1943. The first Dutch *Pride and Prejudice* was published in 1946; in Serbia, the first translation came in 1953; in Iceland, in 1956; and in Slovak, in 1968. In the closing decades of the twentieth century, both retranslations and new foreign editions of *Pride and Prejudice* sprouted like mushrooms. Certainly, the increasing number of translations owes much to the success of the film and television adaptations of the mid 1990s, which of course included the BBC TV adaptation of *Pride and Prejudice* (1996). There is concrete evidence of increased European reception in first translations of *Pride and Prejudice* into the minority languages: Basque (1996), Lithuanian (1997), Latvian (2000) and Galician (2005). And in terms of translations, the 2005 Joe Wright film adaptation prompted even more frenzied activity. Many European publishing houses either re-edited previous translations, or commissioned new ones, in response to this film.

In the twenty-first century, the global dominance of English is virtually uncontested. The impact on translation is striking. In an article published in 1993, Venuti gives some sense of the unequal nature of the terrain: 'only 2–3 per cent of the books published in the US and UK each year are translations, whereas foreign titles, many from English, count for as much as 25 per cent (or more) of the books published annually in other countries'.[12] David Bellos has carried out a study for the period 2000–9, which shows a similar dearth of foreign-language material in Anglo-American publishing. The basic point is obvious: as Bellos pithily puts it, 'translations from English are all over the place; translations into English are as rare as hen's teeth'.[13] Translations of Jane Austen's *Pride and Prejudice* must be read in this context, in foreign countries where translations of Ian Rankin sell alongside Michel Houellebecq, Emily Brontë alongside Goethe and Italo Calvino alongside Paul Auster – in a context, that is, where the English-language novel in translation dominates the literary marketplace.

Yet despite this dominance of the English novel, *Pride and Prejudice* has had few prominent champions to translate it. Writing exclusively on French translations and editions of Austen from 1815 to 2007, Lucile Trunel laments

[12] Lawrence Venuti, 'Translation as Cultural Politics: Regimes of Domestication in English', in *Translation – Theory and Practice: A Historical Reader*, ed. Daniel Weissbort and Astradur Eysteinsson (Oxford University Press, 2006), p. 549.
[13] David Bellos, *Is That a Fish in Your Ear: Translation and the Meaning of Everything* (London: Penguin, 2011), p. 210.

that no 'grand traducteur littéraire' has translated her work into French, despite the fact that many great French writers of the twentieth century admired *Pride and Prejudice*.[14] The same generalisation might be made for translations into other languages. Sigrid Undset (1882–1949), the Nobel Prize-winning Norwegian novelist, admired both Austen, and *Pride and Prejudice*, enormously, as did the influential Italian critic Mario Praz (1896–1992), but neither translated her. And where *Pride and Prejudice* has inspired creativity in great writers in the twentieth century, such as Natsume Sōseki (1867–1916), the Japanese novelist whose unfinished novel *Meian* (1916; Light and Darkness) was influenced by Austen's second novel, such authors seem to have read her only in the original. André Gide, likewise, notes in his journal of 1929 that he has nearly finished the novel, in which Austen reaches 'la perfection': his reference is to *Pride and Prejudice*, and not the French title.[15] One might ask, then, both just what the 'stable' text of *Pride and Prejudice* might be in translation, and exactly how to map what influence it might have had.

The very title has only recently been fixed in many languages. The 1932 Plon edition of the French translation by Valérie Leconte and Charlotte-Marie Pressoir was sold under the title *Les Cinq Filles de Mrs. Bennet*, a title that echoed the title of the translation of Louisa May Alcott's *Little Women*, *Les Quatre Filles de Dr. March*, and was presumably intended to package Austen's novel as literature for female adolescents, by appealing to the same readers. The first Hungarian translation of Austen – a serialisation of *Pride and Prejudice* appearing in a monthly Budapest review between 1934 and 1936 – was entitled *A Bennet család* [The Bennet family].[16] The Dutch translation, now most commonly known as *Trots en vooroordeel*, appeared as *De Gezusters Bennet* [The Bennet Sisters] in 1964. Many languages have selected rival titles for translations of the novel: the first Italian translation of an Austen novel *Orgoglio e prevenzione* [literally, Pride and Prevention] by Guilio Caprin in 1932 remained the preferred title until as late as 1970, when it was replaced by *Orgoglio e pregudizio* [Pride and Prejudice], which saw sixteen different translations using the same name until 2004.[17] Similarly, where most Spanish translations are rendered literally as *Orgullo y prejuicio*, there are exceptions in the mid twentieth century, when a 1945 translation,

---

[14] Lucile Trunel, *Les Éditions françaises de Jane Austen 1815–2007* (Paris: Honoré Champion Éditeur, 2010), p. 497.

[15] Entry dated 24 January 1929, André Gide, *Journal, 1889–1939* (Paris: Gallimard, 1939), p. 909.

[16] Nóra Séllei, 'Jane Austen in Hungary', in *JA in Europe*, pp. 237–56 (p. 240).

[17] Beatrice Battaglia, 'The Reception of Jane Austen in Italy', in *JA in Europe*, pp. 205–23 (p. 216).

and a 1952 reprint of a 1943 translation, are both entitled *Más fuerte que el orgullo* [Stronger than Pride].[18] Gujarati translators opted for *Vahmi venita* in 1919; *Parajta purvagraha* in 1959. Japanese translators have mainly opted for 'Koman to Henken', where 'Koman' means arrogant pride, but 'Jifu to Henken' has also been used, 'Jifu' having the more positive connotations of pride and dignity.

Paratextual presentation has been, likewise, remarkably diverse. The book jacket for the 1954 Tallandier edition of *Orgueil et préjugés* for the collection 'Les Heures bleues' depicts a young woman in the flowered bonnet and high lace collar of *la belle époque* – more George Bernard Shaw's *Pygmalion* (a popular play in France at the time) than a Regency Elizabeth Bennet. Henry and Alberta Burke – Baltimore-based Austen collectors active in the mid twentieth century – were not above incredulity and delight in the misunderstandings that foreign editions can promote through such presentations of the novel. Indeed, Alberta Burke and the bibliographer David Gilson corresponded extensively about translations of Austen's novels in the years leading up to the publication of Gilson's bibliography in 1982, with a friendly exchange about rare copies both had managed to locate: 'Congratulations on your find', Burke wrote to Gilson in February 1973 on the discovery of a hitherto unknown Dutch translation. 'You're now the ultimate authority on translations as well as on so much else in J.A.!'[19] The Burkes' collection is most rich in variant translations of *Pride and Prejudice*, a reflection of the novel's place in the global literary marketplace in the twentieth century. An Italian edition *Orgoglio e pregiudizio* published in Milan in 1958 in the collection has a fifties red-head on the book jacket, complete with blue ribbon tying back a pony tail (see Illustration 10.1); a Spanish *Orgullo y prejuicio* published in Madrid in 1970 contents itself with a large bowler hat in front of a sketch of four women (see Illustration 10.2).

Writing in 1970 of a 1969 Italian edition of *Orgoglio e pregiudizio*, Alberta Burke notes the domesticating tendency of translation and continues: 'the text is very much cut and all Christian names are Italianized – "Giovanna" "Bettina"', which 'certainly does not carry the image which "Lizzy" does'.[20] In an article on translations of Austen, Henry Burke reproduces the front jacket of a 1977 French-Canadian *Pride and Prejudice*, published in

---

[18] Aída Díaz Bild, 'Still the Great Forgotten? The Reception of Jane Austen in Spain', in *JA in Europe*, pp. 188–204 (p. 190).

[19] Alberta Burke, letter to David Gilson, 27 February 1973, Container 1, Folder 18, Goucher College Library.

[20] Alberta Burke, letter to David Gilson, 31 March 1970, Container 1, Folder 15, Goucher College Library.

Illustration 10.1 *Orgoglio e pregiudizio* (Milan: Boschi, 1958). This inexpensive Italian edition of the 1950s was one of ten new translations published in the decade in Italy, and is clearly packaged for the female reader. Image courtesy of Goucher College Library and Special Collections.

Montreal, and packaged in the style of a Harlequin romance.[21] The photographic image shows a darkly brooding Darcy grasping a blonde, bare-shouldered and barely resisting Elizabeth Bennet to his chest. Underneath this image, the words of Sir William Lucas – 'You excel so much in the dance, Miss Eliza, that it is cruel to deny me the happiness of seeing you' – are recast in French, omitting Elizabeth's name. By the positioning on the cover, the reader is misled into believing that the quotation must come from the romantic lead at a moment of barely repressed passion, rather than from a minor

---

[21] Henry Burke, 'Seeking Jane in Foreign Tongues', *Persuasions* 7 (1985), pp. 17–20.

Illustration 10.2 *Orgullo y prejuicio* (Madrid: Narcea/Ediciones Iter, 1970). The bowler hat is enough to signal to the Spanish reader that this is an English classic. Image courtesy of Goucher College Library and Special Collections.

character in the novel, in what is a comic scene. The combination of the text and the image gives an impression of the stock-character of the cruelly dominant Mills and Boon or Harlequin hero, just forceful enough to tame the heroine, even against her will. Such confusions still abound. Editions of Austen's novels produced by the French publishing house 10/18 in the 1990s, and still in print today, all use details of women from Dante Gabriel Rossetti's paintings on their book jackets. The casting of Elizabeth Bennet as a

Pre-Raphaelite beauty of the latter half of the nineteenth century, with independent gaze and twisted mouth, aligns her with the heroines of the Brontë sisters' novels, popular in France from the moment of publication.

The question of the stable text in translation is also a somewhat vexed one. Many European languages have multiple translations of *Pride and Prejudice* in print, and widely available. The French reader who walks into one of the most mainstream Paris bookstores – the FNAC at the Gare St Lazare – as I did myself in June 2011, is confronted with five rival translations. All entitled *Orgueil et préjugés*, and priced between 6.50 euros and 11 euros, on the surface there seems little to choose between them. One might wish to warn the French reader away from the current Archipoche edition of Jean Privat's 1946 translation, which announces boldly on the back cover that Mrs Bennet is a 'femme de pasteur', a clergyman's wife. Further advice, however, must necessarily be subjective: how will the French 'common reader' choose between the Gallimard Folio Classique translation by Pierre Goubert (first published in 2007), and the Flammarion edition translated by Laurent Bury (first published in 2009), the 10/18 edition translated by Valérie Leconte and Charlotte-Marie Pressoir (first published in 1932) and the Motifs edition translated by Béatrice Vierne (first published in 1996)? Should one simply rely on the most prestigious publishing house? Are new translations necessarily better than old? Which translator will best capture the mood and style of the novel?

Pierre Goubert, in his notes to the Gallimard Folio Classique edition, recommends 'caution' to the French reader in the selection of translations: an 'authentic' translation, he points out, requires much more than simply a knowledge of English, it requires an in-depth knowledge of the language, of the history, the morals and indeed the idiosyncrasies of the period.[22] Indeed, the anxiety of translating Austen is something that many contemporary practitioners reflect on in their prefaces, introductions and notes to *Pride and Prejudice*. Naturally, there are considerable linguistic challenges, as there are with any translation of a 200-year-old novel. Soya Michiko, one of Austen's many Japanese translators, sees the family-based and codified world of Austen's fiction as particularly hard to translate. In Japanese, a word such as cousin cannot be translated unless the translator knows whether the cousin is older or younger, male or female. Add to that the fact that Japanese has around ten different words for 'I' and 'you' respectively, and that the correct one must be selected according to both the situation and the relationship between those who are speaking, and one gets a sense of the

---

[22] Pierre Goubert, 'Notice', in Jane Austen, *Orgueil et préjugés* (Paris: Gallimard, Folio Classique, 2007), p. 450.

intricacies of the work of translating any English novel into Japanese. Soya points out, furthermore, that Austen's syntax presents a particular challenge, since her rhetorical style depends frequently on anticlimax, understatement and overstatement in the narrative voice. The Japanese language requires the famous opening sentence of *Pride and Prejudice* to be translated as 'That a single man in possession of a good fortune must be in want of a wife is a truth universally acknowledged.' Once rendered into Japanese, Austen can lose a great deal of her charm.[23] It is an inevitable consequence of such losses that Austen's style is seen to be 'beyond emulation' by many contemporary specialists in literary translation who engage with comparative readings of her novels and their translations into other languages. Many translators themselves are acutely aware of the challenges.

The result is naturally that those who teach Austen abroad are wary of translations of her works. It is true that, on occasion, translation activity has been promoted by the demands of English-language teaching. There are Hindi, Kannada, Marathi, Tamil and Telugu translations of *Pride and Prejudice*, but the number of Indian *English* editions of *Pride and Prejudice* in the twentieth century far outweighs editions in the vernacular. The first translation of Austen into Greek was a translation of *Pride and Prejudice*, *Perifania kai prokatalipsi* (1950). Sponsored by the British Council, this was a clear attempt to promote British literature and culture in Greece. However, the authors of a study of Austen's reception in Greece feel that her novels are best studied in their original language, and point out that Greek 'students are annually supplied with the latest Oxford World Classics or Penguin Classics edition of Austen's novels'.[24] In Spain, the different Spanish universities 'seem to accept the "truth universally acknowledged" that Jane Austen is one of the most important British novelists': *Pride and Prejudice* is the most popular of her novels amongst Spanish students.[25] In France, Laurent Bury and Dominique Sipière focused on the 2005 film adaptation in their collection of essays destined for the classroom. Entitled *Pride and Prejudice: le roman de Jane Austen et le film de Joe Wright* (2006), essays are in French and English, and are written with preparation for the CAPES and Agrégation public examinations in mind: the exam board chose – controversially – to set the novel alongside the adaptation. And in 2009, Slovenian high-school students read *Pride and Prejudice* in translation as a compulsory part of their final examinations. This inclusion followed a November 2007 open letter from

[23] I am grateful to Soya Michiko, who in February 2011 provided me with careful notes on the challenges of translating Austen into Japanese.

[24] Katerina Kitsi-Mitakou and Maria Vara, 'The Reception of Jane Austen in Greece', in *JA in Europe*, pp. 224–38 (p. 238).

[25] Aída Díaz Bild, 'Jane Austen in Spain', in *JA in Europe*, p. 203.

academic representatives of each of the four Slovenian universities to the newspaper *Večer* on the absence of women writers in the school curriculum.[26] *Pride and Prejudice*, then, has clearly achieved the canonical status of a world classic, taught in schools and universities, in translation and in the original.

This omnipresence has come at a price. Where once translations of Austen displayed a remarkable and colourful divergence, a global literary culture dominated by Anglo-Saxon models has to some extent flattened the layers of paratextual and linguistic interpretation of Austen's novels abroad. Now, just as most European high streets have their Starbucks, their McDonalds and their Subways, these same high streets carry translations of *Pride and Prejudice* that are packaged for the global marketplace in remarkably similar ways. One of the most recent, as well as easily available and accessible translations in France, is the 2010 Flammarion edition, *Orgueil et préjugés*, translated and presented by Laurent Bury, and with an introductory interview with Catherine Cusset, a popular French author.[27] The front image on the book jacket – pink floral wallpaper as a backdrop, with a sketch of a hand on which the four fingers have line drawings of young girls with lace veils – is designed to appeal to the French female reader of romance fiction. The two paragraphs of description on the back page emphasise the romance plot – '*Orgueil et préjugés* s'achèvera-t-il par le *happy end* tant attendu?' ['Will *Pride and Prejudice* conclude with the long-awaited happy ending?'] – before mentioning *Bridget Jones's Diary*, *Pride and Prejudice and Zombies* and *Bride and Prejudice*, and referring to television series, films and comic strips. This may be, as the back cover concludes, 'l'un des romans *anglais* les plus lus dans le monde' ['one of the most read *English* novels in the world'] [my emphasis], but it is being deliberately marketed as a global phenomenon, and with reference to films that will be well known to a French audience. In his preface to the translation, Bury has a keen eye on Austenmania in Anglo-American culture, and on popular culture more generally. His introduction concludes with an account of the numerous continuations and re-imaginings of *Pride and Prejudice*, from Dorothy Bonavia-Hunt's *Pemberley Shades* (1949) to Laura Viera Rigler's *Confessions of a Jane Austen Addict* (2007). Since none of these sequels is available in French, the interest for the majority

---

[26] I am grateful to Katja Mihurko Poniz, University of Nova Gorica, for alerting me to this open letter, which she co-authored. See Splošna matura : odprto pismo Državni predmetni komisiji za splošno maturo za slovenščino. *Večer (Marib.)*. [Tiskana izd.], 23. Nov. 2007, letn. 63, št. 270, str. 25.

[27] Jane Austen, *Orgueil et préjugés* (Paris: Éditions Flammarion, 2010), translated and presented by Laurent Bury; interview with Catherine Cusset, 'Pourquoi aimez-vous *Orgueil et préjugés*'.

of readers this edition targets is presumably to document impact and reception. Bury ends his introduction by drawing attention to the forthcoming films '*Pride and Predator*, réalisé par Will Clarke, et un *Orgueil et préjugés et zombies* avec Natalie Portman'.[28] Where early French translators and editors were eager to package Austen in a way that was palatable to their readers, this most recent translation gestures to a global marketplace.

In his 2003 study *What is World Literature*, David Damrosch identifies a 'double process' in the classification of works as world literature. First, such works must be read 'as literature'. Second, they must circulate 'out into a broader world beyond its linguistic and cultural point of origin'.[29] For Damrosch then, as for other specialists of comparative literature, world literature is not simply a European canon of (principally male-authored, principally white) texts, but rather a work that gains in translation, in which our understanding of the text has been formed by this transformative act. Translations of *Pride and Prejudice* have certainly been continuously 'remade' to interpret Austen for new generations of readers abroad, and this process shows no sign of ending. When viewed as 'world literature', however, the trajectory is more circuitous. Most nineteenth-century and early twentieth-century translations of the novel left little mark, and have long been forgotten by all but the most dedicated Austen scholar and/or translation theorist. In the twenty-first century, Austen is re-translated not because of, but rather, in spite of, earlier translations, because *Pride and Prejudice* has been recognised *a priori* as world literature by publishers, editors and translators, and indeed by readers themselves. In this dynamic and ever-shifting climate of translation and reception, it is impossible to predict what will happen to 'the truth universally acknowledged' next.

---

[28] See Bury, *Présentation* [Introduction], p. 31.
[29] David Damrosch, *What is World Literature* (Princeton University Press, 2003), p. 6.

11

JANET TODD

Criticism

According to Jane's sister Cassandra, 'First Impressions', the original story, was begun between October 1796 and August 1797. The manuscript was shared at once with family members and intimate friends, who read, listened and commented. By summer 1799, her friend Martha Lloyd had read it so often that Jane joked that she could almost 'publish it from Memory' (*Letters*, p. 46).

On Austen's own admission 'First Impressions' had been much 'lopt & cropt' by the time it was published as *Pride and Prejudice* in 1813 (*Letters*, p. 210). Changes may have responded to variations in the novel form or have answered Austen's own intellectual development. Or she may have learnt something from the publication of *Sense and Sensibility* in 1811: where this, her first published work, has the clumsiest beginning of the six novels, *Pride and Prejudice* has the fastest paced. When she began revising *Northanger Abbey* in 1816 she pointed out that it had been sent to a publisher thirteen years before and begun many years earlier, and that 'during that period, places, manners, books, and opinions have undergone considerable changes' (*NA*, p. 1). With this kind of sensitivity, it is likely that Austen also modified references to what was topical or of interest in the 1790s but no longer so in the Regency. Whatever she did and for whatever reasons, with *Pride and Prejudice* she fashioned a work more modern sounding than any written by her female contemporaries, Frances Burney, Charlotte Smith or Maria Edgeworth. The gestation of seventeen years allowed her to live up to her own fictional belief that a novelist should revise and not write and publish 'helter skelter'.

On 29 January 1813, Jane Austen wrote excitedly: 'I want to tell you that I have got my own darling Child from London.' She exclaimed over her heroine, 'I must confess that *I* think her as delightful a creature as ever appeared in print' (*Letters*, p. 210). (This became a general but not universal view: on first perusing the novel a year later Mary Russell Mitford found Elizabeth Bennet

'pert' and 'worldly'.)[1] A copy of the book was sent to Godmersham and read at
once by Austen's niece Fanny Knight along with her friend Mary Oxenden,
who scribbled in Fanny's diary 'perfection!!!' Later in the year at a dinner party
the playwright Richard Brinsley Sheridan declared it 'one of the cleverest things
he ever read' and in the following year Jane's brother Charles Austen heard a
nephew of the politician Charles James Fox claim that *Pride and Prejudice*,
together with *Sense and Sensibility*, were beyond compare.[2] Most specific
praise went to the comic characters, especially Mr Collins. Considering the
later elevation of Mr Darcy into the very type of a romantic hero it is apt that an
early admirer should be Lord Byron's future wife, Annabella Milbanke, who
told her mother how superior *Pride and Prejudice* was. She noted, 'It depends
not on any of the common resources of novel writers': it was the '*most
probable*' fiction she'd ever read; the interest is 'very strong, especially for
Mr. Darcy'.[3]

There was little notice in print – novels rarely provoked very serious and
lengthy comment. Two reviews came from the same periodicals as had
remarked *Sense and Sensibility*: the *British Critic* thought the novel 'far
superior to all the publications of the same kind which have lately come
before us' and praised the complex characters and simple plot; the longer
Critical Review concentrated on Mr Collins and Mr Bennet (preferred to
Mr Darcy as literary creations) and compared the heroine to Shakespeare's
Beatrice.[4] Significant public comment on Austen occurred only with Walter
Scott and Richard Whateley a few years later, but neither much mentioned
Pride and Prejudice, although Scott's famous review of *Emma* in 1816
stated that *Pride and Prejudice* showed very clearly the author's talents for
depicting ordinary life. He was more lavish with praise in his journal entry
of 1826, printed in the Lockhart biography, where he claimed that he read
for at least the third time the 'very finely written novel of Pride and
Prejudice'; in Austen he found the 'exquisite touch which renders commonplace things and characters interesting from the truth of the description and
the sentiment'.[5] When Frances Burney's half-sister Sarah Harriet read this,

[1] Revd A. G. K. L'Estrange (ed.), *Life of Mary Russell Mitford, Told by Herself in Letters to her Friends* (New York: Harper & Brothers, 1870), vol. 1, p. 300.

[2] Deirdre Le Faye (ed.), *Fanny Knight's Diaries: Jane Austen through her Niece's Eyes* ([Winchester, Hampshire]: Jane Austen Society, 2000), p. 25; BL MSS cited in Claire Harman's *Jane's Fame: How Jane Austen Conquered the World* (Edinburgh: Canongate, 2010), pp. 60 and 62.

[3] Malcolm Elwin, *Lord Byron's Wife* (New York: Harcourt, Brace & World, 1963), p. 159.

[4] *British Critic* 41 (February 1813), pp. 189–90; *Critical Review*, 4th series, 3 (March 1813), pp. 318–24.

[5] *Quarterly Review* 14 (March 1816), pp. 188–201; J. G. Lockhart, *Memoirs of Sir Walter Scott*, 2nd edn, 10 vols. (Edinburgh: Robert Cadell, 1839), 14 March 1826.

she remarked of the triple reading, '*I have read it as bumper toasts are given – three times three!*'.[6] In 1821 Richard Whateley made the alarming comment that Austen was giving away female secrets by showing in her heroines what women really were.[7]

That same year the novelist and former lover of Byron, Caroline Lamb, wrote to Thomas Malthus that, although she was having trouble with her story, she had a title for it, 'Principle & passion', 'since the fashion is to call every thing in the manner of Pride & prejudice, sense & sensibility'.[8] From this one might conclude that the title was becoming iconic; yet the books were not selling and, in the year of Austen's death, the publisher Thomas Egerton remaindered the third edition of *Pride and Prejudice*. Indeed the decade following 1817 was the lowest period in Austen's fame as one by one the novels fell out of print. In the 1830s Richard Bentley acquired rights to them all and put them back in the marketplace; they sold modestly, with *Pride and Prejudice* no more successful than the other works.

As the century progressed, the title continued to emerge in remarks and private letters. Disraeli claimed he had read *Pride and Prejudice* seventeen times.[9] Yet on the whole the novel was not especially beloved by serious Victorian novelists and readers who tended to appreciate works for their intellectual depth and scope. Austen's greatest champion in mid-century was George Henry Lewes, companion of George Eliot, but even he felt that she was not the highest kind of genius, and, although he claimed he would rather have written *Pride and Prejudice* than the Waverley novels, he did not put it on the same level as Eliot's *Middlemarch* for example.[10] Lewes famously urged a study of Jane Austen on Charlotte Brontë, so giving rise to her damning response to *Pride and Prejudice*: 'what did I find? An accurate daguerreotyped portrait of a common-place face; a carefully fenced, highly cultivated garden, with neat borders and delicate flowers; but no glance of a bright, vivid physiognomy, no open country, no fresh air, no blue hill, no bonny beck. I should hardly like to live with her ladies and gentlemen, in their elegant but confined houses'.[11] Other readers enjoyed the gentle ironic

[6] Lorna J. Clark (ed.), *The Letters of Sarah Harriet Burney* (Athens: University of Georgia Press, 1997), p. 420.

[7] Richard Whateley, Review of *Northanger Abbey* and *Persuasion*, *Quarterly Review* (January 1821), pp. 352–76.

[8] Paul Douglass (ed.), *The Whole Disgraceful Truth: Selected Letters of Lady Caroline Lamb* (New York: Palgrave 2006), p. 177.

[9] Claire Harman, *Jane's Fame: How Jane Austen Conquered the World* (Edinburgh: Canongate, 2010), p. 109.

[10] 'Recent Novels: French and English', *Fraser's Magazine* 36 (December 1847), p. 687.

[11] Margaret Smith (ed.), *The Letters of Charlotte Brontë* (Oxford: Clarendon Press, 2000), vol. II, p. 10.

commentary on ordinary life by a woman partly admired because she knew her limits.

The beginnings of fame

Towards the end of the nineteenth century Jane Austen's fortunes improved. In 1870 James Edward Austen Leigh published his *Memoir of Jane Austen*, in which he presented his aunt as a genteel, modest, Christian spinster. Together with the novels' portrayal of the last and lost pre-industrial era of England, attractive to a new railway and suburban readership in England, this work delivered Jane Austen as national treasure, in time beloved by gentlemanly 'Janeites'. Her books were a nostalgic reminder of a past Britain, prophylactic against modernity and change, and they allowed readers to talk about characters as though they were real people. The image of Austen became associated with 'heritage', a sort of English pastorale. In this milieu *Pride and Prejudice* very much came to the fore.

In 1894 Allen and Macmillan brought out an edition with detailed, rather kitsch line drawings by Hugh Thomson. It sold more than 11,500 copies in the first year and was reprinted many times. The edition had a preface by George Saintsbury, a respected university critic whose critical intelligence rather faltered when he contemplated Elizabeth Bennet, seen as far more than merely a literary character. In a time of challenging female attitudes, she became for Saintsbury a model of what a modern woman should be, an upholder of traditional values: there was in Elizabeth 'nothing offensive, nothing *viraginous*, nothing of the "New Woman" about her'; neither 'impudent' nor 'mannish' she had 'no nasty niceness' and she had 'perfect freedom from the idea that all men may bully her if they choose, and that most will run away with her if they can'.[12]

Saintsbury was not the only gentleman to grow sentimental when contemplating Elizabeth Bennet. A. C. Bradley, a distinguished professor of English at Glasgow and Oxford, said of the heroine, 'I was meant to fall in love with her, and I do.'[13] This sort of response had earlier provoked a famous tiff between William Dean Howells and Mark Twain. In 1890 Howells noted that 'The story of "Pride and Prejudice" has of late years become known to a constantly, almost rapidly, increasing cult, as it must be called, for the readers of Jane Austen are hardly ever less than her adorers: she is a passion and a creed, if not quite a religion.' Twain could not join in what the biographer

[12] Preface to *Pride and Prejudice* (London: George Allen, 1894), repr. in *Prefaces and Essays* (London: Macmillan, 1933).
[13] A. C. Bradley, *Miscellany* (London: Macmillan, 1929), p. 62.

Leslie Stephen called 'Austenolatry', and wrote to a friend, 'I often want to criticize Jane Austen, but her books madden me so that I can't conceal my frenzy from the reader; and therefore I have to stop every time I begin. Every time I read "Pride and Prejudice" I want to dig her up and beat her over the skull with her own shin-bone.' And again: '"When I take up one of Jane Austen's books", he said, "such as *Pride and Prejudice*, I feel like a barkeeper entering the kingdom of heaven. I know what his sensations would be and his private comments. He would not find the place to his taste, and he would probably say so."'[14]

The centenary of her death in 1917 helped associate Austen with war, or, in many cases, an escape from it. Together with *Emma* and *Sense and Sensibility*, *Pride and Prejudice* was considered therapeutic reading matter for wounded and damaged men. The novel became top of a 'Fever-Chart'.[15] In Rudyard Kipling's 1924 short story 'The Janeites' (a term coined by Saintsbury), officers and men used the names of 'The Reverend Collins' and 'The Lady Catherine De Bugg' for their guns. Similar escapist use was later made in Eric Linklater's 1938 novel *The Impregnable Women*, which predicted war and bombs on London and described the Prime Minister going off alone to read *Pride and Prejudice* (in reality the wife of the wartime leader, Winston Churchill, actually did read the book to him during a time of illness in the conflict).[16]

In 1940 when the novel was made into a Hollywood film, the script by Aldous Huxley lost the irony of the original and assumed patriotic resonance. Economically the production used the antebellum costumes that had been such a success in *Gone with the Wind* and avoided portraying a great English house; in future filmic versions the loving presentation of stately homes would add to the association of *Pride and Prejudice* with a National Trust version of England. The Oxford don, Lord David Cecil, president of the Jane Austen Society of the UK, was first introduced to the author by his mother reading *Pride and Prejudice* in an eighteenth-century stately home.[17] Self-consciousness about the reader and reading has marked criticism of *Pride and Prejudice* throughout the decades, and still continues.

If for writers who associated Austen with heritage *Pride and Prejudice* was the salient novel, critics with a more austere literary view tended to prefer *Mansfield Park* or *Emma*. But they continued to comment on the earlier work. Reginald Farrer began the dark trend in 1917 during the First World War, by seeing Austen as a harsh rather than anodyne and nostalgic writer,

[14] Brander Matthews, *Essays on English* (New York: Scribner, 1921), p. 62.
[15] Martin Jarrett-Kerr, letter to *TLS* (3 February 1984), p. 111.
[16] Winston S. Churchill, 'Closing the Ring', *The Second World War* (London: Cassell, 1952), vol. v, pp. 376–7.
[17] David Cecil, *A Portrait of Jane Austen* (London: Constable, 1978), p. 8.

one who resisted contemporary values and survived the horrors of life through her writing. The approach was developed during the Second World War, in 1940, by D. W. Harding, who found a latent hostility in author and text which an unthinking, laughing audience failed to appreciate. *Pride and Prejudice* allowed readers to be amused by characters such as Mrs Bennet, Mr Collins and Lady Catherine, whom the author herself detested since she knew how much real damage they could cause. Marvin Mudrick continued this view of Jane Austen as primarily an ironic writer, critical of her society; meanwhile Geoffrey Gorer applied Freudian analysis to the early novels, finding the oedipal pattern of heroines disliking mothers and marrying father figures – a pattern obvious in *Pride and Prejudice*.[18]

Much credit for securely elevating Jane Austen to canonical status, on a level with George Eliot and Henry James, must go to F. R. and Q. D. Leavis. They agreed with Farrer, Harding and Mudrick in not accepting the author as entirely benign but disagreed with them by insisting on her 'intense moral preoccupation'. Although F. R. Leavis rarely discussed Austen in detail, he had great influence on her reputation when in his critical book on the classic novel, *The Great Tradition*, he made her its inaugurator. For Q. D. Leavis, although *Mansfield Park* was the supreme achievement, all Austen's novels had moral value. The stress was less on what they told of contemporary politics and culture than on their form and style; they were primarily aesthetic objects rather than historical documents and they revealed a timeless author of refined sensibility and irony.[19]

Jane Austen in history

With her canonical position largely assured, Jane Austen entered the period of theory and history in the 1970s. While some commentators insisted on the author's detachment, others saw her fiction mirroring a particular worldview, one however to be interpreted in radically contradictory ways. Using a context of Austen's contemporaries, including the many women writers who had been largely neglected by literary criticism, Marilyn Butler found an author deeply implicated in the ideological struggles of the years following the

[18] Reginald Farrer, 'Jane Austen, ob. July 1817', *Quarterly Review* (July 1917); D. W. Harding, 'Regulated Hatred: An Aspect of the Work of Jane Austen', *Scrutiny* 7 (March 1940), pp. 346–62; Marvin Mudrick, *Jane Austen: Irony as Defense and Discovery* (Princeton University Press, 1952); Geoffrey Gorer, 'The Myth in Jane Austen', *American Imago* 2.3 (1941).
[19] F. R. Leavis, *The Great Tradition* (1948; Harmondsworth: Penguin 1972), p. 16; Q. D. Leavis, 'A Glance Backwards, 1965', in *Collected Essays*, 3 vols. (Cambridge University Press, 1983–9), vol. I, pp. 10–11, 73.

French Revolution. In this context she appeared a conservative Tory at odds with the slightly earlier radical writers Mary Wollstonecraft and Tom Paine, and closer in attitude to the Edmund Burke of *Reflections on the Revolution in France* (1790) and to Anglican theological writers. Butler threw down the gauntlet to those who, when second-wave feminism was flourishing, wanted to align Austen with revolutionary impulses; she wrote of *Pride and Prejudice*: 'the more one examines the novel the more difficult it becomes to read into it authorial approval of the element in Elizabeth which is rebellious'.[20] Much of later criticism has been an effort to refute and moderate this powerful view.

Sandra Gilbert and Susan Gubar opposed it in *The Madwoman in the Attic*. They argued that Austen appeared to accept a patriarchal order that replaced inadequate father figures with more satisfactory husbands to whom, as Gorer had noted, the heroines submitted: 'the necessity for silence and submission reinforces women's subordinate position in patriarchal culture'. In fact this was simply a cover story: Austen was a secret agent, whose books needed to be read against the grain for their true message to be appreciated. Yet the message remained a bleak one, for the process of seeming to submit was psychologically damaging: Elizabeth Bennet was reduced to humility and grief, 'though she hardly knew of what'.[21]

Mediating between extremes, Claudia Johnson in 1988 claimed that in *Pride and Prejudice* the author consented to the conservative myths but only to transform expectations so that women could achieve 'ecstatic personal happiness'; marrying the patriarch, the heroine did not have to renege on her female friendships, her ties with her sister and aunt. Although her novels lacked the bitterness and tension of many of the radical works of the time there was still some ideological affinity between Austen and her more feminist contemporaries.[22] In *Romantic Austen* (2002) Clara Tuite continued to amend Butler's argument of a conservative and regulatory Austen: for her *Pride and Prejudice* displayed a contradictory ethic of allegiance to female-identified writing and reading culture, mediated by an investment in the mystique of aristocratic, paternal culture.[23]

---

[20] Marilyn Butler, *Jane Austen and the War of Ideas* (Oxford: Clarendon Press, 1975), p. 203.

[21] Sandra Gilbert and Susan Gubar, *The Madwoman in the Attic: The Woman Writer and the Nineteenth-Century Literary Imagination* (New Haven: Yale University Press, 1979), pp. 154, 160.

[22] Claudia L. Johnson, *Jane Austen: Women, Politics, and the Novel* (University of Chicago Press, 1988), p. 93.

[23] Clara Tuite, *Romantic Austen: Sexual Politics and the Literary Canon* (Cambridge University Press, 2002), pp. 139–40.

Other critics have gone further in allying Austen with Enlightenment or liberal thinkers. Both Margaret Kirkham in *Jane Austen: Feminism and Fiction* (1983) and Peter Knox-Shaw in *Jane Austen and the Enlightenment* (2004) argued that the author was not a reactionary writer opposing Mary Wollstonecraft, but rather a progressive with much in common with this leading feminist and other radical writers. Knox-Shaw pointed out that *Pride and Prejudice* did not end in perfect harmony as Butler has asserted; clashing attitudes continued beyond the wedding.[24] In 'Conjecturing Possibilities' (2005), Felicia Bonaparte set *Pride and Prejudice* within contemporary debates between empiricists and rationalists, aligning it with the former. The possibility of genuine knowledge was constantly negated: each of the Bennet sisters 'is an experiment in the question of what it is we can rely on for the knowledge we require' while Elizabeth's reading of Darcy's letter extensively used the vocabulary of knowledge to stress epistemological uncertainty. Since she recognised the need for a semblance of truth, Austen avoided the most radical implications of her empiricism; so the narrative became 'a quest for an epistemological principle on which a suitable hypothesis of reality can rest'.[25]

In many such studies Darcy became the touchstone. Sarah Emsley in 'Practising the Virtues of Amiability and Civility in *Pride and Prejudice*' examined his first proposal within the category of social virtue, testing the limits of the protagonists' civility and amiability. In criticising Mary Bennet who studies moral writing, Austen suggested how difficult it was to apply abstract ideas to real life: civility may provide rules for the practice of virtue but does not substitute for it, and amiability is needed. This Darcy achieves. In 'Darcy's Ardent Love and Resentful Temper in *Pride and Prejudice*' Horace Hodges argued that Darcy was used to test current ideas of resentment, such as those discussed by Scottish Enlightenment thinkers Adam Smith and the historian William Robertson, who wrote of 'the strong resentment which calumniated innocence naturally feels'. Darcy's love for Elizabeth lets him put resentment in an epistemological framework and is imbued with 'the Christian concept of a love that is not proud and that seeks to perceive what is good in the loved one'.[26] Putting a different complexion on the change, Rachel Bowlby in '"Speech Creatures"' (2009) found in both

[24] Peter Knox-Shaw, *Jane Austen and the Enlightenment* (Cambridge University Press, 2004).
[25] Felicia Bonaparte, 'Conjecturing Possibilities: Reading and Misreading Texts in Jane Austen's *Pride and Prejudice*', *Studies in the Novel* 37.2 (Summer 2005), pp. 144–5.
[26] Sarah Emsley, 'Practising the Virtues of Amiability and Civility in *Pride and Prejudice*', *Persuasions* 22 (2000), pp. 187–98; Horace Hodges, 'Darcy's Ardent Love and Resentful Temper in *Pride and Prejudice*', *Persuasions* 30 (Winter 2009).

Richardson's Mr B and Austen's Darcy the zeal of a therapied patient in their rejecting of an adulthood malformed by early education and their embracing of a 'humbler selfhood' taught by their future wives.[27]

Marxist criticism has inflected much comment on Austen. Karen Newman, for example, noted that, while marriage, the conservative closure, provided the ending, it was none the less ironised. She related this to the theories of Pierre Macherey and Louis Althusser which suggested that literary texts juxtaposed contradictory meanings, so displaying the faulty nature of the ideology with which they were inspired. Without directly commenting, Austen frequently exposed the interrelation of financial motivation and romantic allure by bringing out the semantic possibilities of a word like 'prudence'.[28] Michael McKeon's demandingly abstract book *The Secret History of Domesticity* was inspired by Jürgen Habermas's schematic model of the emergence of modern civil society in Britain. Habermas postulated an 'intimate sphere' in which bourgeois members of the public sphere might imagine themselves something beyond simply economic and political subjects and could forge self-awareness and sympathy. Modernity was a process of privatisation and internalisation, with feminine subjectivity becoming a fundamental outpost of the realm of privacy. The final case study in the book was *Pride and Prejudice*: here the relationship of family and state structuring much modern thought was 'decisively internalised and privatized within the realm of the family'. The novel became a 'parody of family romance', showing that inner worth was not just a function of patrilineal birth.[29]

Jane Austen in performance

With a flurry of adaptations for the small and large screens, the 1990s saw the beginning of a wave of Austenmania in popular culture (see chapters by Looser and Auerbach). The cinematic treatment gave *Pride and Prejudice* immense and mass popularity: it was a Cinderella story with a simple romantic plot line, gorgeous setting and quick dialogue suited to the new medium. Largely overlooked in favour of Elizabeth – or even Mr Collins – in early criticism, Mr Darcy now emerged as the very type of the brooding romantic hero, with more in common with Charlotte Brontë's Mr Rochester than with

[27] Rachel Bowlby, '"Speech Creatures"': New Men in *Pamela* and *Pride and Prejudice*', in *Theory-Tinged Criticism: Essays in Memory of Malcolm Bowie*, ed. Diana Knight and Judith Still, special issue of *Paragraph* 32.9 (July 2009), pp. 240–51.

[28] Karen Newman, 'Can This Marriage be Saved: Jane Austen Makes Sense of an Ending', *ELH* 50.4 (Winter 1983), pp. 693–710.

[29] Michael McKeon, *The Secret History of Domesticity: Public, Private, and the Division of Knowledge* (Baltimore: Johns Hopkins University Press, 2006), pp. 152 and 692.

Edmund Bertram. The mass popularity did not disturb the academy, which continued to accelerate the amount and complexity of its criticism, drawing still on critical and historical theory. Some of this criticism existed only for the initiated, while some was interestingly interdisciplinary and self-reflecting.

Language, print culture and reading practice became especially fashionable topics, along with the notion of performance / 'performativity': entry into *Pride and Prejudice* came through a study of the various acts of thinking, reading, writing and conversing, as well as the playing out of social and sexual roles. Patricia Michaelson in her prefatory material to *Speaking Volumes* (2002) explained that she read *Pride and Prejudice* silently many times, then, hearing it aloud, realised that 'every sentence had barbs that I had skimmed over'. Eighteenth- and twentieth-century language theorists defined women's language as a 'coherent sociolect' but, using feminist linguistic studies, Michaelson focused not on this symbolic category but on the empirical language used by women, of which gender was only one aspect. *Pride and Prejudice* became an elocution and conversation manual helping women develop 'discourse competence' as well as the manners that negotiated between sincerity and politeness.[30] Bharat Tandon in *Austen and the Morality of Conversation* (2003) continued Michaelson's cultural contextualisation and interest in linguistic theory by studying 'different ways in which people behave in Jane Austen's fiction, and ... different ways in which Austen's fictional language behaves towards them, and towards its readers'. Austen's novels consistently recognised the failure of 'polite conversation' to explain all forms of experience; it even challenged the claim of fiction to provide its own explanatory framework, a notion which enabled Austen to question the meaning and categories of fiction. *Pride and Prejudice* sought to transcend its own genre by 'creating a "sparkling" dramatic comedy out of the eternal possibility of being misunderstood'.[31] Noting Austen's 'evaluative opacity', Massimiliano Morini in *Jane Austen's Narrative Techniques* used pragmatics – the study of how speakers, including narrators, communicate meaning – to examine point of view in the novels as well as their lively and plausible dialogue. This dialogue took up the greatest part of *Pride and Prejudice*: the Bennet family provided an ensemble of different voices where the Bingley/Darcy ménage conversed with greater subtlety and indirection. Some evaluative ambiguity remained through the narrator's refusal always to commit herself to a definitive position.[32] In *The*

---

[30] Patricia Michaelson, *Speaking Volumes: Women, Reading and Speech in the Age of Austen* (Stanford University Press, 2002), pp. xiii and 203.
[31] Bharat Tandon, *Austen and the Morality of Conversation* (London: Anthem Press, 2003), p. 84.
[32] Massimiliano Morini, *Jane Austen's Narrative Techniques: A Stylistic and Pragmatic Analysis* (Farnham, Surrey: Ashgate, 2009), p. 37.

Technology of the Novel (2009) Tony E. Jackson engaged with writing as an 'invented, systematized, tool-using process for representing spoken language in visual signs' that found fullest expression in the novel. He analysed Darcy's first proposal scene and his letter, so revealing the interaction between writing, physical presence and consciousness.[33]

Laughter as a form of performance is a fraught subject. Patricia Meyer Spacks cautioned readers not to laugh too much at *Pride and Prejudice*, lest, like Mr Bennet, they fail to comprehend the emotional lives of the characters to whom they are invited to feel superior.[34] In 1967 Joseph Wiesenfarth had put forward the controversial argument in *The Errand of Form* that *Pride and Prejudice* 'dramatizes the possibility of an ordered world': the Dionysian element represented by Lydia and Mrs Bennet is overshadowed by the Apollonian protagonists who receive a measure of fortune denied everyone else. The argument was complicated by gender: the aesthetic tension between moral conservatism and comic realism was aggravated by Apollo's status as male god – and by the gender status or interest of critics. While Lionel Trilling had spoken of the mutual accommodation of 'female vivacity' and 'strict male syntax' in his essay '*Mansfield Park*' of 1954, critics from Gilbert and Gubar onwards who concentrated on gender had suspected Austen's 'struggles' to 'combine her implicitly rebellious vision with an explicitly decorous form'.[35]

In 'Laughing at Mr. Darcy' Elvira Casal celebrated Elizabeth's laughter, equating it with flirtation and even erotic foreplay, while taking the usual line that any celebration was tempered by connotations of irresponsibility. Paul Goetsch's 'Laughter in *Pride and Prejudice*' allowed less wit than Casal to the 'somewhat pompous' Darcy and was less approving of Elizabeth's sexy laughter. Darcy became a representative of the upper classes which prized gravity as a means of distinguishing themselves from the masses. In Austen's time the seventeenth-century view of humour as 'an aberration demanding satiric attack' was increasingly replaced by a more 'amiable' humour, based on good nature. The laughter of both Elizabeth and Lydia is the 'gift of joyfulness' (Spacks's term), but Lydia's immoderation and pursuit of immediate gratification identify her as thoughtless and threatening, where Elizabeth's self-discipline (suppression of laughter-as-ridicule) gained her the perfect match as her critical laughter gave way to amiable. At the end

33 Tony E. Jackson, *The Technology of the Novel: Writing and Narrative in British Fiction* (Baltimore: Johns Hopkins University Press, 2009), p. 3.
34 Patricia Spacks, 'Austen's Laughter', *Women's Studies* 15 (1988), pp. 71–85.
35 Joseph Wiesenfarth, *The Errand of Form: An Assay of Jane Austen's Art* (New York: Fordham University Press, 1967), p. 82; Lionel Trilling, '*Mansfield Park*', *Partisan Review* 21 (1954), pp. 492–511; Gilbert and Gubar, *The Madwoman in the Attic*, p. 153.

she smiles but ceases to laugh openly at Darcy. Joseph Wiesenfarth seems largely to have won this argument – for the moment.[36]

Gender as a performative category underpinned the discussion of many critics of masculinity, often with a Foucauldian inflection. In the late eighteenth and early nineteenth centuries gender was, it is argued, an apparently stable marker of identity in unstable times, even if pure examples of masculinity and femininity were becoming difficult to find, as Doris Kadish noted in *Politicizing Gender*. The state conceptualised the male citizen as a progressive agent of national modernity (forward-thrusting, potent and historic). Aristocracy having proved itself ineffectual, the patriotic middle class sought to become the mainstay of the English nation and manhood, expressed in hegemony over wife and family.[37] In *Disciplining Love*, Michael Kramp agreed that, generally, Austen's novels helped shape masculinity, allowing the English male to distinguish himself by self-discipline from the uncontrolled French. In *Pride and Prejudice*, the old Burkean model of masculinity was embodied in Darcy, who, through his marriage to Elizabeth and friendship with the rising men of the bourgeoisie – Bingley and Gardiner – was aligned to some extent with the progressive element; so he combined the past with a future coming into being. In her effort to dramatise the destabilising effect of monied wealth, however, Austen made the non-aristocratic wealthy men fall short of the ideal: Bingley's emotions were fluid and unpredictable – rather like new money itself.

Kramp then placed Austen in a later moment of transformation, the crisis of feminism and the perceived decline of male social and sexual roles in late twentieth-century America. Men's movements such as the Promise Keepers used homosocial rituals to reaffirm a traditional masculine identity 'vital to the security of the nation'. The movements coincided in the mid 1990s with the release of popular films based on Austen's novels, which, with a character like Darcy, provided another model of ideal maleness, an integral component of what Kramp called the 'hegemonic structures' of the modern nation.[38]

---

[36] Elvira Casal, 'Laughing at Mr. Darcy: Wit and Sexuality in *Pride and Prejudice*', *Persuasions* 22.1 (Winter 2001); Paul Goetsch, 'Laughter in *Pride and Prejudice*', in *Redefining the Modern: Essays on Literature and Society in Honor of Joseph Wiesenfarth*, ed. William Baker and Ira B. Nadel (Madison, NJ: Fairleigh Dickinson University Press, 2003), pp. 29–43.

[37] Doris Kadish, *Politicizing Gender* (New Brunswick, NJ: Rutgers University Press, 1991).

[38] Michael Kramp, *Disciplining Love: Austen and the Modern Man* (Columbus: Ohio State University Press, 2007), p. ix.

The web is alive with mentions of and variations on *Pride and Prejudice* and every day brings more, usually repetitive, comment in journals, newspapers, reviews, blogs and tweets, both on the brand and on the novel. It is a testament to a remarkable book that the individual reader can, despite all this media and cyber noise, still go away like Cassandra Austen, George Saintsbury, Winston Churchill or Patricia Michaelson to enjoy an intimate relationship with it.

12

JANET TODD

The romantic hero

Jane Austen's hero

Fitzwilliam Darcy enters *Pride and Prejudice* with every advantage of person – large, tall, handsome – and of assets – the round fictional number of £10,000 a year and a very large estate. But he ruins the good impression by boorishness. His manners are extremely poor, and only Mrs Bennet really addresses the problem, accusing him of lacking a 'right disposition'. He is above being pleased; he believes he has a right not to be, accepting that manners are 'natural' and not the result of effort and practice. To be rude is a *droit de seigneur*, part of the gravitas of the upper-class male. He is morose and fastidious, frightening the spirit out of his shy sister. He has no easiness in conversation or letter-writing, studying only to show his superiority – Mrs Bennet says he is one of 'those persons who fancy themselves very important and never open their mouths' (*P&P*, p. 48). 'Haughty, reserved and fastidious' (p. 17), immensely proud of high birth, Darcy assumes he has 'a real superiority of mind' and is among 'the wisest and best' of men, with 'a strong understanding' which he insists must not be ridiculed (pp. 62–3). He knows himself so slenderly as a social being that he thinks he lacks improper pride.

The reader's response to this attitude is complicated by Charlotte Lucas, who has much in common with Edmund Burke, and perhaps with the narrator. Burke sometimes appears to assume that worth encompasses social and moral value as well as birth and riches, while the narrator allows Elizabeth to learn that the riches that have allowed Darcy's arrogance do indeed deliver superiority when used well. Darcy cannot forget or forgive 'follies and vices of others' and admits to being 'resentful' (p. 63), seeing the attribute as perhaps not a virtue, but not quite a vice either. Even taking into account what we later learn of the dastardly Wickham, this remains an uncomfortable aspect. The narrator calls him 'clever' (p. 17) but is it clever constantly to be giving offence, or advantageous to lack what *Persuasion* calls 'elasticity' of mind (*P*, p. 167)?

What does this arrogant man initially think of women? Not much, it seems. He believes his notice gives consequence to any girl and must 'elevate her with the hope of influencing his felicity'. When he follows his devastating critique of the Bennet family with a proposal of marriage, Elizabeth 'could easily see that he had no doubt of a favourable answer. He *spoke* of apprehension and anxiety, but his countenance expressed real security' (*P&P*, p. 212). Where Charlotte Lucas asks only for reasonable humour and financial competence in a *man*, Darcy demands that this subordinate *woman* – she who is to be chosen, not choosing – have every accomplishment, intellectual, social and physical, and still find time for extensive reading. In their attitude to women Darcy and Collins mirror each other: both impose on Elizabeth – and in a private domestic space which should be secure – crude addresses based on a failure to rate the sex as individuals but simply as members of a subordinate group.

Darcy's first movement towards Elizabeth is mastering – he rudely stares at her, then eavesdrops when he will: he has a perfect right to look, to overhear and to perplex. No woman seeking marriage could act like this (though Keira Knightley as Elizabeth Bennet does just this in the twenty-first-century film by Joe Wright, with its continuous tracking of the female look). He may enjoy Elizabeth's 'easy playfulness' but provides no play in return. When she replies wittily to his lumpen remark that poetry is the food of love, 'Darcy only smiled' (*P&P*, p. 49), a social improvement perhaps but no use in promoting the necessary sociability. Why should he be the entertainer? Women are the ones to entertain and flirt – and they do. The word 'archly' is frequently used for Elizabeth, who responds to the condescension of consequence with pertness; the equivalent Darcy adverbs are 'gravely' and 'coldly'. *He* may be silent and wait because all women, even Elizabeth, will in the end try to please. The only time Elizabeth provides coldness is just before his marriage proposal and just after she has learnt of his disgraceful interference in her sister's life; his reaction is 'affected incredulity' (p. 213).

When one woman manages, in her words, to cheat this man of 'premeditated contempt', he falls in love and then blames her for his predicament: he has been 'bewitched' (*P&P*, pp. 56–7) – for all the world as if he were Henry VIII contemplating Anne Boleyn. Now he grows obsessive, even more silent, and conflicted. He gives nothing away of his feelings to his one friend – or anyone else. Meanwhile his effect on the woman he has deigned to love is powerful – and predictable: it diminishes her individual and personal consequence and dents her spontaneity. Faced with his own relative's 'ill-breeding', Darcy simply 'looked a little ashamed ... and made no answer' (p. 195). At the same time he assumes that Elizabeth will be mortified by a portrayal of the manners of her family.

To suit her man, Elizabeth may retain what is unusual but likeable. There is always present in Elizabeth and Darcy something of the attractive but hierarchical heterosexual balance, the one so supremely caught in Shakespeare's Beatrice and Benedict from *Much Ado About Nothing*. Elizabeth always retains her critical intelligence; however, she sheds her 'conceited independence' (*P&P*, p. 39), her earlier refusal to see herself as a marriageable commodity, and she exchanges the verbal impertinence of Rosings for the maidenly and silent confusion of Pemberley, despite the fact that she is a heroine who has supremely constructed herself through language. Soon after meeting Darcy she is described as checking a laugh, hiding a smile, very much as Frances Burney's Evelina learns to do before her upwardly mobile marriage to Lord Orville in the popular 1778 novel that so influenced Jane Austen. Under Darcy's gaze Elizabeth controls further what Miss Bingley describes as 'that little something, bordering on conceit and impertinence' (p. 57) and subdues her individualistic tendencies in the interest of traditional social harmony.

Her egalitarian political views soften too. At first she had noted that Wickham's guilt seemed equal to his humble descent, and, musing over Darcy's treatment of Jane, considered his objection must have been her 'having one uncle who was a country attorney, and another who was in business in London' (*P&P*, p. 218). However, the Darcy letter, delivered with 'haughty composure' (p. 218) and providing an explanation about Wickham which is owed not primarily to Elizabeth but to himself and in which he declares he must state again the defects of her nearest relations, starts a transformation directed towards her social and economic interests. On first perusal of the letter she saw only 'pride and insolence' (p. 226); on second she was mortified at *herself*. Darcy's reproach became merited and 'her sense of shame was severe' (p. 231). In the past (especially at Netherfield) Elizabeth had shown herself embarrassed by her family when publicly displayed, but now, with one unmannerly letter this 'squeamish' youth (p. 256), to use Mr Bennet's resonant phrase, has made her utterly ashamed of a family of lawyers and tradespeople she had laughed at – and with – for all her adult years.

Having spied Pemberley Elizabeth finds man and property coalescing. As Alistair Duckworth has argued, in the classic English novel the logic of the metonym influences how estates and landscapes are presented, so that houses play a variety of coded social and political roles.[1] Big, handsome Darcy is expressed by his house described as 'large, handsome' and 'standing well' (*P&P*, p. 271). As the book's habitual irony falters before the estate, so it does before the owner; the adjective 'handsome' is used by the housekeeper for the

[1] Alistair Duckworth, *The Improvement of the Estate: A Study of Jane Austen's Novels* (Baltimore: Johns Hopkins University Press, 1971).

master, and here it extends over physical, social and moral qualities. Despite her earlier determination to note distant landscape in detail, Elizabeth aids the coalescing by seeing only the newly admirable Darcy in the stones of his estate.[2] With renewed hopes, she is insisting on herself as a gentleman's daughter, not the niece of a tradesman and country lawyer. Now she seems to crave a mastering man, lord of all he surveys, one who will allow her to be mistress of grand rooms and elegant furniture, and also to be the student of a benefactor and teacher with superior 'judgment, information, and knowledge of the world' (*P&P*, p. 344). It is convenient that knowledge, property and virtue so nicely coincide.

The generic hero

Of all her novels, *Pride and Prejudice* departs most thoroughly from the probabilistic fiction with which Jane Austen has been most credited by her serious critics from Walter Scott in 1816 to present commentators who find real history and socio-economic comment in her pages. Although it is only part of an otherwise realistic novel, uniquely among her works *Pride and Prejudice* evokes fantasy; in recent years its lovers – with the aspects I have outlined above – have become archetypal figures, its luxurious upper-class setting the theatre of romance. But the contemporary attention has been due less to Jane Austen's heroine, so beloved of the author and early twentieth-century male readers, than to the hero, who is now freighted with the crudeness of repeated and culturally supported female dreams. This figure evokes both an enjoyable masochistic dread of the overbearing male *and* a utopian exultation at the feminine erotic power that can bring the monster to heel with minimal effort. Popular art does not much question itself any more than do folk tales. The myth critic Northrop Frye noted that 'the uninhibited imagination ... produces highly conventionalised art': he was talking about structure but the remark works for character in popular fiction where stylised formulaic narratives are demanded to support it.[3] A reader of *Pride and Prejudice* can let her mind or imagination reproduce and luxuriate in the central wish-fulfilling element that is in the novel, despite the fact that it is delivered under a probabilistic carapace and riddled with irony: not just the Cinderella story of a humble girl marrying a prince but the worthy lowly girl catching or taming a deliciously arrogant master.

[2] Elizabeth's looking is as themed as any modern National Trust leaflet introducing a property according to the assumed desires of current visitors.
[3] Northrop Frye, *Fables of Identity: Studies in Poetic Mythology* (New York: Harcourt, Brace and World, 1963), p. 27.

Romance in some form is as old as narrative, the 'tale of wild adventures in war and love' in Dr Johnson's phrase. The early printed romance of heroic adventure and chivalric love, perfect damsels and adoring knights, demanded protagonists of high birth and purpose. It provoked identification: Renaissance men jousted as Arthurian knights out of courtly romance, and coteries of ladies wrote to each other under the names of characters from the popular early seventeenth-century French romance *L'Astrée* by Honoré d'Urfé. Chivalric heroic tales maddened Cervantes's hero Don Quixote, while courtly-love romance associated with the French writers Madeleine de Scudéry and the Seigneur de la Calprenède turned the head of the heroine of Charlotte Lennox's *Female Quixote* (1752), who expected real life to conform to this (by now old-fashioned) romantic fiction and confused an ideal with a real world. Clara Reeve in *The Progress of Romance* (1785) described this ideal type of romance as making young women 'deport themselves too much like Queens and Princesses'. Discussing the newer, more realistic romances exemplified by Samuel Richardson's *Pamela* (1740), again she assumed that the female reader – and it is with the woman consumer that eighteenth-century commentators were most concerned – would be influenced by the book to become an obsessive scribbler like the heroine. Reeve made little reference to the effect of the romance hero on the female reader.[4]

Austen's Darcy has at the start of the novel no sense of the enlightened civic duty which was becoming a public virtue in British culture in eighteenth-century fiction and reality as dominant men were socialised out of old-fashioned *laissez-faire* ways in sexuality and social life.[5] 'I am ill qualified to recommend myself to strangers' is his boast; 'We neither of us perform to strangers', he says to Elizabeth (*P&P*, pp. 196–7). But in the new English civic society no citizen is a 'stranger' and accommodation to all companions was the goal. In the first proposal scene Darcy puts truth-telling above ordinary politeness, as if the feelings of another cannot defeat an urge to self-expression. '[D]isguise of every sort is my abhorrence', he declares. But disguise is, as eighteenth-century social philosophers were never tired of declaring, necessary for civil society to function (p. 215). Bingley is truly civil and he forces his sister 'to be civil also, and say what the occasion required' (p. 49). He gets nowhere with his friend: Darcy makes degrading assumptions about others every time he opens his mouth, and he accepts that a rich man, whether himself or Bingley, has a right to consider his own appetite only and has no

[4] Clara Reeve, *The Progress of Romance through Times, Countries and Manners ...* (Colchester, 1785), vol. I, pp. 67 and 137.
[5] John Brewer, *The Pleasures of the Imagination: English Culture in the Eighteenth Century* (New York: Farrar Straus Giroux, 1997), p. 102.

responsibility to a neighbourhood. In short Darcy has, before his conversion, no concern for 'the convenience of the world' (p. 63). The pride of aristocracy trumps the affability of the gentleman demanded in realistic romance from Samuel Richardson's Mr B to Burney's Lord Orville. In fact Darcy in the early pages is so bad he is almost comic. Maybe in the original, probably far more satiric, 'First Impressions' he may have been as straightforwardly ridiculous as the dazzling Charles Adams from the juvenile 'Jack and Alice', who cannot be looked on by ordinary people because he is – and knows he is – so perfect. Darcy, however, realises his error where Charles Adams does not.

In narrative outline Richardson's *Pamela* seems to have much in common with *Pride and Prejudice*. The heroes of both novels learn some social con-formity and respect for impressive women. In both, a young girl markets herself in marriage without her family and finds a man to value her mind and virtue and raise her rank – without the commodification implied in Mr Collins's proposal to his cousin, but with all the compromises a social rise demands. So it might be argued that, between them, Darcy and Elizabeth have followed the old trajectory of the eighteenth-century hero and heroine, Mr B and Pamela, acting out a conservative ideology whereby the dominance of the rigid ruling class is softened by some energy and virtue rising from below; the inheritance is renovated, not reformed. It is a fantasy beloved of the literate middle orders in the eighteenth century – hence the huge popular-ity of *Pamela*. Towards the close of *Pride and Prejudice* Mr Darcy takes on the mantle of the polite eighteenth-century gentleman, Mr B and Richardson's later ideal, Sir Charles Grandison, or the female-created equivalent, Lord Orville. In all these novels social and individual come resoundingly together, uniting a civil and semi-feudal society of best master and landlord within a satisfying denouement that solves all the problems of the heroine.[6]

If this were all, then *Pride and Prejudice* would be stuck in its period of genesis, the eighteenth century, and be as little read now as *Pamela* and *Evelina*; even by 1813 it would have seemed hopelessly old-fashioned. For, late in the previous century, a new kind of male character had entered the novels of Mrs Radcliffe and her followers, one who was largely unknown from the inside, a man who treated the heroine with cruelty – but with whom she and the reader were nonetheless fascinated, as Emily famously was by her persecutor Montoni

---

[6] *Pride and Prejudice* differs substantially from the didactic courtship novel written by Burney and Mary Brunton, which, while allowing some enjoyment of romance, tends in the end to oppose a romance that allows love to trump all other considerations. Ashley Tauchert in *Romancing Jane Austen: Narrative, Realism, and the Possibility of a Happy Ending* (Basingstoke and New York: Palgrave Macmillan, 2005) argues that Austen's novels, while they do allow the 'rescue fantasy', are real love stories in which women struggle to gain and retain identity and happiness.

in *The Mysteries of Udolpho*: she finds herself inadvertently looking for him from the castle window and her would-be seducer Morano actually accuses her of loving the villainous man.

The gothic male character was much implicated in the arrogant and enthralling Romantic hero born in the next century, round about the time Jane Austen was first publishing: Childe Harold (beginning 1812) and the Giaour (1813) in the first of the *Oriental Tales*. In these works the poet Lord Byron combined gothic villain and hero, creating in himself and in his work the image of a new kind of man: a sexy, moody aristocrat with great charisma. From him derived a whole line of similarly stern, powerful, self-obsessed and fascinating men for whom the 'implacability of ... resentments' and 'unforgiving temper' of the early Darcy were almost mandatory and need not be surrendered. In all of them a proud temper might lead to some acts of feudal generosity – as the cynical Wickham notes for Darcy. Wickham himself has a 'very pleasing address' and 'a happy readiness of conversation', but the romantic hero should keep his distance, his mastery and his mystery: he would be better frightening the world with his 'high and imposing manners' than engaging in small talk. (Although appreciating easy manners in women, Jane Austen herself seems increasingly to dislike them as the main defining mark of her fictional menfolk – as is evident in her demolition of Frank Churchill in *Emma* and, even more, of the easy gentleman, Mr Elliot of *Persuasion* – although she does not again create a rude and overbearing hero such as the early Darcy.) The new hero does not seek to please; he does what he likes, not what another likes. He does so, because, as Colonel Fitzwilliam notes of his cousin, he has the means and the power. In this sort of romance the obstacles that create and then obstruct desire – the romantic story line – reside in the hero as much as in the external world.

Charlotte Brontë wrote that in *Pride and Prejudice* she found 'a carefully-fenced, highly cultivated garden with neat borders and delicate flowers'.[7] It is an ironic response since later readers ensured that Mr Darcy at least stepped out of this garden and travelled beyond Mr B, Lord Orville and Austen's other heroes including Henry Tilney and Mr Knightley to find some generic resemblance to the Brontës' own Heathcliff and Mr Rochester, as well as to Grandcourt in George Eliot's *Daniel Deronda*. However, Darcy's arrogance is not as thoroughly assaulted and humbled as most of his successors' and there is far less anguish in the process. And he is not quite like these men any more than he is quite like Mr B or Lord Orville. His distinction in the novel is

[7] Margaret Smith (ed.), *The Letters of Charlotte Brontë* (Oxford: Clarendon Press, 2000), vol. II, p. 10.

to promise a combination of the old social and civic progress with the new sexual charisma of the romantic hero. The novel makes the types consecutive – romantic hero, then polite gentleman – but in the popular imagination they may coalesce.[8]

Mr Darcy's heirs

Part of the fantasy that Mr Darcy embodies drove Jane Austen's near contemporary, the feminist Mary Wollstonecraft, almost wild with irritation. '[B]ut why is virtue to be always rewarded with a coach and six?' she complained.[9] She knew the problems of romance for women, its materialistic aspect and fixation on a magical provider, as of course did Jane Austen – most of the time. But neither Austen nor Wollstonecraft could have foreseen that two subsequent waves of feminism with their different emphases on gender sameness and equality would make no dent in the mass phenomenon of the modern cultural idea of romantic 'true love', the utopian desire of female readers for a special kind of romance and special kind of hero. One could argue that this fantasy has conquered the globe. In our culture and many others, the idea of romance has, as the Jungian critic Robert A. Johnson argued, supplanted religion as an arena in which men and women seek meaning, transcendence, wholeness and ecstasy: the interest and human instinct for wholeness is projected on to love.[10]

As Jane Austen's novel is subsumed into the culture of mass romance, Darcy gains in the popular imagination a more transparently passionate inner life and comes to fit the stereotype of the irrationally loving lover, out of control. He becomes the Jungian male who has to overcome his masculine ego to gain his feminine side: even in the Austen novel he sees his love as something happening to him from outside, hence his awkward contorted marriage proposal. Johnson relates this motif to the Tristan myth where the love is from a potion: that is, it is involuntary. However, the cleverness of Austen in *Pride and Prejudice* is to combine some outline of this with the female story in which the heroine, who ends up loving the hero, is not caught in that kind of romantic love: here the

---

[8] In *Self-Control* (1811), which Jane Austen read just before publishing *Pride and Prejudice*, Mary Brunton made her heroine choose between the unruly imperious man and the virtuous, polite one. Jane Austen was kinder.

[9] Wollstonecraft, Review of *The Mental Triumph*, in *The Works of Mary Wollstonecraft*, ed. Janet Todd and Marilyn Butler (London: William Pickering, 1989), vol. VII, p. 174.

[10] Robert A. Johnson, *The Psychology of Romantic Love* (London: Routledge and Kegan Paul, 1984), pp. xi and 60–1.

playful conceit of Elizabeth's love mediated through the magnificent grounds of Pemberley does its work well.[11]

Some of the outlines of *Pride and Prejudice* may be discerned in many of the later classic romances of the twentieth century. I shall mention only a few out of numerous potential examples. E. M. Hull's *The Sheik* (1919), with the independent heroine and dangerous hero, adds overt erotic and sexual elements – the arrogant hero actually rapes the heroine, who accepts the emotional risk loving such a man entails: 'you will have a devil for a husband', he tells her. Daphne du Maurier's gothic romance *Rebecca* (1938) provides an arrogant rich older man, Maxim de Winter, dominating a poorer young woman socially beneath him; he is the owner of a great mansion, Manderley, that expresses his psyche and past as well as his purse. Margaret Mitchell's *Gone with the Wind* (1936) displays characters who begin by living the archetypal plot of overbearing man and ingénue.

The prolific kitsch British queen of twentieth-century mass-market romance, Barbara Cartland, declared herself influenced by *The Sheik* when she began writing four years after its publication. The influence of Jane Austen, or rather the simplified image of Austen, is evident in the formulaic reworking of conventional *Pride and Prejudice* plot of rich, usually noble and at first unattainable male, and submissive female who catches him, the story usually placed in a costumed Regency setting. By her death in 2000 Cartland had written over 700 short romances and far exceeded Jane Austen in sales.

The simplicity and naïveté of Cartland's plots did not prevent her from being accused of plagiarism in the 1950s by a more middlebrow queen of historical romance, Georgette Heyer.[12] In 1921 at the age of nineteen Heyer published her first romance, *The Black Moth*, and from then until her death in 1974 she averaged one or two historical novels a year, many echoing *Pride and Prejudice* in situations of courtship and betrothal, attraction and barriers overcome. Like many of Cartland's short fictions, Heyer's novels were usually set in a Regency period associated with Jane Austen but, far more than in Austen's spare works, filled with the consumer items that kept the settings alien for the twentieth-century reader, if not quite as exotic as the deserts of the sheik. In *Pride and Prejudice* Mr Darcy impressed with his 'fine, tall person, handsome features, noble mien' and his 'ten thousand a year'. Heyer's character, Mr Beaumaris in *Arabella* (1949), has all this as well as the same attributes of boredom and arrogance, but far more is made of his costume, his tight jacket, pantaloons and polished boots, and in many

[11] Ibid., p. 57.
[12] Jennifer Koestler, *Georgette Heyer: Biography of a Bestseller* (London: William Heinemann, 2011).

respects he seems closer to the conventional notion of a Regency buck than to Mr Darcy. In other novels the hero has to submit to rather more independent-minded girls than would inhabit Jane Austen's world: in *The Grand Sophy* (1950), for example, the hero is matched by a woman who can do the shooting and kidnapping as well as any man.

British Mills and Boon romances and the North American counterpart, Harlequin, are series of short formulaic novels in simple predictable language, issued each month. They proved hugely popular from the 1930s, peaking in the post-war period of consumer expansion. Aimed at millions of readers no longer buying books in conventional bookshops or using the serious section of lending libraries, they were far removed from the subtleties and style of Jane Austen, yet claimed some inspiration from a popularised version of her novels, and the Darcy figure of power and property tamed by the humbler less technicolour girl was a constant feature. Violet Winspear, a prolific Mills and Boon author, said of her heroes that she wrote them as if they were 'capable of rape', a comment that led to her receiving hate mail.

In much of this mass-market material the formula comes close to the skeleton of *Pride and Prejudice*. As Tania Modleski expressed it in *Loving with a Vengeance* in 1982, a work that discussed the hold which romantic ideology and narrative have over women's conscious and unconscious: a young, inexperienced, poor to moderately well-to-do woman is involved with a handsome, rich older man whose behaviour confuses her: though he is 'obviously interested in her, he is mocking, cynical, contemptuous, often hostile, and even somewhat brutal'. Fredric Jameson had argued that mass art often contains many specific criticisms of everyday life, and that it works on real anxieties manifesting themselves in texts; these anxieties can then be repressed or dealt with. Modleski uses the idea to argue for a double perspective: the contemptuous treatment might confuse the heroine in the novel but it does not confuse the reader because the reader has 'retrospective illumination' from her knowledge of the Harlequin formula. Unlike the heroine, the reader is able to read back from the formula ending in which all misunderstandings are cleared away and the hero reveals he has loved the girl all along. The reader may identify emotionally with the heroine without suffering her confusion.[13]

In this distancing, Modleski also sees a potential for expressing a female fantasy of revenge on the men who so treat women, while stifling guilt at the hostility the heroine is allowed to feel. This reader response may be related to psychoanalytical theories of hysteria and feminine masochism, but Modleski

[13] Tania Modleski, *Loving with a Vengeance: Mass Produced Fantasies for Women* (Hamden, CT: Archon Books, 1982), p. 28.

has reversed the usual Freudian psychoanalytical approach (women's anxieties about rape conceal a desire to be taken by force) so that, in romance fantasies, the desire to be taken by force may conceal anxiety about rape and wish for power and revenge. '[P]opular feminine texts do not ... question the myth of male superiority or the institutions of marriage and the family', although they do provide 'outlets for women's dissatisfaction' with those conditions.[14] They may also guide women to accept and interpret enigmatic male behaviour in a comforting way and so dampen female anxieties about men.

The achievement of the heroine remains problematic. As Elizabeth Bennet rather ill-naturedly describes her success in *Pride and Prejudice*: 'I roused, and interested you, because I was so unlike *them*' (*P&P*, p. 421): that is, not like women looking for male approbation. The mass-market romances are open to the kind of criticism levelled at *Pamela* in the eighteenth century: that they may be seen as tales not of virtue rewarded but of sly female manipulation and necessary hypocrisy. *Pride and Prejudice* may provoke a similar response, except that Elizabeth's change from hostility to admiration is presented as progress and a process of self-discovery, proof not of betraying an original spirited independence but of achieving a proper self-awareness. Marriage is of course essential to romance, but its use to indicate self-improvement may seem less convincing when, unlike in Austen's age, there are many alternatives, and the basic institution is left unquestioned.[15]

The kind of romance fiction that *Pride and Prejudice* has helped to spawn feeds female readers, largely powerless in real life, with the enduring romantic fantasy of complete fulfilment through heterosexual love. Popular literature is conventionally popular because it allows the latent potential of the primitive to emerge. Northrop Frye relates the fantasy of romance to the human unconscious.[16] Romance signifies emotionally in a manner appealing to the unrealistic primitive feelings of childhood.[17] Taking another approach Jan Cohn in *Romance and the Erotics of Property* states that the 'deep flaw of romance fiction ... lies in the ultimate failure of romance to provide even in fantasy a satisfying answer to the problem of women's powerlessness'. Perhaps, however, women largely without adult agency can find in *reading* romance fiction a regressing to infantile comfort and a way of transcending their exclusion from male preserves since a gendered cultural consciousness

[14] Ibid., p. 106.
[15] See Pamela Regis, *A Natural History of the Romance Novel* (Philadelphia: University of Pennsylvania Press, 2003), pp. 73–4.
[16] Northrop Frye, *The Secular Scripture: A Study of the Structure of Romance* (Cambridge, MA: Harvard University Press, 1976), p. 57.
[17] Anne Williams, *Art of Darkness: A Poetics of Gothic* (University of Chicago Press, 1995).

can emerge that imaginatively empowers them. At the same time it can provide compensatory consolation in a changing world. It is no accident that the fictional mass-romance boom paralleled second-wave feminism. As Anne Barr Snitow commented of Harlequins: they offered an archetypal, fixed image of the exchange between men and women as well as a counterpoint to shifting and confusing social actualities.[18]

If mass romance had a second peak during second-wave feminism, then chick lit, its offshoot, entered with postfeminism and tended to mock or deflate the beliefs and hopes of second-wave feminism. Aimed at younger readers, it mirrored the rise in recent years of singles culture. The book often credited with its beginning, *Bridget Jones's Diary* (1996) by Helen Fielding, was loosely modelled on *Pride and Prejudice* with Austen's Fitzwilliam Darcy becoming the knitted-jumper-wearing lawyer Mark Darcy and the overweight Bridget reprising Austen's heroine. But the resemblance doesn't reach far: as Stephanie Harzewski argued in her book on chick lit, 'the supremely static nature of Bridget's character – a chief difference from Elizabeth Bennet and her acknowledgement of pride and misjudgement – offers a perverse resistance to feminism's ideals of achievement and liberation'.[19] Fielding's hero is less attractively overbearing than dysfunctional in an entirely contemporary way. Nonetheless the image of Austen's Darcy remains implicated: *Bridget Jones's Diary* appeared at the same time as the mass enthusiasm greeting the BBC's 1996 serialisation of *Pride and Prejudice*, which made the actor Colin Firth into *the* Mr Darcy for many viewers. When a film was made of Fielding's novel, Firth played Mark Darcy.

---

[18] Jan Cohn, *Romance and the Erotics of Property: Mass-Market Fiction for Women* (Durham, NC: Duke University Press, 1988), p. 176; Anne Barr Snitow, 'Mass Market Romance: Pornography for Women Is Different', *Radical History Review* (Spring / Summer 1979), p. 150.

[19] Stephanie Harzewski, *Chick Lit and Postfeminism* (Charlottesville: University of Virginia Press, 2011), p. 76.

13

LAURA CARROLL AND JOHN WILTSHIRE

Film and television

One index of the popularity of *Pride and Prejudice* is the number and frequency of stage, film and television adaptations of the novel. A West End stage play in 1936, made into a Hollywood film in 1940, a Broadway musical in 1959, and filmed for BBC television no less than five times, in 1952, 1958, 1967, 1980 and 1995, its main characters are known by name even to many who have never thought to open the book itself. A lavish British film followed the very successful 1995 serial in 2005; another is rumoured to be in the works (one is always rumoured to be in the works). Almost as many visual adaptations of *Pride and Prejudice* have been made, in fact, as of all the other Jane Austen novels put together.

Does this suggest little more than that each generation needs to see, if not read, the novel in a different light, or that new technical possibilities in the visual media stimulate new inspirations? Perhaps. But surely it means more importantly that over the last two centuries *Pride and Prejudice* has continued to speak to its readers, and the need to recapture or remake its magic is what sends so many writers as well as film and television directors to the novel. *Pride and Prejudice* has not just retained its power to amuse and delight; it has seemed to demonstrate something our culture finds powerful and true.

Pride and Prejudice tells a story with a fairy-tale quality: an attractive young woman (virtually penniless) meets a handsome and rich gentleman (practically a prince) who falls in love with her. Eventually, though they face many impediments, they marry, and he whisks her off to his imposing home, far from her inconvenient, if not downright horrible, family. Elizabeth is spirited and appealingly unconventional, Darcy is 'the perfect romantic hero ... aloof, withdrawn, but hot as well' (as the scriptwriter Andrew Davies puts it in his commentary on the 1995 series).[1] However implausible in historical terms is this romance

---

[1] The 'restored' DVD edition of 1995 *Pride and Prejudice* (2007) includes a commentary by Davies; the '10th Anniversary Limited Collector's Edition' DVD (2005) includes a bonus

between a great landowner and a woman from the lesser gentry, what *Pride and Prejudice* does so remarkably is convince its readers that this romantic love and its promises exist within reality. Film and television adaptations for a broad contemporary audience seize upon this romantic narrative as the heart of the novel.

In this chapter we suggest rather that *Pride and Prejudice* is centred not so much on romantic love, as upon the nature of true marriage, and we treat the films largely in the light of this belief. The novel's argument about marriage is worked through the exceptionally unusual device of the double proposal. When he makes his first proposal, Darcy is passionately in love; on the other hand Elizabeth hates him – more or less. They say insulting and wounding things to each other, things that seem unforgivable. Even when Elizabeth reads Darcy's letter, and recognises how wrong she has been, all she can (apparently) feel is compassion for his disappointment: 'His attachment excited gratitude, his general character respect; but she could not approve him; nor could she for a moment repent her refusal, or feel the slightest inclination ever to see him again' (*P&P*, p. 236). It's over, then – but whether such adamant statements conceal something else is a question. As far as the reader knows, Darcy, angrily nursing his wounds, feels the same. But by the time Darcy proposes again both have learned better, partly as a direct result of the bitter confrontation that has appeared to put an end to any relationship. The second proposal and its acceptance not only completes the romantic narrative, it leads to a renewal of energetic conversation between the two that allows them now to enjoy the company of each other as adults. As people who have learned a lot about each other, they talk as equals, which promises that their marriage will overcome conventional expectations.

This reading of *Pride and Prejudice* follows from the philosopher Stanley Cavell's famous treatment of seven screwball comedies of the 1930s, *Pursuits of Happiness: The Hollywood Comedy of Remarriage* (1981).[2] Cavell argued that these films are not lightweight entertainments, but serious works of art, and proposed that they together form a new genre, that he calls, with a distinction from Shakespearean comedy in mind, the romantic comedy of remarriage. Usually in these films, but not always (as in *It Happened One Night* (1934)), a man and a woman have been married, but whether or not they have been married, they have quarrelled badly; the action brings them

disc including interviews with cast members and brief comments by Davies, the producer Sue Birtwistle and others.

[2] Stanley Cavell, *Pursuits of Happiness: The Hollywood Comedy of Remarriage* (Cambridge, MA: Harvard University Press, 1981). Cavell comments briefly on *Pride and Prejudice* in *Philosophy the Day After Tomorrow* (Cambridge, MA: Harvard University Press, 2005), pp. 127–8, but in a different context. Ann Gaylin refers to Cavell's book in her chapter on *Pride and Prejudice* in *Eavesdropping in the Novel from Austen to Proust* (Cambridge: Cambridge University press, 2002), pp. 37–8.

together again, and with much witty, intelligent and fast-moving talk leads to their discovery, or re-discovery, of their love for each other and to their mutual forgiveness. As Cavell writes of this comedic genre, the 'drive of its plot is not to get the central pair together, but to get them *back* together, together *again*'.[3] The goal of the action in both these comedies and *Pride and Prejudice* is the legitimation of marriage, and the hero and heroine's survival of their quarrels, and their learning from them, suggests how successful that marriage will be.

A main feature of these films, and crucial to Cavell's account, is the brilliance of their dialogue. To explain its significance he draws on Milton's claim that 'a meet and happy conversation is the chiefest and noblest end of marriage'.[4] 'Conversation', in his interpretation, wraps together the older sexual meaning of the word with its more modern one of continued verbal exchange. It is their 'capacity, say a thirst, for talk' that brings the couple together, their flirtatious, audacious and even aggressive reaching out to each other, that distinguishes the pair from the mundane world around them (including, often, the new man the heroine thinks she loves). The sequence of dialogues in the first volume of *Pride and Prejudice* is famously scintillating; they can be read in different lights. But whether or not we feel that Darcy is as unbending, or herself as unengaged with him, as Elizabeth thinks, these exchanges lay the foundation for the reunion in the second volume. If Cavell assigns a moral value to conversational engagements that go beyond, as well as include, attractive and witty talk, so of course does Jane Austen.

The films Cavell writes about share other characteristics with Austen's novel. The figures in them are often from 'high society' and are people with leisure enough to enjoy the pleasures of talk; but more importantly they are comedies set in the modern world, where their audience also lives. Jane Austen's novels are similarly focused, with exceptional comic acuity, on the manners and society in which she was writing. Because she expects her readers to know that world, she can practise an art that reduces appearances and settings to a minimum. But in contrast to both the comedies of remarriage and Austen's novels, the film and television adaptations of her texts are set in the past, and must visualise that past. They belong to the genre of period or costume drama, or what has been called the 'heritage' film.[5] With its picturesque villages and grand houses, its elaborate costumes and décor, its

[3] Cavell, *Pursuits of Happiness*, p. 2.
[4] John Milton, *Doctrine and Discipline of Divorce* (1643), quoted in Cavell, *Pursuits of Happiness*, p. 87. The later quotation in this paragraph is from Cavell, *Pursuits of Happiness*, p. 182.
[5] Andrew Higson, *English Heritage, English Cinema: Costume Drama Since 1980* (Oxford University Press, 2003).

candle-lit interiors, the past depicted in the period drama is selective and seductive. Fantasies of a past time, it differs completely from Austen's unremitting attention to the contemporary.

The category of period drama is a broad one, and the adaptations of Jane Austen's novel are distinct from each other. Each of them, though set in the past, speaks of its own time, and interacts as much with previous versions as it does with the originating text. The first film of *Pride and Prejudice* was directed by Robert Z. Leonard in 1940, with Greer Garson and Laurence Olivier. It has many elements of the screwball comedies then popular (and also present in the movies Cavell discusses): 'warring lovers, witty dialogue, class differences, opportunity for elaborate costumes, and comic minor characters', along with a rapidly cascading plot, and two coolly glamorous stars.[6] Yet in coming closer to screwball comedy the adaptation moves away from the specific features of the novel that ally it with the comedies of remarriage. Garson's Elizabeth has the complete air of 'self-sufficiency' Caroline Bingley jealously accuses her of (*P&P*, p. 299), and her teasing is sometimes more like baiting. 'Oh, if you want to be really refined you have to be dead', she unfunnily tells Caroline. 'There's no-one as dignified as a mummy.' She projects an outspoken assurance and polish belonging more to the spunky Hollywood heroine than to Austen's Elizabeth, who is not yet too hardened to be unsettled, and eventually changed, by contact with Darcy. The film's speedy compression of events collapses scenes together – Lydia and Wickham's return to Longbourn is followed seconds later by Lady Catherine barging in, which in turn brings Darcy instantly to Elizabeth's door – and leaves little room for the critically important processes of revision and working through that Elizabeth and Darcy undertake, together and apart, silently and in conversation. Cavell writes that 'the quarrel, the conversation of love, takes lavish expenditures of time, exclusive, jealous time',[7] and this commodity is in short supply in a film that runs for only ninety minutes.

But it does offer one sequence in which something like the novel's dynamic is recreated. It occurs at a moment when Elizabeth's assurance has been cracked by the viciousness of Caroline Bingley's attack on her family, and she has retired from the dance to wipe her tears in private. Darcy follows, and coming close, attempts to console her. The intimacy of the scene is heightened by Elizabeth's also having for once discarded the preposterous bonnet she is

[6] Sue Parrill, *Jane Austen on Film and Television: A Critical Study of the Adaptations* (Jefferson, NC: McFarland & Company Inc., 2002), p. 49.
[7] Cavell, *Pursuits of Happiness*, p. 30.

condemned to wear through so much of the movie. She turns to Darcy, gazing into his face:

ELIZABETH: You're very puzzling, Mr Darcy. At this moment it's difficult to believe that you're so – proud.

DARCY: (smiling) At this moment it's difficult to believe you're so – prejudiced. (He bends towards her.) Shall we not call quits and start again?

As he smiles, she looks at him in full face, also smiling. She is about to respond – to agree? – when they are interrupted. He takes her arm and they move towards the dance floor. But they overhear Mrs Bennet boasting of Jane's marriage to Bingley and how it will boost the chances of her other daughters to marry rich men; Lydia and Kitty cut across them, tipsy from punch and fooling with officers; and Mr Collins thrusts himself on Darcy's acquaintance. Distressed again, Elizabeth would still like to dance, but this is too much for Darcy who withdraws with disdain and hands her over to 'other men'.

No other film of the novel was made until 2005, and three of the television series made before then seem to have vanished.[8] But the 1980 serial, with a script by the novelist Fay Weldon, and made in the midst of second-wave feminism, remains an interesting treatment of *Pride and Prejudice*, largely because of its sceptical, anti-romantic emphasis. It suggests that a successful marriage is a rare event indeed. This is partly achieved by using dialogue from the novel but moving it into different parts of the story. Elizabeth from the beginning grasps the full emotional poverty of her parents' relationship. The serial opens with an intimate conversation between Elizabeth and Charlotte Lucas in which the novel's first two sentences are effectively reshaped into a playful exchange between these friends who share a wryly amused consciousness of the feminine excitement Mr Bingley's arrival at Netherfield is going to produce, no matter what his own plans should turn out to be. But then Charlotte advances the opinion that 'it is best to know as little as possible of the defects of the person with whom you are to pass your life'. Elizabeth replies more or less as she does in another scene on which this exchange draws, that Charlotte knows it is not sound – 'you would never act this way yourself – never'. She implies that there is nothing more to be said.

In this version, though, Charlotte presses the point, asking Elizabeth if her parents knew each other before marrying. 'You are too shrewd, Charlotte', Elizabeth replies, and then proceeds to describe her father's and mother's characters in the language and with the Olympian detachment of the narrator's summary descriptions at the end of Chapter 1. This produces the

---

[8] *Bride and Prejudice*, a Bollywood treatment of the novel, directed by Gurinda Chadha, was released in 2004.

disturbing effect that Elizabeth sees her parents from a psychological position detached from her own relation to them. The scene then cuts to the conversation between Mr and Mrs Bennet that opens the novel. Primed by Elizabeth and Charlotte's discussion, the viewer notices their discordant unattractiveness. Mrs Bennet is a vapid, fidgeting creature making whining requests and her husband frowns crossly and barks his refusals. This is not a 'sparkling', amusing dialogue, as in the novel: instead the scene has a heavy, claustrophobic feeling, augmented by the dark interior in which it takes place.

Pride and Prejudice does render the pairing of Darcy and Elizabeth the more satisfying because of the other relationships that play against it, but in this version, unsatisfactory and unromantic marriage receives a steady attention until the final moments. In the novel, once Charlotte is married to Collins, Elizabeth 'could never address her without feeling that all the comforts of intimacy were over' (*P&P*, p. 165), but here Elizabeth with mock solemnity informs Mrs Collins that her husband 'will look very strange' in the bizarre hat he has purchased on the advice of Lady Catherine, and when Charlotte despairingly replies 'I know', the friends burst into conspiratorial laughter. Weldon's Elizabeth does not appear to feel that Charlotte's marriage is beyond a joke, and she displays that tendency of her father to take a detached ironic attitude to everything that the novel suggests is potentially disastrous. This serial gives Mr Bennet the last word. The final scene is an exchange between him and his wife where she expresses her raptures at Mr Darcy's wealth and he tells her to send in any young men who call for Kitty or Mary, 'for I am quite at leisure'. Since we know Mrs Bennet is incapable of appreciating the playfulness in this remark, in the novel shared with Lizzy, the serial ends on the same slightly sour note of matrimonial disharmony, vulgarity at cross-purposes with cynicism, with which it began.

By contrast, the adaptation directed by Joe Wright released in 2005 and starring Keira Knightley as a youthful Elizabeth is the most alluringly romantic treatment the novel has received. This widescreen film announces its difference from the television serials by exploiting the mobility of the camera and conspicuously utilising camera work to suggest emotion and atmosphere. It features one compellingly unromantic scene concerning Charlotte's marriage. Elizabeth has rejected Collins, and is swaying idly on a swing outdoors. Charlotte, plainly dressed, arrives to break the news of her engagement, evidently nervous; when her friend is appalled, her nervousness turns to anger, and she delivers a passionate defence of her decision: 'I'm twenty-seven years old . . . and I'm frightened. So don't judge me Lizzy, don't you dare judge me.' She leaves, and the camera, panning slowly backwards and forwards across the farmyard, reproducing Elizabeth's desultory swinging movement, suggests the grim future that might face her too.

Despite their evident dislike of each other, Wright's film depicts an Elizabeth Bennet and Fitzwilliam Darcy who are hypnotically drawn together from the start. In a surreal sequence at the Netherfield ball, the two are observed from a distance as they move in and out and up and down the crowded avenue of dancers, speaking in coldly terse tones. Abruptly, they come to a standstill in the middle of the set, inches apart, eyes fixed on each other's face. As they begin to move again, they are suddenly alone in the room and the single violin to which the assembly has been dancing is joined by the saturated sound of a string quartet. The uncanny auditory effect is heightened by the camera, rhythmically tracking inwards to the dancers and then out again, at right angles to the transverse movement of the dancing, as well as against the tempo of the dance. They move now without speaking, they look intensely but unsmilingly at each other. The spiralling, overlapping arcs traced by dancers and camera echo a celebrated shot in Alfred Hitchcock's *Vertigo*, and, as in the 1958 film, the effect is to suggest a magnetic attraction between the man and woman. Whereas in the novel their conversation at the Netherfield ball is crucial to the rendering of their relationship, here – as in so much of this film – the couple are 'stunningly inarticulate'.[9]

In the 1995 television series, the Netherfield dance had been filmed in a very different way. Elizabeth and Darcy's dialogue at Netherfield is stretched out for the duration of a lengthy country dance. The real conditions of dance, the music and movements unrepresentable in the novel, become actors in the drama, as in the 2005 film, but here the presentation is entirely naturalistic. A seventeenth-century tune with an unusual 3/2 time signature and strong beat pulsates to stress the painfully long pauses between speeches in a dialogue that closely follows the novel. The couple rotate through one complete 16-bar dance figure before Elizabeth prods Darcy to speak. 'Do you talk by rule, then, when you are dancing?' he asks her, and Elizabeth's assent confirms that she means the conversation they are having to be rule-governed and closed, exactly analogous to the complex but predictable patterns of the dance in which they are partners. As they move down the set, though, tension between them builds as Elizabeth deflects, with increasing urgency, each of Darcy's verbal attempts to break through her pose. Just at the moment she accuses him of mistreating George Wickham, they arrive at the bottom of the set and must stand still face to face; the sudden removal of the social framework of the dance reveals the power each one has to summon strong feeling from the other.

---

[9] Rachel M. Brownstein, *Why Jane Austen?* (New York: Columbia University Press, 2011), p. 52.

This 1995 television serial remains the most important and popular adaptation of the novel, and as the filming of this scene suggests, for good reasons. But its most famous sequence, at Pemberley, presents all adaptations with a challenge, though the 1940 film omits the visit altogether. (Its origins were in the 1936 stage play by Helen Jerome where the omission is more explicable.) For several chapters in the second volume of *Pride and Prejudice* following his rejected proposal Darcy has virtually disappeared from the text. At Pemberley he returns but only at first by proxy, in mediated terms, through the housekeeper's encomium, and then in the portrait that triggers Elizabeth's memories of his earlier smiles. Several important paragraphs are given to her thoughts as she views and reviews the image of the man she now can almost admit to herself she loves. The three more recent adaptations acknowledge the need to give some kind of representation to this turning point which, though featuring a portrait, is entirely a matter of introspective process. (The 1980 serial gives a précis of Elizabeth's thoughts in voice-over; the 2005 film substitutes a sequence in Chatsworth's sculpture gallery culminating in Elizabeth's confrontation with a marble bust of Darcy, its eyes, as if repudiating Austen's portrait, blank.) Outside Pemberley, Elizabeth soon encounters the man himself, whose changed demeanour now promises reconciliation. But no sooner is an approach to the novel's goal in sight, than another barrier, this time the scandalous elopement of Elizabeth's headstrong sister Lydia, arises to prevent it.

Avowedly refashioning the narrative balance between the main figures, the 1995 series insistently reminds the viewer of Darcy in those intervals the novel almost allows him to be forgotten. At the same time Elizabeth's change of heart is patchily, even inadequately, represented. In this version of Pemberley Elizabeth looks at the portrait appreciatively, but this is repeatedly intercut by shots that show Darcy riding, dismounting from his horse, unbuttoning his jacket, and then diving into an uninvitingly weedy lake. He is back on the scene, though Elizabeth has tried to make sure that he would be absent; the suspense is underscored by the theme music rising to a crescendo. In the novel, Elizabeth returns to the portrait, and returning to it allows her to recognise and appreciate the Darcy – both family man and great landowner – that her prejudice had previously obscured. Darcy's whole being, she can now understand, is bound up with his family, his social role and responsibilities. But this crucial development in Elizabeth gets literally swamped by the new focus on the 'natural man' (as Davies says he conceives of Darcy here) leaping away from responsibility. The documentary released with the 'restored' DVD of the series (2007) demonstrates how critical to the scriptwriter and director's conception was the filming of Darcy's dip. Their efforts were amply rewarded, of course, by the sequence's subsequent fame.

A more important reward is the scene that follows. Darcy is seen striding towards the house; Elizabeth comes down a slope, turns, and is amazed to see him. Both are embarrassed and disconcerted. She feels she has no business to be there; he is half-dressed and wet through. Metaphorically, if not literally naked, they are bereft of the usual social resources, both vulnerable. These two intelligent and witty people are reduced to the halting exchange of commonplaces. It might bring to mind Cavell's insistence that the process towards reunion requires 'the metamorphosis of death and revival'.[10] Attended by a gentle, understated humour, this meeting is not threatening, but hopeful. Though leaving the viewer still in doubt about Darcy's feelings, the encounter puts in motion the process through which their relationship can be remade. It successfully captures in dramatic terms what in *Pride and Prejudice* is a series of awkward silences.

Its paradoxically invigorating effect draws power from revisioning as comic the stuff of earlier disconcerting tête-à-tête encounters. This is the negative of the earlier vigorous conversations that have portrayed a man and a woman problematically intertwined with each other. Here their reaching out is frustrated not by preconceptions but by circumstances.

Yet it is the second proposal, which the Pemberley encounters initiate, and the renewal of conversation to which the proposal immediately leads, that marks out *Pride and Prejudice* as akin to the comedies of remarriage, and measures its distance from an ordinarily romantic conception of love. The handling of this second proposal in the screen versions is therefore especially interesting. In Wright's 2005 film, as in the 1940 movie, the second proposal follows almost immediately after Lady Catherine's invasion, here made melodramatically in the middle of the night. Elizabeth is seen, wakeful in the dark, hearing the dawn chorus. The camera, moving from right to left, unveils her full-face, staring outwards, a candle burning at her side. Wrapping herself in a shawl, in the misty dawn she ventures outside into the garden. Then, in close-up, Elizabeth is staring towards the right. In the distance, to a gasp on the sound-track, the figure of Mr Darcy walks purposefully across the fields, his morning gown floating behind him, towards the camera. The way he moves creates the sense that he is almost a phantom, the magical fulfilment of all that Elizabeth has dreamed. Music (solo piano and strings) increases in volume as he nears her. Now they are together in the dawn: 'I couldn't sleep'; 'Nor I.' They speak quietly about Lady Catherine's visit. In words here hardly changed from the novel, Darcy says 'You are too generous to trifle with me. If your feelings are still what they were last April, tell me so at once. My affections and wishes have not

[10] Cavell, *Pursuits of Happiness*, p. 19.

changed, but one word from you will silence me ... for ever.' Elizabeth is silent; and then Darcy says quietly, and with aching emotion, 'You have bewitched me body and soul. I love – I love – I love you. I never wish to be parted from you from this day on.'

The words 'Darcy had never been so bewitched by any woman as he was by her' occur early in the text (*P&P*, p. 57). Transferring the word from the beginning of the relationship to its climactic conclusion undercuts Darcy's development, which consists in his unbewitching, or bewitchment's release into genuine love. Elizabeth responds again wordlessly, only moving closer to him. The difference in their heights emphasises the childlikeness of her gesture of acceptance: 'Your hands are cold.' The amber light of dawn is now filmed glowing behind their heads bending together. Nothing more is said, and this is virtually the end of the film. The sequence is beautifully and expertly crafted, but it could not be more unlike the novel's handling of the second proposal. There the moment is treated with characteristic mischievous reticence, the narrator only remarking dryly that Darcy expressed himself 'as warmly as a man violently in love can be supposed to do' (*P&P*, p. 407).

It is interesting that this proposal scene in the 1995 television series is the only one that Andrew Davies singles out in 2007 as a comparative failure. On a walk, as in the novel, the two find themselves side by side. Darcy asks Elizabeth, apparently not looking at her, if her views have changed. In close-up, Elizabeth, smiling, says, 'They are in fact quite the reverse.' Darcy's face, as he continues walking, shows signs of relief and pleasure. As they amble side by side, their shoulders touch, and this slight easy physical contact suggests their reconciliation. (In the 1980 series, this intimacy between the couple is signalled less subtly by Darcy's removing his top hat!) 'I should have written them standing still', Davies says in the DVD commentary, so that there would be eye contact, as, for instance, when Mr Knightley, similarly walking out with Emma Woodhouse, 'stopped in his earnestness to look the question, and the expression of his eyes overpowered her' (*E*, p. 468). Darcy, still looking forward, not at Elizabeth, now relates how much her accusation of ungentlemanlike manners has tormented him, but the terrible earnestness with which in the novel he speaks at length of the 'torture', the 'inexpressibly painful' shame and distress he has long endured at the accuracy of her assessment of him seems largely thrown away here. None of the adaptations, produced for a modern audience, tries to make real how much Darcy's pride, his 'character' as responsible landowner and public figure means, both to him, and to the novel's narrative. A long shot from behind shows the pair continuing together on their walk: if they talk more, it is inaudible.

In the novel Elizabeth and Darcy together work over their past. Darcy must, it seems, tell Elizabeth of his suffering and regrets, his need for moral reformation, and receive a kind of absolution from her. In turn Elizabeth, though she is less inclined to self-castigation and regret, confesses her own long-standing 'shame' at what she said to him, and later admits that 'my spirits might often lead me wrong'. She tells him in effect that it is better to forget, but Darcy is not to be deterred: he presses on with a retrospect of his upbringing and education, since he is the kind of person who must bring to consciousness and full awareness the self that he has been in order to solidify and confirm the self he has become. His turning to her with tender frankness: 'Such I was, from eight to eight and twenty; and such I might still have been, but for you, dearest, loveliest Elizabeth' (*P&P*, p. 410) is more than a romantic moment, it is the apotheosis of trust, reconciliation and forgiveness. This conversation is what Jane Austen in *Mansfield Park* calls 'unchecked, equal, fearless intercourse' (*MP*, p. 273). But it is more: each is now able to recognise the other's difference, and to know the other for what they are, rather than as a denizen of their own imagination or fantasy. Neither sacrifices their distinct narrative identity: he remains introspective and serious, she continues to be wary, witty and amused. They walk together 'several miles in a leisurely manner' (they talk then, for well over an hour). Their 'conversation of love' is indeed shown to require 'expenditures of time, exclusive, jealous time'.

At the end of the chapter Elizabeth can still be privately amused at Darcy, but after the interval provided by Chapter 17, 'her spirits soon rising into playfulness again', she begins asking impertinent or at least cheeky questions of him. This is that 'capacity, say a thirst, for talk' which Cavell celebrates in the comedies of remarriage, as Darcy and Elizabeth continue analysing their past behaviour, appearances and mutual misunderstandings. Their reminiscences conjure up a past whose mistakes they admit they shared, and a forgiveness they grant each other. Elizabeth tells Darcy that 'in spite of the pains you took to disguise yourself, your feelings were always noble and just', and the reader is invited to reread the novel and to join with the pair in their celebration. These extensive dialogues in Chapters 16 and 18 of the third volume of *Pride and Prejudice* convey the comfort with each other, the capacity to work over the past without resentment, the laughing grace of mutual forgiveness of people who, even though they are not literally married, demonstrate what a good marriage might be like.

Pride and Prejudice is taught all round the world, and in many classes the films and television serials are used to introduce students to Jane Austen. Accessible and pleasurable, they have been the means of bringing vast numbers of readers to Austen, but they do not provide an aesthetically or psychologically equivalent experience. They belong to a genre at odds with the novel they seek to reproduce, with the almost inevitable consequence that they scant the radical core of *Pride and Prejudice*: its affirmation of the possibility, developed through the double proposal, of a romantic marriage that is also a marriage of adults.

14

DEVONEY LOOSER

The cult of *Pride and Prejudice* and its author

Although the word 'cult' may seem a loaded one to describe the afterlife of Jane Austen's most recognised novel, in many ways it is an apt term. What other label could make sense of the outpouring of attention to *Pride and Prejudice* in the past century and a half of popular literature, film and culture? How else might we explain a text that has attracted everything from paper dolls and board games to zombies and vampires? 'Cult' best applies to *Pride and Prejudice* in one of its eighteenth- and nineteenth-century meanings: 'devotion or homage to a particular person or thing, now esp. as paid by a body of professed adherents or admirers'. (The meaning of 'cult' as 'a relatively small group of people having religious beliefs or practices regarded by others as strange or sinister' emerged in the early twentieth century, according to the *Oxford English Dictionary*.) *Pride and Prejudice* has reached near ubiquity, having become a long-term 'media event'.[1]

The remarkable cultural history of this novel is impossible to tell succinctly. Entire books have been – and should be – written to describe the twists and turns in its afterlife. In this chapter, I provide broad brushstrokes designed to prompt us to recognise how it has carried different meanings for changing sets of readers at discrete historical moments. *Pride and Prejudice* may or may not deserve the term often used to describe its appeal: 'universal'. Nevertheless, the ways the novel has been imagined, used and reinterpreted over the past 200 years have been far from uniform. Whether these trends proved transitory or gained significant traction, they deserve to be better known.

As we now recognise, Austen and her most famous novel were 'practically overlooked for thirty or forty years after her death'.[2] Landmark studies by

I am grateful to Ruth Knezevich for her invaluable research assistance.

[1] William Warner refers to Samuel Richardson's *Pamela* and its reception in 1740–1 and thereafter as a 'media event' in *Licensing Entertainment: The Elevation of Novel Reading in Great Britain, 1684–1750* (Berkeley: University of California Press, 1988). It is difficult to imagine a higher-profile 'media event' novel than *Pride and Prejudice*.

[2] Claire Harman, *Jane's Fame* (Edinburgh: Canongate, 2010), p. 2.

Kathryn Sutherland, Claire Harman, John Wiltshire, Emily Auerbach and Deidre Lynch have tackled aspects of Austen's posthumous treatment. Still, plenty of work remains to make sense of how and why *Pride and Prejudice* has captured commercial, popular and critical attention from decade to decade, generation to generation, whether in relation to readers' gender, class, age, race, sexuality or national origin. For instance, we do not yet know when *Pride and Prejudice* came to be considered an appropriate book for young readers, although it appeared in 1908 in 'a series of English texts, edited for use in elementary and secondary schools' and in 2011 in a counting primer board book for toddlers.[3] We also ought to ask more questions about the class associations of *Pride and Prejudice* and its actual or purported readers. We need to know more about late nineteenth-century debates over Austen as the Shakespeare of the novel. We need additional information to make sense of *Pride and Prejudice* as a global phenomenon, although we know that by 1970 *Pride and Prejudice* had been translated into more than thirty languages, from Arabic and Bengali to Tamil and Thai.[4] We are also just beginning to chart how and when *Pride and Prejudice* came to be understood as so-called 'chick lit'.

Jane Austen in the Men's Club: 1880s–1940s

Pride and Prejudice was not always considered 'chick lit', because Austen was once the darling of elite male readers. This is an association she held from the late nineteenth to the mid twentieth centuries, when her fiction was said to cover an 'infinitely smaller field than any of her later rivals' (as author G. K. Chesterton (1874–1936) wrote) but to have done so to perfection. Austen was the idol of educated, tasteful men, akin to one of her own heroines for her worshipping male hero-readers; they often described her and her characters as living people. Critic George Saintsbury (1845–1933) believed that there were several female protagonists with whom it might be a pleasure to fall in love, but to live with and marry, none ranked for him above Elizabeth Bennet. In this period, it was said that men who criticised Austen were engaging in a dangerous activity, or so Arnold Bennett (1867–1931) put it in 1927/8:

---

[3] David Gilson, *A Bibliography of Jane Austen*, new edn (Winchester: St Paul's Bibliographies, and New Castle, DE: Oak Knoll, 1997), p. 287; Jennifer Adams, *Pride and Prejudice: Little Miss Austen* (Layton, UT: Gibbs Smith, 2011). Andrew Wright's 'Jane Austen Adapted', *Nineteenth Century Fiction* 30.3 (1975), pp. 421–53) includes a list of *Pride and Prejudice* editions both abridged and retold for schoolchildren.
[4] Gilson, *Bibliography*, pp. 186–207.

The reputation of Jane Austen is surrounded by cohorts of defenders who are ready to do murder for their sacred cause. They are nearly all fanatics. They will not listen. If anybody 'went for' Jane, anything might happen to him. He would assuredly be called on to resign from his clubs. I do not want to resign from my clubs. I would sooner perjure myself.[5]

Bennett, not willing to label Austen 'great' but seeing her instead as a 'great little novelist', admits he once thought *Persuasion* her masterpiece but concludes: 'Now I am inclined to join the populace and put *Pride and Prejudice* in the front.'[6] He believes that his elite private men's clubs are filled with members who think 'Jane Austen was the only estimable author who ever lived.'[7]

Bennett's dismissive description of the knight-errant, Austen-loving male reader was a caricature, but there were in fact many highly placed male champions of Austen. Henry James traced Austen's popularity to her 'first slightly ponderous amoroso', Thomas Babington Macaulay (1800–59), but he also includes himself among those who had 'lost our hearts to her'.[8] Notable among Austen's male supporters were her first scholarly editor, R. W. Chapman (1881–1960) and Oxford fellow Lord David Cecil (1902–86), who came to like Jane Austen so much in the course of writing a biography of her that he writes that he wants very much to please her. There were also, of course, famous men who found reading Austen not to their taste. American novelist Mark Twain wrote in a private letter, 'Every time I read Pride and Prejudice I want to dig her up and beat her over the skull with her own shin-bone!'[9] But the widely held belief that Austen and her signature novel were the rightful property of educated males held force from before the turn of the century to after the Second World War.

Rudyard Kipling's short story 'The Janeites' represents this phenomenon in full colour, as a fictional soldier recounts his past exploits during the First World War.[10] The unnamed narrator describes his indoctrination by officer-superiors into a secret society, The Janeites. The soldier read all of Austen's books and was quizzed on them, made to defend why he renamed their unit's guns after Lady Catherine de Bourgh (called De Bugg) and Reverend Collins. When an enemy bomb kills all of the Janeites except the narrator, he tells how

[5] Arnold Bennett, *Arnold Bennett: The 'Evening Standard' Years: 'Books and Persons' 1926–1931*, ed. Andrew Mylett (Hamden, CT: Archon, 1974), p. 68.
[6] Ibid. [7] Ibid., p. 215.
[8] Henry James, *The Question of Our Speech; The Lesson of Balzac: Two Lectures* (Boston: Houghton Mifflin, 1905), p. 62.
[9] Mark Twain, letter (13 Sept. 1898), quoted in Robert Morrison, *Jane Austen's 'Pride and Prejudice': A Sourcebook* (New York: Routledge, 2005), p. 64.
[10] Kipling's short story was first published in *Debits and Credits* (London: Macmillan, 1926).

his knowledge of Austen won him better treatment among the survivors. Austen was so highly valued by the women ministering to the wounded that the narrator got special attention. The narrator's line that 'there's no one can touch Jane when you are in a tight place' has been interpreted in many ways, but on the face of it, it is an indication of how Austen had become a male touchstone for sanity and survival – for comic realism – in wartime.

If *Pride and Prejudice* was literary sustenance for men in the trenches, trying to make order and find humour in their chaotic world (as in Kipling's version of her 'cult'), Prime Minster Winston Churchill's Austen fulfilled a different nationalist fantasy. Churchill recounted that when bedridden with pneumonia during the Second World War, he was told not to work or worry; he chose to have *Pride and Prejudice* read aloud to him. Doing so made him reflect of the novel's characters, 'What calm lives they had, those people! No worries about the French Revolution, or the crashing struggle of the Napoleonic Wars. Only manners controlling natural passion as far as they could, together with cultured explanations of any mischances.'[11] Churchill emphasises that novel's escapist, rather than realist or humorist, potential. These examples demonstrate that Austen's novel had, for a time, special appeal for real and imagined male (and martial) readers. As Austen scholar Claudia Johnson puts it, 'Austen's novels appear often to have facilitated rather than dampened conversation between men.'[12] She troubles over an emerging undercurrent of these conversations that contextualises the male 'Austen-haters'. Such men (like Twain) may imply that enjoying Austen is an un-manly activity that marks one out as a 'pansy'.[13] In elite circles in the early twentieth century, however, that was apparently a minority view.

Loving Jane Austen was more than a litmus test for masculine good taste. Scholars today are beginning to document how *Pride and Prejudice* appealed more widely, extending to 'middlebrow' and working-class reading audiences of both sexes. The rich data in popular periodicals of the time (now searchable in digital formats) may paint a different or more complicated picture, once it is more thoroughly assessed. We might compile more evidence of *Pride and Prejudice*'s being of consequence to the first wave of feminists, active in the years leading up to women's suffrage. This group understood the novel on far different terms from the male literati. Looking to these writers, we discover that there was a simultaneously circulating feminist or proto-feminist version of Austen.

[11] Winston Churchill, 'Closing the Ring', *The Second World War* (Boston: Houghton Mifflin, 1951), vol. v, p. 425.

[12] Claudia L. Johnson, 'The Divine Miss Jane: Jane Austen, Janeites, and the Discipline of Novel Studies', *boundary 2* 23.3 (1996), p. 145.

[13] Ibid., p. 150.

The 'New Woman' and Austen: 1880s–1940s

Feminists of the first wave appreciated Austen's satire, social criticism and professional success as much as or more than her artistry and good taste. They tended to see her not as a token, lovable female among great male novelists but as the linchpin in a tradition of struggling female authors. This would prove the beginning of a pattern that envisioned Austen as the happy culmination of her literary historical foremothers, with *Pride and Prejudice* as a kind of fictional pinnacle; we might call the phenomenon that of the New Woman Austen. Novelist and critic Virginia Woolf (1882–1941) thought Austen 'the most perfect artist among women, the writer whose books are immortal'.[14] In *A Room of One's Own*, Woolf laid out her theory that

> When the middle-class woman took to writing, she naturally wrote novels ... one may go even further, I said, taking *Pride and Prejudice* from the shelf, and say that they wrote good novels. Without boasting or giving pain to the opposite sex, one may say that *Pride and Prejudice* is a good book. At any rate, one would not have been ashamed to have been caught in the act of writing *Pride and Prejudice* ... Here was a woman about the year 1800 writing without hate, without bitterness, without fear, without protest, without preaching ... If Jane Austen suffered in any way from her circumstances it was in the narrowness of life that was imposed upon her. It was impossible for a woman to go about alone. She never travelled; she never drove through London in an omnibus or had luncheon in a shop by herself. But perhaps it was the nature of Jane Austen not to want what she had not. Her gift and her circumstances matched each other completely.[15]

The skewed pronouncements of the Men's Club Janeites about Austen's personal and fictional limitations are echoed here by Woolf but for entirely other ends. By contrast, author Rebecca West (1892–1983) worked to turn the tide against such qualified, even if well-meaning, praise. West found ridiculous the 'comic patronage' of assigning littleness of scope to Austen's fiction, arguing, 'To believe her limited in range because she was harmonious in method is as sensible as to imagine that when the Atlantic Ocean is as smooth as a mill-pond it shrinks to the size of a mill-pond.'[16] West used the word 'feminism' to refer to the political thrust of Austen's fiction as early as 1932, arguing, 'It is surely not a coincidence that a country gentlewoman

---

[14] Virginia Woolf, *The Common Reader* (New York: Harcourt, Brace & World, 1953), p. 149.
[15] Virginia Woolf, *A Room of One's Own* (San Diego: Harcourt Brace Jovanovich, 1957), pp. 70–1.
[16] Rebecca West, *The Strange Necessity: Essays* (Garden City, NY: Doubleday, Doran & Co., 1928), p. 289.

should sit down and put the institutions of society regarding women through the most gruelling criticism they have ever received, just at the time when Europe was generally following Voltaire and Rousseau in their opinion that social institutions not only should but could be questioned.'[17] West imagines Austen as quite intentionally writing novels of energetic, proto-feminist critique.

If the Men's Club Jane was depicted as a worthy lover, in need of cultural protection, the New Woman Austen was a strong, inspirational model-author-heroine. The emphasis was on Austen's spirited achievement as a *woman* writer. As critic Sarah Tytler [Henrietta Keddie] (1827–1914) concludes of *Pride and Prejudice* in 1880, 'Thus ends a novel which has for nearly a century been viewed, with reason, as one of the best novels in the English language, which has been the delight of some of the greatest geniuses of this and other countries. It must always remain a marvel that it was the work of a country-bred girl in her twenty-first year.'[18] Tytler gave voice to a counter-vision of Austen as a marvel, because – not in spite – of her being a *young woman* author. This view had currency until the second wave of feminism of the 1960s and 1970s, when Austen's class affiliations and heterosexual marriages came to be seen as more politically problematic. For a time, and well into the 1980s, Austen's fiction was dismissed out of hand by a cadre of feminists because of its lack of identification with the working classes and its apparently unapologetic heteronormativity.

Popularising *Pride and Prejudice*: continuations, dramatisations and adaptations, 1890s–1970s

Both of these early twentieth-century 'cults', the Men's Club Jane and the New Woman's Austen, came out of intellectual circles. But *Pride and Prejudice* had, over the same period, begun to gain a foothold among more popular audiences as well. One might go about showing this by cataloguing the publication of its new mass-marketed editions or its expanding readership. But nowhere is *Pride and Prejudice*'s intensifying popular appeal more clear than in the adaptations and continuations that came into print, on stage, and to film and television, from the 1890s to the 1970s. Dramatisations of *Pride and Prejudice* appeared earliest. *Duologues and Scenes from the Novels of Jane Austen, Arranged and Adapted for Drawing Room Performance*

---

[17] Rebecca West, 'Preface' to Jane Austen, *Northanger Abbey* (London: Jonathan Cape, 1940), pp. vii–viii.

[18] Sarah Tytler, *Jane Austen and Her Works* (New York: Cassell, Petter, Galpin, 1880), p. 128.

(1895) by Rosina Filippi was quite successful, and was republished in 1929.[19] Two of its seven scenes are from *Pride and Prejudice*. Phosphor Mallam's *Mr. Collins Proposes* (1912) and *Lady Catherine is Annoyed with Elizabeth Bennet* (1912) are brief dramatic dialogues or scenes, with notes appended on costuming and setting. Throughout the 1910s and 1920s, *Pride and Prejudice* was repurposed for use in works such as *Scenes for Acting from Great Novelists* (1913) and other dramatic readers.[20]

The novel also came in for more extended dramatic treatment, as Laura Carroll and John Wiltshire describe in this volume (Chapter 13). Playwright Mary Medbery MacKaye wrote a full-length version of the story in *Pride and Prejudice: A Play* (1906), which claimed in its new edition (1928) to have been often staged for two decades in Britain and the United States and to have become the darling literary object of university professors, students and amateur actors. Dramatisations appeared in other languages, too. A five-act play written in Marathi by Gopal Chimanji Bhate was published in India as *Vichar-vilasit* (1912). From the 1920s to the 1940s, dramatic adaptations of the novel appeared with stunning frequency, including Helen Jerome's *Pride and Prejudice* (1935), which follows its predecessors in attempting to stage the novel with some faithfulness. Its dialogue is by turns breezy, melodramatic or stilted, as Jerome's Elizabeth voices climactic short speeches, such as this one, to Darcy: 'Enjoy your triumph! *(With bowed head.)* I am abased! And I never wanted to see you again!'[21] Another dramatic version, *Miss Elizabeth Bennet* (1936), was written by A. A. Milne, of Winnie the Pooh fame. Jane Kendall's (Anne Louise Coulter Martens's) play *Pride and Prejudice* (1942) includes appendices with directions for lighting, properties and costumes, suggesting its design for amateur theatricals, school performances and community theatres. It was increasingly possible to gain exposure to *Pride and Prejudice*'s plot and characters not through Austen's novel itself but through other popular media.

Most of these early dramatisations strove for faithfulness to the original, just as assuredly as they did not escape their own time and place of composition.[22] Popular fiction appears to have earliest experimented with extending or elaborating on the novel's events. Sybil Brinton's *Old Friends and New Fancies* (1913) takes characters from the major novels and throws them in

---

[19] For information about Filippi's [Mrs Dowson's] *Duologues*, see Gilson, *Bibliography*, p. 406.

[20] Gilson, *Bibliography*, p. 408.

[21] Helen Jerome, *Pride and Prejudice: A Sentimental Comedy in Three Acts* (London: Samuel French, 1936), p. 80.

[22] Wright argues that 'no version escapes its time or place. English, American, Australian, and South African renderings each bear the mark of its origins' ('Jane Austen Adapted', p. 439).

with the Darcys, a mix that has led to its being identified as the first published Austen continuation, a subject Emily Auerbach considers in detail in this volume (Chapter 15).[23] The focus in these early continuations is on imagining beyond the happy ending and emulating Austen's style, filling in details such as what Elizabeth calls her husband (e.g., 'dear Darcy', 'Will' or 'Fitz'), whether there are Darcy offspring, and which further marriages occur. These texts fulfil the reader's desire to know what happens next, to obviate the fact that Austen's story has an end. Continuation dramatisations, too, worked in this vein, as in Arthur Russell's play *A Wedding at Pemberley* (1949) or Cedric Wallis's *The Heiress of Rosings* (1956).

Other chapters in this volume describe in greater detail the history of Jane Austen on stage, television and film. The first film adaptation, following a UK television version (1938), was Robert Z. Leonard's *Pride and Prejudice* (1940). Its screenplay was written by Aldous Huxley and Jane Murfin, featuring Greer Garson (Elizabeth) and Laurence Olivier (Darcy).[24] Film, radio and television adaptations appeared regularly thereafter. On television, an NBC adaptation aired in 1949, and three BBC mini-series versions in 1952, 1958 and 1967. A BBC2 mini-series in 1980 featured a screenplay by Fay Weldon and aired in the United States on *Masterpiece Theatre*, which went on, over its forty-year history, to feature Austen adaptations with regularity. Most recently, *Masterpiece Theatre* televised *The Complete Jane Austen* (2008), adaptations of the six novels and a biopic, *Miss Austen Regrets* (2008). It produced a *Complete Guide to Teaching Jane Austen* for its website, answering the question, 'Why Austen? Why Now?' At least ten books on Jane Austen on film and/or television have assessed these adaptations, looking for continuities and discontinuities from the 1940s to the present, comparing novel to films, and making sense of the elements adapted, transformed, emphasised and de-emphasised. There is no doubt that these adaptations widened, deepened and complicated Austen's cult status.

Beyond masterpiece to Darcymania: the 1990s to the present

By the late twentieth century, both fanciful continuations and largely faithful Austen adaptations were widely available, with *Pride and Prejudice* gaining the distinction of being Austen's 'novel with the greatest number of

---

[23] Jennifer Scott, *After Jane: A Review of the Continuations and Completions of Jane Austen's Novels* (Lincolnshire: West Street Copying Services, 1998), p. 14 (privately published). 'Continuation' here is distinct from 'completion'. Published completions of Austen's unfinished texts appeared earlier.

[24] Wright suggests that this film adaptation was based on a successful stage adaptation by Helen Jerome, *Pride and Prejudice* (1936) ('Jane Austen Adapted', p. 430).

sequels'.[25] At the beginning of this period, most of these works centred on Elizabeth – or on Elizabeth and Darcy together – imagining futures for the principal and minor characters that included births, deaths, marriages and many new relationship-based hurdles. By the mid 1990s, newer trends emerged and solidified. On the big screen, once-dominant historical costume dramas of Austen gave way to versions featuring present-day settings. Perhaps nowhere was the contemporary repurposing of Austen's novels laid more bare than in the spate of self-help books purporting to use her fiction to help today's women find mates, such as Laura Henderson's *Jane Austen's Guide to Dating* (2005).

A stunning number of precious pocket-sized books on Austen also appeared in the 1990s and 2000s. Most of them consist of charming quotations from the fiction and letters, taken entirely out of context and collected as witty or profound aphorisms. This became a popular genre in the eighteenth century, called 'Elegant Extracts', after Vicesimus Knox's selections of verse by that title. (Austen referred to Knox in *Emma* and poked fun at the genre in *Northanger Abbey*; there is now an Austen fan fiction website, 'Elegant Extracts': www.elegantextracts.com.) In the worst of these miniature Austen books, the words of her most flawed or wicked characters are attributed to the author herself. These books feature simultaneously grand and diminutive titles, such as *Jane Austen's Little Advice Book* (1996), *Bite-Size Jane Austen* (1999), *Jane Austen's Little Instruction Book* (1995), *Jane Austen Speaks to Women* (2000) and *The Jane Austen Companion to Life* (2010). The sheer number of these titles in this format suggests that some of them must have sold in profitable quantities.

The watershed moment for *Pride and Prejudice* during this era came from a filmic costume drama. Andrew Davies's 1995 six-part BBC adaptation, starring Colin Firth, singlehandedly transformed Austen's cultural stock. Firth's jumping into the lake at Pemberley became a cultural sensation. It was said that British women held 'Darcy parties' to watch that scene over and over, ogling the character's tan jodhpurs and wet white shirt clinging to his chest. To date, that four-minute excerpt has been viewed a stunning 2 million times on YouTube. This scene has made Darcy loom larger than all of Austen's other characters, leading to what one critic calls 'Darcy's escape to iconicity', noting how it prompted his 'cutting himself away from the source novel'.[26] Although some critics called this mid-1990s period 'Austenmania', others

[25] Marilyn Sachs, 'The Sequels to Jane Austen's Novels', in *The Jane Austen Companion*, ed. J. David Grey et al. (New York: Macmillan, 1986), p. 374.
[26] Sarah Caldwell, 'Darcy's Escape: An Icon in the Making', in *Fashion Cultures: Theories, Explorations, and Analysis*, ed. Stella Bruzzi and Pamela Church Gibson (London: Routledge, 2000), p. 243.

accurately dubbed it 'Darcymania'. It is of significance because it marked the moment that Darcy became for many readers and viewers the imaginative centre of *Pride and Prejudice*, taking that role over from Elizabeth. This change in focus also flourished in continuation fiction told from Darcy's perspective. The signal features of Darcymania – strong, silent, sensitive masculinity; the objectification of male bodies; the emphasis on the courtship plot to the exclusion of almost all else – bear little resemblance to those of either the Men's Club Jane or the New Woman Austen. Neither camp would ever have imagined *Darcy* as the centre of the novel! Yet then, as now, readers consult very similar versions of the original text. As a result, we might conclude that *Pride and Prejudice* functions more like a cultural Rorschach test than a 'universal' work of fiction.

Everywhere, everyone's Austen

Darcymania is just one strand of a cornucopia of *Pride and Prejudice* patterns and products. The 1990s and 2000s women's book club craze, and Austen's centrality to it, was documented in its own work of fiction (and then film) in Karen Joy Fowler's *Jane Austen's Book Club* (2004). In the past five years, at least five versions of *Pride and Prejudice* as a musical have been staged, a phenomenon that apparently got its start decades earlier with an American musical version (1959) and a South African one (1964), according to Andrew Wright.[27] Today, it seems every genre and medium – and every fictional subgenre from Western to Christian to pornographic – has its *Pride and Prejudice*. Some of these adaptations and continuations capitalise on the novel's signature irony and humour, while others approach the subject with deadpan seriousness. From 2009 to 2011, at least 130 *Pride and Prejudice*-inspired novels appeared in print. (Some of these were no doubt self-published, and this is by no means an exhaustive count.) Even the 'Dummies' series added Joan Klingel Ray's *Jane Austen for Dummies* (2006) to its list of titles.

The *Pride and Prejudice* explosion has long been internet based as well. The Republic of Pemberley, a self-described web haven for Austen addicts, has been going strong since 1996, calling itself the largest Austen website on the internet. AustenBlog is devoted to news about Austen in popular culture. Countless similar sites have followings of various sizes and audiences. Every so often, a Jane Austen clip goes viral on YouTube, as with the humorous 'Jane Austen Fight Club' from July 2010. Austen now has her own glossy magazine, too. Since 2004, *Jane Austen's Regency World* has been published

[27] Wright, 'Jane Austen Adapted', pp. 422, 438–9.

bimonthly, out of the Jane Austen Centre in Bath. The Jane Austen Society of North America boasts 3,000 members, 500 of whom meet for an Annual General Meeting of scholarly lectures, entertainments and a costume ball. Jane Austen societies now flourish worldwide, with branches on every continent but Antarctica. Several *Pride and Prejudice* trivia games and board games have been produced in recent years, as well as action figures, tea towels and every manner of gewgaw imaginable.

How do we make sense of this proliferation of all things *Pride and Prejudice*? The reasons that critics have offered are as varied as the vehicles forwarding that popularity. Some point to economics; classic novels like *Pride and Prejudice* – because out of copyright, cheap and available – have built-in cachet and are therefore poised for cultural exploitation and likely profit. Other critics suggest Austen's popularity signals a post-feminist moment, with overworked women longing not for equitable treatment but for a return to an imagined past when strong, handsome men with lots of money fell into the paths of deserving women and put them on pedestals. (This resonates with previous versions of Austen's escapist appeal that see her as popular because her fiction prompts us to forget our real problems.) A post-feminist Austen would explain the popularity of many of the aforementioned *Pride and Prejudice*-inspired dating guides. For instance, Sarah Arthur's *Dating Mr. Darcy: The Smart Girl's Guide to Sensible Romance* (2005) promises to help women find their own 'ideal gentleman' by gauging a guy's Darcy Potential – that is, by evaluating his relationships with family, friends and God. This version of Austen's fiction does more than document Regency women's courtship experiences; it can help you get a husband today, too! (Such readings conveniently overlook the fact that almost all of the marriages depicted in Austen's fiction are anything but rosy.)

If some see Austenmania and Darcymania as harbingers of a conservative turn, others locate more progressive promise in *Pride and Prejudice*'s contemporary efflorescence. These theories see in Elizabeth and Darcy's popularity the celebration of heterosexual relationships that bring together strong-willed, intellectual equals; such interpretations would also point up the novel's not-so-veiled criticisms of unjust economic pressures, divided by sex as well as by class, and focus on the ways that recent adaptations and continuations recognise and comment on them, particularly through comedy and irony. Still others, however, conclude that Austen's popularity has little to do with either conservative or progressive gender politics, attributing *Pride and Prejudice*'s popularity to the contemporary love of Regency fashion; to the flowering of neo-nationalisms or other fantasies of order, particularly those buttressed by moral philosophy; or to garden-variety nostalgia or anglophilia. What is fascinating in the case of each of these versions is the extent to which some scenes, characters and qualities of the novel (and even its newer permutations) are emphasised, while others are downplayed or ignored.

So how ought we to make sense of the proliferation of *Pride and Prejudice* cults and cultures? At the present moment, it might be most credible to acknowledge that we simply cannot. The novel's reincarnations have become far too diffuse to understand through any particular interpretive lens. Jane Austen has, according to one critic, been 'pimped' or customised into a kind of 'Have it Your Way' author.[28] Austen has become 'an infinitely exploitable global brand', with *Pride and Prejudice* poised as the 'representative Austen title'.[29] In other words, Austen serves as everyone's everything. She and her most popular novel have become what Marjorie Garber called the first line of *Pride and Prejudice* ('It is a truth universally acknowledged'): a cultural bromide.[30] Garber compares the rabid love of Austen of today – which she labels 'a syndrome', or a non-pathological symptom – with that of Shakespeare in the eighteenth century. We might say that the signifier 'Jane Austen' serves, depending on one's perspective, as either a tabula rasa on which an individual's desires are written or as a collective cultural cipher to which every manner of desire is opaquely attached.

We are wont to see ourselves today as unusual or special for loving Jane Austen and her remarkable novel. Looking across a wider swath of time, however, we must locate continuous interest in and attachment to her and her fiction, albeit with differing emphases and concerns. Although we live in a time when cult-like activity around *Pride and Prejudice* has a far greater reach than in previous eras, we may have outdone our predecessors more in saturation than in innovation. Does this mean that Jane Austen's reputation has, to employ television lingo, finally jumped the shark? Or are the writers at Masterpiece Theatre onto something by predicting that 100 years from now we'll still be asking 'Why Austen? Why Now?' The mercurial reputation of Sir Walter Scott's fiction ought to prompt our serious reflection on this question. Where *Pride and Prejudice* is concerned, though, it seems unfathomable to imagine its celebrity petering out, even if we ought not to be surprised to see its ubiquity fade in the coming decades, if only out of sheer popular cultural fatigue.

[28] Brandy Foster, 'Pimp My Austen: The Commodification and Customization of Jane Austen', *Persuasions On-Line* 29.1 (Winter 2008), www.jasna.org/persuasions/on-line/vol29no1/foster.html, accessed 15 September 2011.
[29] Claire Harman, *Jane's Fame: How Jane Austen Conquered the World* (Edinburgh: Canongate, 2010), p. 3.
[30] Marjorie Garber, *Quotation Marks* (New York: Routledge, 2002), p. 204.

15

EMILY AUERBACH

Pride and proliferation

Elizabeth and Darcy as zombie-slayers, bisexuals or twitter partners, Mrs Bennet as a Jewish mother ('Oy!'), Mary Bennet inflicting a cobra dance on visitors to her parents' home in India and Charlotte Lucas dressed up as Lady Catherine whipping Mr Collins into an orgiastic frenzy: these are but a few of the hundreds of variations on the theme of *Pride and Prejudice* since its publication in 1813 (see Illustration 15.1). Any discussion will be out of date, unable to keep up with the extraordinary global proliferation of the novel's progeny in print, online, on the screen or stage, and in other media.

The process of extending characters' lives beyond the novel began immediately – and by the author herself. Austen's nephew reports in his 1870 *Memoir* that his Aunt Jane 'would, if asked, tell us many little particulars about the subsequent career of some of her people', including the fates of the two unmarried sisters of *Pride and Prejudice*: 'Kitty Bennet was satisfactorily married to a clergyman near Pemberley, while Mary obtained nothing higher than one of her Uncle Philips' clerks' and became an admired personage in Meryton.[1]

What would Jane Austen think, however, of the 200 years of adaptations and permutations, prequels and sequels, dramatisations and cinematic versions of *Pride and Prejudice*? Would she, like her heroine Elizabeth Bennet, 'dearly love a laugh', or would she lament her inability to share in the profits? A *Newsweek* cover story entitled '181 Things You Need To Know Now' featured Jane Austen's face sandwiched between Barack Obama and Beyoncé, referred to 'Jane Austen's commercial viability', and observed, 'Like BMW, Prada, and Martha Stewart, Austen is now a brand.'[2] A later *Newsweek* story entitled 'Not-so-Plain Jane' concluded, 'In the economic

---

[1] James Edward Austen Leigh, *Memoir of Jane Austen*, 2nd edn (London: Bentley, 1871), p. 376.
[2] *Newsweek* (9 July 2007), p. 71.

186

Illustration 15.1 Examples of recent proliferation. Photograph Keith Meyer.

doldrums, it is the eminently bankable Austen's blessing and curse to be constantly applied and misapplied. Jane-anything sells out.'[3] As *Bridget Jones's Diary* author Helen Fielding observed, 'I just stole the plot from *Pride and Prejudice*. I thought it had been very well market-researched over a number of centuries.'[4]

Authors have expanded *Pride and Prejudice* in many directions, capitalising on the fact that readers simply cannot get enough of Austen's characters and settings. Marilyn Sachs observed over two decades ago in 'The Sequels to Jane Austen's Novels', 'Followers of Jane Austen have an incurable addiction to the fate of her characters and greedily, if disdainfully, gobble up sequels to her novels', with *Pride and Prejudice* easily winning the contest for the Austen novel with the most continuations.[5] Sequels such as Sybil Brinton's *Old Friends and New Fancies* (1913) and the anonymous 'Memoir's' *Gambles and Gambols: A Visit with Old Friends* (1983) explore Elizabeth and Darcy's married life and throw in characters from other novels as well, for instance pairing *Pride and Prejudice*'s Kitty Bennet with James Morland from *Northanger Abbey* or hitching Georgiana Darcy to William Price from *Mansfield Park*. (Writing in JASNA's *Persuasions*, Kathleen Glancy

---

[3] Sarah Ball, 'Not-so-Plain Jane', *Newsweek* (8 March 2010), p. 53.
[4] Quoted in Natalie Tyler, *The Friendly Jane Austen* (New York: Viking, 1999), p. 274.
[5] Sachs, 'The Sequels to Jane Austen's Novels', in *The Jane Austen Companion*, ed. J. David Grey et al. (New York: Macmillan, 1986), p. 374.

scathingly indicts *Gambles and Gambols* as 'a large pile of the waste product from the digestive systems of male bovines'.[6]) Laurence Fleming's *The Heir to Longbourn* (2003) and *The Will of Lady Catherine* (2010) similarly find spouses for the unmarried characters of *Pride and Prejudice* by merging the story with other Austen novels. Other authors simply keep the story of *Pride and Prejudice* moving forward. Dorothy A. Bonavia Hunt's *Pemberley Shades* (1949) presents a happily married Elizabeth calling Darcy 'Fitz' and welcoming into the world their second son; in this version, Kitty marries Darcy's neighbour. The ever-growing collection of *Pride and Prejudice* continuations includes titles such as Jane Dawkins's *Letter from Pemberley: The First Year* and *More Letters from Pemberley*, explored through Elizabeth's letters (1999; 2007), Diana Birchall's *Mrs. Darcy's Dilemma* (2008), examining Elizabeth and Darcy after twenty-five years of marriage, and Juliette Shapiro's *Excessively Diverted: The Sequel to Jane Austen's 'Pride and Prejudice'* (2011).

Why not pick a character and flesh out his or her portion of the story? Mr Darcy reigns supreme in this regard, generating titles such as *The Diary of Henry Fitzwilliam Darcy* (1997), beginning when Darcy is ten years old, *The Confession of Fitzwilliam Darcy* (2003), *Fitzwilliam Darcy's Memoirs* (2004), *Mr. Darcy's Diary* (2005), *Darcy's Story* (2006), *Darcy's Passions* (2008), *The Private Diary of Mr. Darcy: A Novel* (2009), *Mr. Darcy's Obsession* (2010), *To Conquer Mr. Darcy* (2010), *Mr. Darcy's Undoing* (2011), *Mr. Darcy's Letter* (2011), *Darcy and Fitzwilliam* (2011) and *Dialogue with Darcy* (2011). This abbreviated list represents only the tip of the icily mannered, initially aloof Darcy iceberg. Such Darcy sequels and prequels often add his childhood background, fill in gaps in the novel (dialogue showing Darcy convincing Wickham to marry Lydia), thaw his reserve, follow him into the bedroom and add his tormented internal thoughts.

Pick just about any character from *Pride and Prejudice* and one may find a novel with him or her at the centre. Examples include Elizabeth Newark's *Consequence, or Whatever Became of Charlotte Lucas* (1997) or Jennifer Beckins's *Charlotte Collins* (2010), Patrice Sarath's *The Unexpected Miss Bennet: A Novel* (2011), focusing on Mary Bennet and her new beau, C. Allyn Pierson's *Mr. Darcy's Little Sister* (2010), Anna Elliot's *Georgiana Darcy's Diary* (2010), Sharon Lathan's *Miss Darcy Falls in Love* (2011) , following Georgiana on a musical tour of Europe, Skylar Burris's *The Strange Marriage of Anne de Bourgh* (2010), Joan Aiken's *Lady Catherine's Necklace* (2000) and Jane Odiwe's *Lydia Bennet's Story* (2007), billed as 'a breathtaking

[6] Kathleen Glancy, 'What Happened Next? Or the Many Husbands of Georgiana Darcy', *Persuasions* 11 (1989), p. 110.

regency romp!' Amanda Grange's *Wickham's Diary* (2011) boasts that it allows 'Jane Austen's Quintessential Bad Boy' to 'have his say'. An envy-ridden Wickham muses, 'Why should I be beneath Fitzwilliam? I am just as handsome as he is.'[7]

Or one can invent new characters to insert into the story. Children and grandchildren of various *Pride and Prejudice* characters offer a whole new source of possibilities for authors in search of a plot, as with Jane Gillespie's *Teverton Hall* (1983), starring the adult children of Mr Collins, or Elizabeth Aston's *Mr. Darcy's Daughters* (2003). New cousins and half-siblings pop up everywhere as well. The cover of Monica Fairview's *The Other Mr. Darcy* (2009) observes, 'Unpredictable courtships appear to run in the Darcy family'; Darcy's American cousin, Robert Darcy, makes his move after witnessing Caroline Bingley collapsing to the floor at Darcy's wedding. New faces also appear in Monica Fairview's *The Darcy Cousins: Scandal, Mischief, and Mayhem Arrive at Pemberley* (2010), introducing an incorrigible American cousin named Clarissa Darcy. Grégoire Darcy, an illegitimate half-brother ensconced in a French monastery, takes centre stage in Marsha Altman's *The Ballad of Grégoire Darcy: Jane Austen's 'Pride and Prejudice' Continues* (2011). One can even fuse characters from *Pride and Prejudice* with figures from other novels, as with *Fitzwilliam Ebenezer Scrooge: 'Pride and Prejudice' Meets 'A Christmas Carol'* (2011); in this novel by Barbara Tiller Cole, ghosts help a despondent and embittered Fitzwilliam try to woo Elizabeth.

Dozens of authors have in fact been able to build an entire industry around *Pride and Prejudice*, inventing stories occurring before, after or during the action of Austen's novel. Kara Louise has produced *Pemberley Celebrations – the First Year, Darcy's Voyage* (a 2010 'tale of uncharted love and the open seas'), and many others. Carrie Bebris offers an entire series of Mr and Mrs Darcy Mysteries featuring Elizabeth and Darcy as sleuths untangling intrigues involving other characters, beginning with her *Pride and Prescience* (2004). Abigail Reynolds has generated at least eight *Pride and Prejudice* variations. Regina Jeffers also keeps the sequels coming, touting *Christmas at Pemberley: A 'Pride and Prejudice' Holiday Sequel* (2011) as 'a festive holiday novel in which personal rivalries are resolved, generosity discovered and family bonds renewed', and promising readers a blend of romance and crime in *The Phantom of Pemberley: A 'Pride and Prejudice' Murder Mystery* (2010).

Why not fuse an Austen novel with a murder mystery, profiting from the enormous success of both genres? At the age of ninety-one, acclaimed British

---

[7] Amanda Grange, *Wickham's Diary* (Naperville, IL: Sourcebooks, 2011), p. 4.

detective novelist P. D. James released *Death Comes to Pemberley* (2011), placing a murder in the middle of *Pride and Prejudice*, her favourite Austen novel. James told the BBC she apologised to Jane Austen 'for involving her beloved Elizabeth in a murder investigation', but found great joy through 'this fusion of my two enthusiasms – for the novels of Jane Austen and for writing detective stories'.[8] *Death Comes to Pemberley* imagines Elizabeth and Darcy in 1803, six years after their marriage and with two sons, their lives suddenly turned upside down when Lydia Wickham arrives screaming that her husband has been murdered; shortly afterwards, the drunken Wickham is revealed to be alive but suspiciously covered with the blood of his slain friend, Captain Denny. While working to unravel the murder mystery, readers familiar with *Pride and Prejudice* will also appreciate the way James weaves in many strands from Austen – continuations of characters' quirks, references to other Austen novels, and period-appropriate crime-solving methods (no DNA evidence). Mary Bennet, now married to a rector, remains 'a frequent deliverer of platitudes which had neither wisdom nor wit', and Lady Catherine is 'fonder of visiting Pemberley than either Darcy or Elizabeth were anxious to receive her'.[9] Although James lovingly recreates Regency England and occasionally delivers ironic lines reminiscent of Austen's wit, she gives Elizabeth Bennet little sparkle: as one reviewer noted, 'marriage has made Elizabeth Bennet, Austen's smartest, sharpest-tongued and most beloved character, a little dull'.[10] In the same year, under the pen-name 'Ava Farmer', Sandy Lerner self-published *Second Impressions* aiming to offer readers 'an historically-accurate sequel to Jane Austen's *Pride and Prejudice*'.

Rather than staying in England or even Europe, other authors have moved the characters across continents and oceans, as well as into different eras. Nogami Yaeko's *Machiko*, a novel serialised in Japan in 1928–30, features a kimono-clad heroine initially refusing a proposal from the haughty head of the Kawai Financial Group.[11] In *The Sheik of Araby: 'Pride and Prejudice' in the Desert* (2010), Lavinia Angell creates 'a torrid desert romance' complete with a Muslim Darcy in Arab garb wooing an abducted Elizabeth.

American adventures abound, as in Paula Cohen's *Jane Austen in Boca* (2003) set in a retirement community with widowers on Viagra, Mary Lydon

---

[8] 'P.D. James Writes Pride and Prejudice Crime Novel', BBC News, 22 September 2011, www.bbc.co.uk/news/entertainment-arts-15023862.

[9] P. D. James, *Death Comes to Pemberley* (New York: Knopf, 2011), pp. 11 and 156.

[10] Charles McGrath, 'A Look Back, and Ahead, at Pemberley', *New York Times* (26 December 2011), p. C6.

[11] Hisamori Kazuko, 'Elizabeth Bennet Turns Socialist: Nogami Yaeko's *Machiko*', *Persuasions On-line* 30.2 (Spring 2010), www.jasna.org/persuasions/on-line/vol30no2/hisamori.html.

Simonsen's *Darcy on the Hudson: A 'Pride and Prejudice' Reimagining* (2011) taking Darcy and Bingley to America just before the War of 1812, and Heather Rigaud's *Fitzwilliam Darcy, Rock Star* (2011), featuring Darcy as a virtuoso guitarist, Elizabeth as lead singer in a girl band called Long Borne Suffering, and Lady Catherine as the owner of De Burgh Records.

Or why not give Darcy a ten-gallon hat? Jack Caldwell bills *Pemberley Ranch* (2010) as '*Pride and Prejudice* meets *Gone with the Wind*'; the line 'Frankly, Darcy, I don't give a damn!' graces the back cover. Union supporter Beth Bennet moves from Ohio to Texas after losing her only brother in the Civil War, so she naturally dislikes former Confederate officer Will Darcy, owner of Pemberley Ranch. Balding, oily Billy Collins manages Rosings Bank, Wickham-like George Whitehead is a 'carpetbaggin' piece o' scum' and Mrs Catherine Burroughs forecloses on families and occupies a pretentious plantation house formerly run by the labour of slaves. With a play on Austen's name, *Pemberley Ranch* ends with Darcy going to Austin, Texas, to take a seat in the Legislature.

Another American recasting comes in Karen Cox's *1932* (2010), placing Mr Bennet as a professor of English Literature at Northwestern University who loses his job and must move his family during the Great Depression. Bingley hires Jane as clerk at Netherfield's Dry Goods store, Wickham turns out to be a drunken bigamist and Lydia becomes a country back-up singer in Nashville. An Epilogue takes readers to 1970 with an update of the careers (paediatrician, architect, etc.) of Elizabeth and Darcy's adult children.

Moving back and forth between eras proves lucrative. Formerly titled *Pemberley by the Sea* (2008), Abigail Reynolds's *The Man Who Loved 'Pride and Prejudice'* (2010) gives us 'a modern love story with a Jane Austen twist'; an Elizabeth-like heroine works as a marine biologist in Cape Cod. In *The Man Who Loved Jane Austen* (2009), Sally Smith O'Rourke asks, 'What if a modern man had traveled back in time, fell in love with Jane Austen, and became the inspiration for her Darcy character?' O'Rourke's time-travelling Darcy watches Austen undress, noting 'her slender, full-breasted figure limned in the dancing firelight'; once he departs, Jane Austen begins revising 'First Impressions' into *Pride and Prejudice*, having encountered her real-life modern model for Mr Darcy.[12] Karen Doornebos's *Definitely Not Mr. Darcy* (2011), dedicated 'To Jane Austen, may you rest in peace', transports 39-year-old divorcee Chloe Parker into a Jane Austen-inspired reality dating show that is set in 1812, competing with other women for Mr Wrightman, heir to an estate. Nostalgically longing to 'banter with a

---

[12] Sally Smith O'Rourke, *The Man Who Loved Jane Austen* (New York: Kensington, 2006), p. 201.

gentleman in his tight breeches and riding boots, smoldering in a corner of the drawing room', Chloe describes herself as so 'twenty-first century weary' from 'all the social networking, Twittering, emailing, and texting' that she 'can't wait to escape to the 1800s and slow things down for awhile'.[13]

Alas for the length of this chapter, there is so much more. Melissa Nathan's 'Pride and Prejudice' and Jasmin Field (2001) casts a modern-day Elizabeth in a Pride and Prejudice theatre production opposite the Darcy-like Harry Noble. In First Impressions (2004), Christian-romance author Debra White Smith adds a tornado and imagines Elizabeth as a feisty lawyer starring in a production of 'Pride and Prejudice' opposite a handsome but arrogant rancher. Sarah Angelini's The Trials of the Honorable F. Darcy (2009) envisions Darcy as a British-born judge encountering young lawyer Elizabeth Bennet in a San Francisco courtroom. Aimée Avery's A Little Bit Psychic: 'Pride and Prejudice' with a Modern Twist (2009) transforms Elizabeth Bennet into a twenty-first-century Ph.D. student dreaming of princesses and knights. In Alexandra Potter's Me and Mrs. Darcy and Shannon Hale's Austenland, both from 2007, Austen-obsessed modern heroines (one a bookstore manager, the other a graphic designer) encounter contemporary versions of Darcy and Wickham. As Marilyn Francus notes, Potter and Hale 'not only demonstrate that Austen and her plots are applicable to modern society, but they argue that we live in Austen's world, whether we are aware of it or not'.[14] Hale has produced a sequel called Midnight in Austenland (2012) for fans who seem never to tire of buying books about the fusion of Austen's England and our own times.

An additional target seems to be middle-school and high-school audiences, or grown-ups longing to revisit those peer-pressured times in their lives. Mandy Hubbard's Prada and Prejudice (2009), marketed as 'a must read for Austen junkies' and appropriate for grades seven to ten, opens, 'It is a truth, universally acknowledged, that a teen girl on a class trip to England should be having the time of her life ... Instead I'm miserable.' The novel narrates the time travels of Callie, a 'clumsy geek-girl' trying to impress the popular girls on a high-school trip to London. When she tries on her new Prada heels, she trips, smacks her head and wakes up in the year 1815. Simon & Schuster marketed Pies and Prejudice (2010) as part of their Mother Daughter Book Club for girls in grades six through nine and their mothers. In this novel by Heather Vogel Frederick, a book group of girls about to start high school read Pride and Prejudice, try to stay in touch with one group

[13] Karen Doornebos, Definitely Not Mr. Darcy (Berkeley, CA: Berkeley Trade, 2011), pp. 1, 3.
[14] Marilyn Francus, 'Austen Therapy: Pride and Prejudice and Popular Culture', Persuasions On-line 30.2 (Spring 2010), www.jasna.org/persuasions/on-line/vol30no2/francus.html.

member now living in England and hold bake sales featuring pies; their lives mimic the literature they are reading as they meet characters resembling Mr Darcy, Mr Collins and others. Jenni James sets *Pride and Popularity* (2011) in Farmington, New Mexico, and features the feisty, outspoken Chloe Elizabeth Hart doing battle with high-school cliques. In *Prom and Prejudice* (2011), Elizabeth Eulberg sends Lizzie, a scholarship student from Hoboken, New Jersey, off to boarding school. Graced with a shimmering prom dress on its pink cover, the book opens, 'It is a truth universally acknowledged, that a single girl of high standing at Longbourn Academy must be in want of a prom date.'[15] Caroline Bingley wants to talk about fancy vacation spots and 401 Ks, while Lydia mars her speech with 'like', hopes as a freshman to be taken to the prom and has a dancing video of herself uploaded to the internet. Charles breaks off a date with Jane by text messaging, while Darcy explains himself via email.

Some writers have spiced up *Pride and Prejudice* by adding a third P: pornography. In *Pride and Promiscuity: The Lost Sex Scenes of Jane Austen* (2001), the co-authors pretend to have found missing R-rated manuscript pages from Austen's novels. A cover illustration shows Charlotte Lucas costumed as Lady Catherine and flagellating Mr Collins into an erotic ecstasy. Readers learn later, 'The pleasure that each reaped in the giving and receiving of punishment cannot be underestimated.'[16] Louisa and Caroline climb into bed naked with an ill Jane at Netherfield, while during Elizabeth's visit to Pemberley 'Darcy . . . reached beneath her undergarments and began to touch her most sensitive part'.[17]

Erotic moments find their way into many of the sequels, giving readers a chance to indulge in the guilty pleasure of undressing their favourite literary characters. Fans label as 'Definitely R-rated' Linda Berdoll's *Mr. Darcy Takes a Wife* (2004) and *Darcy and Elizabeth: Nights and Days at Pemberley* (2006). Fusing time travel with eroticism and showing a lot of skin on its cover, Gwyn Cready's *Seducing Mr. Darcy* (2008) features a divorcee suffering from 'carnal deprivation' who enjoys a one-night stand with Mr Darcy. Books such as Mitzi Szereto's *'Pride and Prejudice': Hidden Lusts*, Enid Wilson's *My Darcy Vibrates: A Collection of 'Pride and Prejudice'-Inspired Steamy Short Stories* and Michelle Pillows's *'Pride and Prejudice': The Wild and Wanton Edition*, all three from 2011, make no secret of their thrust, so to speak. Admit it, Pillows notes on her website: we have all wanted to see

[15] Elizabeth Eulberg, *Prom and Prejudice* (New York: Point, 2011), p. 1.
[16] Arielle Eckstut and Dennis Ashton, *Pride and Promiscuity* (New York: Fireside, 2001), p. 40.
[17] Ibid., p. 27.

Mr Darcy '*sans* knickers'. Fans can climb in bed with Elizabeth and Darcy in dozens of such offerings, or they can imagine them in pulsing, throbbing same-sex affairs (Elizabeth with Charlotte; Darcy with Bingley and Wickham) in Ann Herendeen's *Pride/Prejudice: A Novel of Mr. Darcy, Elizabeth Bennet, and Their Forbidden Lovers* (2010).

Mash-ups, or creative combinations from different sources, offer another genre for reworking *Pride and Prejudice*. Acknowledging Jane Austen as the co-author, a mash-up writer reprints large portions from the original novel but dots it here and there with original and often startlingly incongruous material. A digitally published mash-up called *Pride and Prejudice, or The Jewess and the Gentile* (2011) envisions the Bennet family as Jews struggling against their society's anti-semitism. Lev Raphael adds Hebraic touches to Austen's novel, beginning with an extra clause inserted in the opening sentence: 'It is a truth universally acknowledged, not least by a Jewish mother, that a single man in possession of a good fortune must be in want of a wife.' Mrs Bennet passes her life with 'visiting, news, and kugel'. Raphael sprinkles his mash-up with Yiddish phrases, from Mrs Bennet's '*Oy!*' and 'I could *plotz*!' to the labelling of the idiotic Mr Collins as a *nudnik* and a *nebbish*. Raphael links Mr Bennet's wit to his religion, as he notes, 'Why should a Jew *not* answer a question with a question?'

Raphael adds an additional layer to Austen's characterisation of the disdainful, snobbish Mr Darcy by depicting him as initially 'so prejudiced against Jews'. In the famous early scene in *Pride and Prejudice* where Darcy slights Elizabeth ('She is tolerable, but not handsome enough to tempt me'), Raphael's Darcy objects to the 'Levantine cast' to Elizabeth's features. Lady Catherine cannot stomach the notion of her nephew's marriage to a Jew, insisting, 'No Darcy has ever disgraced the family name by marrying even a Catholic.' Though superficially silly, this mash-up hints at the devastating effects of intolerance and religious prejudice. With the majority of the words taken directly from *Pride and Prejudice*, Mr Bennet might ask rhetorically what's *not* to like about this mash-up?

Pride and Prejudice and Zombies, a 2009 mash-up 'by Seth Grahame-Smith and Jane Austen', made the *New York Times* best-seller list with its book jacket illustration of a fanged Regency heroine dripping in blood and its promise to deliver 'all new scenes of bone-crunching zombie mayhem'. Capitalising on the modern taste for sensational potboilers and exposing our distaste for literary classics, the back cover boasts, 'Complete with romance, heartbreak, swordfights, cannibalism, and thousands of rotting corpses, *Pride and Prejudice and Zombies* transforms a masterpiece of world literature into something you'd actually want to read.'

Grahame-Smith opens *Pride and Prejudice and Zombies* with an altered first sentence: 'It is a truth universally acknowledged that a zombie in possession of brains must be in want of more brains.'[18] To visit her ill sister, Austen's Elizabeth must walk several miles, arriving with dirtied clothes and a face glowing with the warmth of exercise. To this walk Grahame-Smith adds the fact that on her way Elizabeth must kill three 'unmentionables' (blood-thirsty zombies risen from the grave), therefore arriving at Netherfield not only with muddy petticoats but also with 'pieces of undead flesh upon her sleeve'.[19] Elizabeth's verbal battle with Lady Catherine becomes a literal swordfight, and Darcy and Elizabeth unite as a couple able to share in their talent for zombie combat. Mixing the refined with the disgusting, Grahame-Smith describes an attack that leaves behind 'a delightful array of tarts, exotic fruits, and pies, sadly soiled by blood and brains, and thus unusable'.[20] Further parody comes in the form of a pseudo Reader's Discussion Guide, complete with a final question mocking the commercial motivation of the whole venture: 'Some scholars believe that the zombies were a last-minute addition to the novel, requested by the publisher in a shameless attempt to boost sales. Others argue that the hordes of living dead are integral to Jane Austen's plot and social commentary. What do you think?'[21]

The New Yorker's Mary Halford called Pride and Prejudice and Zombies 85 per cent Austen, 15 per cent Grahame-Smith and 100 per cent terrible, but sales figures helped propagate more of the same, including Steve Hockensmith's Pride and Prejudice and Zombies: Dawn of the Dreadfuls (2010) featuring a cover that shows Elizabeth hugging a skeleton.[22] Visit any bookstore and find grotesque titles from 2009 undoubtedly capitalising on the popularity of Stephanie Meyer's Twilight series: Mr. Darcy, Vampyre ('A married man in possession of a dark fortune must be in want of an eternal wife'), Vampire Darcy's Desire (starring a Darcy 'tormented by a 200-year-old curse and his fate as a half-human/half-vampire'), Jane Bites Back ('It is a truth universally acknowledged that Jane Austen is still alive today ... as a vampire') and Moonlighting ('Will Elizabeth discover Darcy's secret identity as the head of the Pemberley pack of werewolves?'). More werewolves can be found in Mr. Darcy's Bite (2011), and in Mrs. Darcy vs. the Aliens (2011) Elizabeth and Wickham team up to fight hordes of tentacled aliens. Horror fusions have spawned graphic novels, a video game boasting 'the perfect blend of zombie slaying action and touching romance narrative', and movie deals, including promises from 'Pride and Predator' promoters that their film will slaughter the cast of the novel.

[18] Seth Grahame-Smith. Pride and Prejudice and Zombies (Philadelphia: Quirk, 2009), p. 7.

[19] Ibid., p. 31.   [20] Ibid., p. 80.   [21] Ibid., p. 319.

[22] Macy Halford, 'Jane Austen Does the Monster Mash', New Yorker (8 April 2009), www.newyorker.com/online/blogs/books/2009/04/jane-austen-doe.html.

In *The Five-Minute Iliad and Other Instant Classics: Great Books for the Short Attention Span*, Greg Nagan quips about Austen, 'At the end of the eighteenth century despite the liberal tendencies of the age, women were still discouraged from writing books. British writer Jane Austen was therefore compelled to write screenplays, and subsequently languished in obscurity until the invention of cinematography.'[23] *Pride and Prejudice* has furnished rich material for numerous adaptations to the stage and to the screen (see the chapters in this volume by John Wiltshire, Laura Carroll and Devoney Looser).

Screenwriters have also mined *Pride and Prejudice* for characters, plot and themes. Movie versions of Helen Fielding's *Bridget Jones's Diary* and its sequel *Bridget Jones: The Edge of Reason* capitalise on Darcy/Colin Firth fever. Caroline Bingley becomes a cold-hearted barrister, Wickham sexually harasses his employees at Pemberley Press and Mrs Bennet (Bridget Jones's mother) serves gherkins at a party and sells jewellery on a TV shopping network.

Transporting the novel to modern India, Gurdiner Chadha's 2004 *Bride and Prejudice* adds Bollywood colour to the story while keeping many of Austen's themes and characters intact. Unctuous Mr Kholi sells real estate, Will Darcy displays American condescension towards rural India and Mrs Bakshi embarrasses her sari-clad daughters through her shameless attempts at matchmaking. When Mr Kholi proposes to Lalita (Elizabeth) and Mrs Bakshi insists to her husband that he must make his recalcitrant daughter accept the offer, Mr Bakshi echoes Austen's Mr Bennet directly by giving her a choice between alienating one or the other of her parents through her decision. Lalita's younger sister Lakhi runs off with Johnny Wickham, while her beautiful older sister Jaya despondently waits for an email from Balraj, Darcy's friend. *Bride and Prejudice* concludes in over-the-top splendour with Austen's two happy wedded pairs riding on elephants through the streets of Amritsar, complete with Bollywood song and dance.

Another cinematic retelling is *Lost in Austen* (2009), imagining twenty-first-century London bank employee Amanda Price swapping places with Elizabeth Bennet. The film is permeated with what Laurie Kaplan calls 'multiple cross-cultural, cross-class, cross-text, cross-media, and cross-linguistic references'.[24] Disillusioned with her uncouth boyfriend's lack of panache ('Marry me, babes!' he drunkenly requests between burps), Amanda nostalgically time-travels into the more courteous, elegant world of her favourite novel. Once there, her use of slang ('jeepers'), modern garb and immodest

[23] Greg Nagan, *The Five-Minute Iliad* (New York: Simon & Schuster, 2000), p. 65.
[24] Laurie Kaplan, '*Lost in Austen* and Generation-Y Janeites', *Persuasions On-line* 30.2 (Spring 2010), www.jasna.org/persuasions/on-line/vol30no2/kaplan.html.

behaviour (as when she kicks Collins in the groin) marks her as hopelessly unable to accept the confines of Regency England. Screenwriter Guy Andrews achieves an additional layer of irony by having Amanda recreate scenes not only from Austen's novel but also from recent film versions, as when she asks Darcy to please emerge from a pool *à la* Colin Firth.

Other media offer additional possibilities for adaptation. Apparently it is never too soon for a human being to encounter Austen, as the Baby Lit Board Book series introduces infants and toddlers to *Little Miss Austen's Pride and Prejudice* (2011), a counting primer complete with two rich gentlemen, five sisters and nine fancy ball gowns. Need cartoon-like pictures? Try the illustrated Marvel *Pride and Prejudice* (2010), a five-instalment graphic novel boasting bits such as 'Lizzy on Love, Loss, and Living' and 'Bingleys Bring Bling to Britain' on its cover. Musicals, Broadway versions and light operas have also been reported. Internet sites, blogs and fan clubs have begotten an astonishing number of variations, with Elizabeth and Darcy communicating by cell phone, email, Facebook or Twitter (Darcy: 'One tweet from you will silence me forever').[25] Amateur cyber-authors contribute a never-ending series of inserted tales. Any mention of websites in a book can be risky because of the rapidly changing nature of the medium, but at the time of this printing, numerous sites such as www.janeaustenprequel sandsequels.com, www.pemberley.com/janeinfo/austseql.html, http://bestja neaustensequels.com, http://austenprose.com and www.austenauthors.net keep fans informed of new additions.

Let me close with a note of disclosure. I am by no means a fan of fan fiction, vampire stories, salacious Regency romps with heaving bosoms or time-travel adventures. I fear I have barely scratched the surface of this material. Nearly every version I read as part of my research for this chapter (or for my *Searching for Jane Austen* book) left me longing for the witty and wise novels of Jane Austen herself. How sad that an author so full of promise died before her forty-second birthday, with untold stories buried with her.

That said, I do confess to finding this journey through hundreds of permutations exhilarating. Wickham can become a carpetbagger, Lady Catherine an American hotel CEO and Mr Bennet a Midwestern college professor precisely because Austen has created universal characters who transcend all boundaries. Elizabeth and Darcy can match wits in the desert, at a high-school dance or over the corpses of the undead. The global proliferation of *Pride and Prejudice* spin-offs, mash-ups and knock-offs, though alarming and overwhelming, proves the power of Jane Austen's sparkling novel to capture the imagination of its readers, again and again.

[25] 'Pride and Twitterverse', Madhattermommy.blogspot.com/2009_05_01_archive.html.

GUIDE TO FURTHER READING

Primary editions

The Cambridge Edition of the Works of Jane Austen.
Austen, Jane, *Pride and Prejudice*. Ed. Pat Rogers. Cambridge University Press, 2006.
Le Faye, Deirdre, ed. *Jane Austen's Letters*. 4th edn. Oxford University Press, 2011.

On the text

Bodenheimer, Rosemarie. 'Looking at the Landscape in Jane Austen.' *SEL: Studies in English Literature, 1500–1900* 21 (1981), pp. 605–23.
Bonaparte, Felicia. 'Conjecturing Possibilities: Reading and Misreading Texts in Jane Austen's *Pride and Prejudice*.' *Studies in the Novel* 37.2 (2005), pp. 141–61.
Bradbrook, Frank W. *Jane Austen and Her Predecessors*. Cambridge University Press, 1966.
Brownstein, Rachel M. *Why Jane Austen?* New York: Columbia University Press, 2011.
Butler, Marilyn. *Jane Austen and the War of Ideas*. Oxford: Clarendon Press, 1975; 2nd edn, 1987.
Byrne, Paula. *Jane Austen and the Theatre*. London and New York: Hambledon and London, 2002.
Collins, Irene. *Jane Austen and the Clergy*. London: Hambledon Press, 1994.
Copeland, Edward and Juliet McMaster, eds. *The Cambridge Companion to Jane Austen*. Cambridge University Press, 1997.
Duckworth, Alistair M. *The Improvement of the Estate: A Study of Jane Austen's Novels*. Baltimore: Johns Hopkins University Press, 1971.
Emsley, Sarah. *Jane Austen's Philosophy of the Virtues*. New York and Basingstoke: Palgrave Macmillan, 2005.
Fulford, Tim. 'Sighing for a Soldier: Jane Austen and Military Pride and Prejudice.' *Nineteenth-Century Literature* 57 (2002), pp. 153–78.
Gallop, David. 'Jane Austen and the Aristotelian Ethic.' *Philosophy and Literature* 23.1 (1999), pp. 96–109.
Garside, Peter. 'Jane Austen and Subscription Fiction.' *British Journal for Eighteenth-Century Studies* 10 (1987), pp. 175–88.
Giffin, M. *Jane Austen and Religion: Salvation and Society in Georgian England*. Basingstoke, Hants, and New York: Palgrave Macmillan, 2002.

Gilson, David. *A Bibliography of Jane Austen*, new edition. Winchester: St Paul's Bibliographies, and New Castle, DE: Oak Knoll Press, 1997.

Harris, Jocelyn. *Jane Austen's Art of Memory*. Cambridge University Press, 1989.

Heydt, Jill. '"First Impressions" and Later Recollections: The "Place" of the Picturesque in *Pride and Prejudice*.' *Studies in the Humanities* 12.2 (1985), pp. 115–24.

Heydt-Stevenson, Jill. 'Liberty, Connection and Tyranny: The Novels of Jane Austen and the Aesthetic Movement of the Picturesque.' In *Lessons of Romanticism: A Critical Companion*. Ed. Thomas Pfau and Robert F. Gleckner. Durham: Duke University Press, 1998, pp. 261–79.

Hothem, Thomas. 'The Picturesque and the Production of Space: Suburban Ideology in Austen.' *European Romantic Review* 13 (2002), pp. 149–62.

Jenkyns, Richard. *A Fine Brush on Ivory*. Oxford University Press, 2004.

Johnson, Claudia. *Jane Austen: Women, Politics, and the Novel*. University of Chicago Press, 1988.

Knox-Shaw, Peter. *Jane Austen and the Enlightenment*. Cambridge University Press, 2004.

Macpherson, Sandra. 'Rent to Own; or, What's Entailed in *Pride and Prejudice*.' *Representations* 82 (2003), pp. 1–23.

Mandal, Anthony. *Jane Austen and the Popular Novel: The Determined Author*. Basingstoke and New York: Palgrave, 2007.

Mooneyham White, Laura. *Jane Austen's Anglicanism*. New York and Farnham, Surrey: Ashgate, 2011.

Pascal, Roy. *The Dual Voice: Free Indirect Speech and Its Functioning in the Nineteenth-Century European Novel*. Manchester University Press, 1977.

Rawson, Claude. *Satire and Sentiment, 1660–1830: Stress Points in the English Augustan Tradition*. New Haven: Yale University Press, 1994.

Ryle, Gilbert. 'Jane Austen and the Moralists.' In *Critical Essays on Jane Austen*. Ed. B. C. Southam. London: Routledge and Kegan Paul, 1968, pp. 106–22.

Sutherland, Kathryn. *Jane Austen's Textual Lives: From Aeschylus to Bollywood*. Oxford University Press, 2005.

Tanner, Tony. *Jane Austen*. Basingstoke and New York: Macmillan, 1986.

Todd, Janet. *Introduction to Jane Austen*. Cambridge University Press, 2006.

On the context and criticism

Andrews, Malcolm. *The Search for the Picturesque: Landscape Aesthetics and Tourism in Britain, 1760–1800*. Stanford University Press, 1989.

Archer, John. *Architecture and Suburbia: From English Villa to American Dream House, 1690–2000*. Minneapolis: University of Minnesota Press, 2005.

Armstrong, Nancy. *Fiction in the Age of Photography: The Legacy of British Realism*. Cambridge, MA: Harvard University Press, 1999.

Auerbach, Emily. *Searching for Jane Austen*. Madison: University of Wisconsin Press, 2004.

Austen-Leigh, J. E. *A Memoir of Jane Austen and Other Family Recollections*. Ed. Kathryn Sutherland. Oxford University Press, 2002.

Bautz, Annika. *The Reception of Jane Austen and Walter Scott: A Comparative Longitudinal Study*. New York: Continuum, 2007.

Bellos, David. *Is That a Fish in Your Ear? Translation and the Meaning of Everything*. London: Penguin, 2011.

Bray, Joe. *The Epistolary Novel: Representations of Consciousness*. London: Routledge, 2003.

Brewer, John. *The Pleasures of the Imagination: English Culture in the Eighteenth Century*. University of Chicago Press, 1997.

Copeland, Edward. *Women Writing About Money: Women's Fiction in England, 1790–1820*. Cambridge University Press, 1995.

Copley, Stephen and Peter Garside, eds. *The Politics of the Picturesque*. Cambridge University Press, 1994.

Cossy, Valérie. *Jane Austen in Switzerland: A Study of the Early French Translations*. Geneva: Slatkine, 2006.

Courtemanche, Eleanor. *The 'Invisible Hand' and British Fiction, 1818–1860*. New York and Basingstoke: Palgrave Macmillan, 2011.

Dadlez, E. M. *Mirrors to One Another: Emotion and Value in Jane Austen and David Hume*. Oxford: Wiley-Blackwell, 2009.

Damrosch, David. *What Is World Literature?* Princeton University Press, 2003.

Downie, J. A. 'Who Says She's a Bourgeois Writer? Reconsidering the Social and Political Contexts of Jane Austen's Novels.' *Eighteenth-Century Studies* 40 (2006), pp. 69–84.

Erickson, Lee. *The Economy of Literary Form: English Literature and the Industrialization of Publishing, 1800–1850*. Baltimore: Johns Hopkins University Press, 1996.

Fabricant, Carole. 'The Literature of Domestic Tourism and the Public Consumption of Private Property.' In *The New Eighteenth Century: Theory, Politics, English Literature*. Ed. Felicity Nussbaum and Laura Brown. New York: Methuen, 1987, pp. 254–75.

Fergus, Jan. *Jane Austen: A Literary Life*. Basingstoke: Macmillan, 1991.

Gilpin, William. *Observations, Relative Chiefly to Picturesque Beauty, Made in the Year 1772*. London: R. Blamire, 1786.

Harding, D. W. 'Regulated Hatred.' In *Jane Austen: Critical Essays*. Ed. Ian Watt. New Jersey: Spectrum Books, 1963.

Harman, Claire. *Jane's Fame: How Jane Austen Conquered the World*. Paperback edn. Edinburgh and New York: Canongate, 2010.

Knight, Richard Payne. *The Landscape: A Didactic Poem*. London: W. Bulmer, 1794.

Le Faye, Deirdre. *Jane Austen: A Family Record*, 2nd edition. Cambridge University Press, 2004.

Louden, Robert B. *Kant's Human Being*. Oxford University Press, 2011.

Lynch, Deidre, ed. *Janeites: Austen's Disciples and Devotees*. Princeton University Press, 2000.

Mandal, Anthony and Brian Southam, eds. *The Reception of Jane Austen in Europe*. London: Continuum, 2007.

Mazzeno, Laurence W. *Jane Austen: Two Centuries of Criticism*. Rochester, NY: Camden House, 2011.

Mellor, Anne K. *Mothers of the Nation: Women's Political Writing in England 1780–1830*. Bloomington: Indiana University Press, 2002.

Michie, Elsie B. *The Vulgar Question of Money: Heiresses, Materialism, and the Novel from Jane Austen to Henry James*. Baltimore: Johns Hopkins University Press, 2011.

Modleski, Tania. *Loving with a Vengeance: Mass Produced Fantasies for Women*. Hamden, CT: Archon Books, 1982.

Moir, Esther. *The Discovery of Britain: The English Tourists, 1540–1840*. London: Routledge and Kegan Paul, 1964.

Price, Martin. 'The Picturesque Moment.' *From Sensibility to Romanticism: Essays Presented to Frederick A. Pottle*. Ed. Frederick W. Hilles and Harold Bloom. Oxford University Press, 1965, pp. 259–92.

Price, Uvedale. *An Essay on the Picturesque, as Compared with the Sublime and the Beautiful; and, On the Use of Studying Pictures, for the Purpose of Improving Real Landscape*. London: J. Robson, 1794.

Reeve, Clara. *The Progress of Romance through Times, Countries and Manners* ... Colchester, 1785.

Repton, Humphry. *Sketches and Hints on Landscape Gardening*. London: W. Bulmer, 1794.

Schellenberg, Betty. *The Professionalization of Women Writers in Eighteenth-Century Britain*. Cambridge University Press, 2005.

Todd, Janet, ed. *Jane Austen in Context*. Cambridge University Press, 2005.

Turner, Cheryl. *Living by the Pen: Women Writers in the Eighteenth Century*. London and New York: Routledge, 1994.

Valihora, Karen. *Austen's Oughts: Judgment after Locke and Shaftesbury*. Newark: University of Delaware Press, 2010.

Venuti, Lawrence. *The Translator's Invisibility: A History of Translation*. London: Routledge, 1995.

Vickery, Amanda. *The Gentleman's Daughter: Women's Lives in Georgian England*. New Haven, CT: Yale University Press, 1998.

Wainwright, Valerie. *Ethics and the English Novel from Austen to Forster*. New York and Aldershot: Ashgate, 2007.

Wall, Cynthia. 'Gendering Rooms: Domestic Architecture and Literary Acts.' *Eighteenth-Century Fiction* 5 (1994), pp. 349–72.

Weissbort, Daniel and Astradur Eysteinsson, eds. *Translation – Theory and Practice: A Historical Reader*. Oxford University Press, 2006.

Wiltshire, John. *Recreating Jane Austen*. Cambridge University Press, 2001.

Wollstonecraft, Mary. *A Vindication of the Rights of Woman*. In *Mary Wollstonecraft: Political Writings*. Ed. Janet Todd. London: William Pickering, 1993.

  The Works of Mary Wollstonecraft. Ed. Janet Todd and Marilyn Butler. London: William Pickering, 1989.

Woodworth, Megan A. *Eighteenth-Century Women Writers and the Gentleman's Liberation Movement*. New York and Farnham: Ashgate, 2011.

Wright, Andrew. 'Jane Austen Adapted.' *Nineteenth-Century Fiction* 30.3 (Dec. 1975), pp. 421–53.

INDEX

Cambridge companions to...

AUTHORS

TOPICS

13874236R00131

Printed in Great Britain
by Amazon.co.uk, Ltd.,
Marston Gate.